Praise for *The Love Producer*

"*The Love Producer* provides the ultimate peek behind the cameras with this refreshingly raw, honest take on romance, ambition, self-love, and producing your own happily ever after. As a longtime Bachelor franchise fan, I gobbled up every juicy morsel of it!"

—Amy Lea, international bestselling author of *Set on You*

"From my time with Julie I am not surprised that her memoir brings us honesty and humor. Julie invites readers into stories of heartbreak, moments of turmoil, aging, dating, and spiritual renewal all leading to a place of feeling less alone and confident in our journey to love ourselves. A gifted and compassionate storyteller, Julie encourages us to question the narratives we've inherited and discover a love far richer and more lasting."

—Ben Higgins, former star of *The Bachelor* and author of *Alone in Plain Sight*

"I've always thought that the drama that happens in Bachelor Nation off camera is just as juicy as what happens on camera and *The Love Producer* proves it. This book is brain candy for the pop culture–loving, romantic millennial. Julie wrote the ultimate page-turning chick lit . . . except it's her true story."

—Ashley Iaconetti, star of Bravo's *Real Housewives of Rhode Island* who found love through *The Bachelor* franchise

"*The Love Producer* is a sparkling, behind-the-curtain romp through the chaos of modern romance, where text messages matter more than limos and the real twist isn't the edit—it's vulnerability. Charming, self-aware, and deliciously fun, this is the love story the producer never saw coming."

—Hannah Pittard, author of *If You Love It, Let It Kill You*

"Using the familiar arc of everyone's favorite dating show, Julie LaPlaca writes the unscripted truth in this gem of a book. Brave, vulnerable, and messy, *The Love Producer* is a beautiful reminder to become our own permission slip, quiet our inner a**hole, lose shame, and to finally own our story, with all its perfect imperfections."

—Jennifer Pastiloff, national bestselling author of *Proof of Life* and *On Being Human*

"*The Love Producer* gave me goosebumps from the go—think Renée Zellweger in Jerry Maguire: 'you had me at hello.' It's both relatable and aspirational; hopeful and heartbreaking; easy to read yet emotionally deep. I don't know any pop culture lovers who won't instantly melt into these pages. And if you like reality TV, Julie's stories are pure heaven! But mostly, it's sweet, charming, and feel-good, all the way, and that's exactly what we want and need right now."

—Alyssa Shelasky, author of *New York* magazine's *Sex Diaries* book and column and star of HBO's *Sex Diaries* docuseries

"From behind the scenes of reality TV's most iconic love story machine comes a juicy, deeply honest memoir about heartbreak, awakening, and choosing herself."

—Amber Rae, *USA Today* bestselling author of *Loveable*

"*The Love Producer* is a real-life rom-com come to life. As a former love producer on the Bachelor franchise who got to work with Julie first-hand, I can confidently say that the best and juiciest moments of love and heartbreak all actually take place off-camera, behind-the-scenes. No one has been brave enough to talk about it or share about it until now. Julie's book speaks to a very real thing I have felt myself: why are we so good at getting people to open up and be vulnerable on national television and yet can't find the courage to tell people in our own lives how we feel? The irony and paradox is fascinating. *The Love Producer* made me laugh and weep and is for anyone out there who is afraid to tell the one person they love, how they actually feel. Sometimes our own lives can feel like a movie, and this is a story that should be made into one. To all the people who love fearlessly, and to all those who are scared of opening their hearts, *The Love Producer* is for you."

—Naz Perez, cultural conversationalist, television host, and former *Bachelor* producer

"Julie LaPlaca went from helping singles on their journeys to find love in the glitzy, globe-trotting world of *The Bachelor* to embarking on her own journey of finding love within. In *The Love Producer*, we get to tag along on her heartwarming, wild ride, and it's nothing short of marvelous. I was totally captivated, staying up way too late to get to the book's refreshing, empowering happily ever after. As vulnerable as it is glamorous and unexpected, reading this felt like talking with a best friend I'd known for years."

—Isabelle Engel, author of *Most Eligible*

"Woah! I feel like we really needed this book as Bachelor Nation Fans. Julie being one of the OG and main producers on the ICONIC show for so long, she is really spilling so much tea from an angle that hasn't been done before. And she also had a love story saga with Pilot Pete? I mean who hasn't, but like a producer being on a Bachelor's roster? I am intrigued."

—Zachary Weinberg, @ZacharyReality and media personality

"This book is a quiet unraveling of the love stories we're taught to chase. When we can move beyond the fantasy and into the tender terrain beneath it, *The Love Producer* traces one woman's journey from scripted romance to self-listening. With humor, vulnerability, and spiritual depth, Julie reminds us that love isn't something to be produced or 'perfected,' it's something to be remembered. It's an invitation to turn our attention inward and let a truer love story reveal itself."

—Rosie Acosta, author and associate producer of *Balance: A Perimenopause Journey*

"What an accurate description of the vulnerability, honesty, and radical self-acceptance that leads to the most amazing journey there is . . . authenticity. The rawness of the spiritual awakening explored in Julie's story begs the reader's soul to join in the quest for oneself, as the universe provides alternate plans to our own productions."

—Mystic Michaela, author of *What's My Aura* and podcast host

"*The Love Producer* is a vulnerable, honest, and often comedic story of love, loss, and healing. Julie shares her history producing reality TV love stories while personally seeking her own happily ever after. I felt invested and on the edge of my seat to see how the stories would unfold. For any Bachelor franchise fans or inner romantics, this book details how we all can be the authors of our own love story."

—Michelle Maros, *USA Today* bestselling author of *Dear Friend*

"There's a lot of tea being spilled throughout these pages, but there is so much more beneath the surface that readers will find relatable and inspirational. **Come for the gossip but stay for the lessons** . . . You will be compelled to laugh and to cry, but more importantly, to look in the mirror and ask yourself some very serious questions that will lead you to a better life."

—Chris Harrison

The LOVE PRODUCER

LOVE PRODUCER

My Unscripted Journey from a Reality TV Career to My Own Happily Ever After

BenBella Books, Inc.
Dallas, TX

BenBella Books, Inc.
8080 N. Central Expressway
Suite 1700
Dallas, TX 75206
benbellabooks.com
Send feedback to feedback@benbellabooks.com

BenBella is a federally registered trademark.

Printed in the United States of America
10 9 8 7 6 5 4 3 2 1

Library of Congress Control Number: 2026000723
ISBN 9781637748862 (trade paperback)
ISBN 9781637748879 (electronic)

Editing by Rebecca Pillsbury
Copyediting by Michael Fedison
Proofreading by Cheryl Beacham and Lisa Story
Text design and composition by Jordan Koluch
Cover design by Morgan Carr
Cover image by Boris Brenman (headshot); image © Adobe Stock / Artem (rose),
    biancaoddi (stars)
Printed by Lake Book Manufacturing

To all the men who became my muse,
and to my parents for their unconditional love.

Contents

Author Disclaimer   xiii

Note to Readers   xv

Foreword by Chris Harrison   xvii

PART ONE: THE BACKSTORY

Teaser: My Final Two Men   3

1. Fairy-Tale Dreams   9
2. Career Dreams   17
3. If You Can Make It Here, You Can Make It Anywhere   27
4. City of Dreams   33
5. Dream Man   41
6. Dream Job   45
7. The Breakup   55
8. Bless the Distress   63
9. Bachelorettes, Proposals, Wrinkles, and Catching Bouquets   71

PART TWO: THE DRAMA

10. Pilot Pete   77
11. The Cinderella Story That Could Have Been   91

12. Forever a Bachelorette   105

13. Fantasy Suite   111

14. The Grand Finale   117

15. Stillness of the Face, Mind, and World   127

16. Return to Chaos   131

17. Home Is Where the Heart Is   137

18. Final Goodbyes   145

PART THREE: THE HEALING JOURNEY

19. The Supporting Characters   153

20. Carl, Hypnotherapist to the Stars   163

21. Thomas, the Toad   169

22. Ayahuasca Bros   173

23. My First Love   181

24. Return of the Exes   187

25. Henry, the Leading Man   195

26. The Warning   205

27. 'Til Death Do Us Part   213

28. The Villains   219

29. Drama and Decisions   225

30. The Breakup of Our Burning Love   237

31. The Not So Hollywood Ending   243

32. My Final Rose   247

Epilogue   253

Resources That Supported My Journey   259

Acknowledgments   261

Author Disclaimer

Memory is the diary that we all carry about with us.

Oscar Wilde

This is my story, told through my lens. Memory is inherently imperfect and subjective. Others may remember events differently, and I acknowledge my perspective is not the only one. Some names and identifying details have been changed or omitted to protect the privacy of individuals. While efforts have been made to preserve the accuracy of events, certain details have been reordered or condensed for narrative clarity. What follows reflects my personal experience and the truths I discovered on my journey for love. If my story seems a bit dramatic, just remember—I'm a reality TV producer.

Note to Readers

Before we get into it, we must start with a speech, of course! This speech is for you, my readers.

First of all, thank you for taking time out of your busy lives to be a part of this journey with me. Words can't express how grateful I am to have you along for the adventure to come.

If you're looking for love, I know how it can feel to lose hope that you'll ever find the connection your heart yearns for. Whether you're someone who puts others' needs before your own, have gone on one too many bad dates, or are healing from a broken heart, I'm here to tell you to not give up. If you go into this journey with an open and curious mind, wearing your heart on your sleeve, and staying true to yourself, I promise you'll be one step closer to the unconditional love you deserve.

The journey that you're about to read will look a little different than stories in fairy tales, but I've learned that when you step into the unknown and lead with your heart, true transformation begins. I encourage you all to do the same as you follow along. Because, after all, this journey isn't just about me. It's for all of us yearning for deeper love in our lives.

So go ahead—grab a glass of champagne (or tea), buy yourself a dozen roses, and find your favorite reading nook. Now, let's raise our glasses and do a toast. Cheers to the start of an amazing journey. Cheers to love.

Foreword by Chris Harrison

As host of *The Bachelor* franchise for nineteen years, I saw many young producers come and go. There are a lot of cookie-cutter people in this business, and I became good at seeing people who were different—the diamonds in the rough. Julie was one of those diamonds—a brilliant, kind, wonderful woman, ready to explode into life. It was my pleasure to get to know her and to watch her grow into an amazing producer.

Julie rose through the ranks very quickly, to the point where she was producing the Bachelors and Bachelorettes, which is a coveted position and a difficult job. Julie had to balance being a friend to the contestants with being parent-like; she was a confidante but also had to be tough because she had a job to do. She was expertly able to walk that line and find a way to connect with even the more challenging contestants.

Reality TV devours a lot of people; the job can easily become your life. It's a "kill or be killed" environment that causes many to put on a protective shell. Julie managed to remain vulnerable, empathetic, and caring throughout it all; as much as the show tried to kill that human side of her, she didn't let it. One of the things I admire most about her is that she got out of the business while her sanity was still intact. The easy decision would have been to stay; she was making a good living, working on one of the most popular shows in the world. Instead, she bravely chose to break away into the unknown and learned to appreciate, love, and heal herself, and I will always respect her for that.

Through the pages of this book and beyond, she can do the same for you. A good producer asks good questions and truly listens to the answers so they can help the contestants avoid hurdles other people have stumbled over. The importance of listening is browbeaten into producers in reality TV; most people, out of insecurity or nervousness, are instead thinking, *What's the next thing I'm going to say?* Producers—or guides—must ebb and flow with what the situation is giving them and what a particular person is giving them on that day. Sometimes they need to be a cheerleader and sometimes they need to give tough love, and it's their job to know which will motivate someone in that moment. Given at the wrong moment, tough love could break someone, resulting in a loss of a whole day or even week of production. It's very rare to find someone who has all these qualities and skills, and Julie does.

As a producer, she saw people stumble over hurdles of epic proportions. I have personally sat and watched Julie for hundreds of hours, interviewing, listening, breaking people down, and literally picking them up off the floor of a closet to get them back in the game of life. If she can do that in the most extreme circumstances, just think what she can do for you—by example, and as a "love producer" or guide.

The show we gave so much of our life and soul to is successful because it is relatable. The moments we were producing were microcosms of what we all go through in life. That's what makes the show so good. It isn't a game show; it is life. And yes, on a grand scale…maybe on a glacier in the Swiss Alps, or on a beach in the Maldives. But when the extravagance is stripped away, the show is about real-life issues that we all deal with. Julie was in the trenches every day at the deepest levels, gaining the skills and learning the lessons that have gone into this book.

There's a lot of tea being spilled throughout these pages, but there is so much more beneath the surface that readers will find relatable and inspirational. Come for the gossip but stay for the lessons . . . You will be compelled to laugh and to cry, but more importantly, to look in the mirror and ask yourself some very serious questions that will lead you to a better life.

And now, coming up next, the most dramatic read ever. Julie, when you're ready ...

Chris Harrison

THE BACKSTORY

Teaser: My Final Two Men

The setting: Stagecoach, 2023. A weekend of country music fun in the desert, turned reality star mecca of the world.

I had been an original attendee during the festival's early days, but work had me traveling in recent years, causing me to miss out on all the fun. For *Bachelor* alumni, the drama doesn't stop once the cameras are done rolling. Stagecoach, just outside of Palm Springs, California, was the unofficial pregaming destination to see which contestants might pair up for the summer show I had previously worked on, *Bachelor in Paradise*. One of my shining moments as a producer was when a contestant turned friend, Kristina, spilled the tea about the real-life drama that ensued in the desert: She hooked up with Blake, a *Bachelorette* contestant, on Friday night. He then went and slept with another contestant on Saturday. All three of them were set to attend *Bachelor in Paradise* the following month. Blake trying to cover his tracks became the main source of drama at the beach that summer.

Ironically, I was now in a dark, smoky honky-tonk dance hall watching Blake DJ to a fully packed crowd. The Stagecoach powers that be had loved the press and invited him to play a gig once he transitioned from reality TV star to DJ. How about that for taking an embarrassing experience and turning it into a thriving business?

The tent had been transformed into a nightclub, with strobe lights and smoke machines taking over the space. The music was a blend of country and electronic dance that somehow worked. My friends and I made our way through the crowd and found a spot to the right of the stage. We had just enough room to show off our dance moves.

I was thriving. Happily unemployed, I was excited to be back in my element, with cowboy boots and a cowboy hat on in place of a walkie-talkie and Converse. I'd opted for an all-black ensemble, with a dash of sparkle on my crop top and snake print leather shorts. Quitting my job had really done wonders for me, and I may have possibly de-aged myself from the relief of stress and getting normal hours of sleep. I also had a spray tan and fresh blonde highlights for spring, adding to my glow and confidence.

What felt like right on cue, there he was standing directly in front of me. My Prince Charming. He had on a white T-shirt and blue jeans, like a true cowboy. So simple, yet so sexy. I could feel the nerves bubbling up inside, like a bottle of champagne ready to pop. I leaned forward and tapped his shoulder. As he turned around and processed who he was looking at, a big smile came across his face.

"Jules!!!" he exclaimed.

"Peter!!!" I yelled back, my excitement matching his. We embraced in a hug that lasted the entirety of the song. He smelled so damn good.

Yes, it was Peter as in Peter Weber, the former Bachelor who I produced on his journey for love during season twenty-four of *The Bachelor*.

"Oh my God, it's so good to see you," he said. "Do you have any idea how much I think about you, Jules?"

"No, I don't, considering your girlfriend won't let you speak to me," I said, raising my eyebrows with a look that read, *I can't believe you're with her.*

"I think about you all the time, especially considering the bullshit I'm going through. We broke up. I'm done," he said with certainty.

A quiet thrill ran through me. "Can't say I didn't see that one coming."

Peter had been dating the fifth runner-up from his season of *The Bachelor*, someone I never thought was right for him.

"You know," he continued, "no one will ever have a relationship like you and I have." As the words came out of his mouth, I sensed a heartfelt sincerity to what he was saying. I felt the same, yet couldn't help but laugh.

"Very true, Mr. Weber," I stated, with a smug smile only he and I understood.

He introduced me to his friends and sang my praises as he kept his arm wrapped around me. I felt at home in his embrace. I sensed his excitement at seeing me, as he continued to say how much he had been thinking about me lately. If only he knew how much I had been thinking about him for the past three years—since our last night together.

When I introduced him to my bestie, Adam, Peter turned to him and declared, "Do you have any idea how much I love this girl, Adam?"

How much? Inquiring minds wanted to know. I wanted to know. Did he love me more than he had loved Kelley? Madison? Hannah Ann? Hannah Brown? Where was I on the love scale of all the cast members he had expressed his feelings to? Was I even on the same scale, or did I fall into the category of older-sister-type love? Had he realized that it should've been me all along? Had he fantasized of our future together, with a house in Westlake Village and a loft in New York City, two kids, and a life full of travel, adventure, and trips to all the places we exclaimed we wanted to go to together? Had he thought about how perfectly our families got along and how seamlessly our lives would merge into one? How much did he really love me?

Pick me, choose me, love me . . . Like Meredith Grey expressed to McDreamy in *Grey's Anatomy*, I had so desperately wanted to say those words to him in the weeks leading up to his finale of *The Bachelor*, yet fear and denial got in the way.

I was no longer working at the show, so fear of judgment from my coworkers had diminished, for the most part. Peter was single again, so what better time than now? Well, there was one tiny problem . . . I, for the first time in over six years, was not.

I had a boyfriend. A wonderful boyfriend who I loved and adored.

Henry wrote me sweet notes, made playlists, enjoyed cooking, and even washed the dishes afterward. He was a real man who knew how to fix things with his bare hands, unlike the men of LA. Henry was funny, smart, sexy, passionate, and oh so charming. He was my real-life Prince Charming, complete with an English accent that quite literally had me at hello. The thing is, Henry currently lived outside of London, and I hadn't seen him in over two months.

Morgan Wallen's "Last Night" started playing. Peter grabbed me and we began to dance with each other, singing along. There was an old familiarity with Peter, a comfort. We were always silly, goofy, and fun together. We were a bit reckless as well.

The flashing strobe lights bounced across our faces as we danced. We belted out the lyrics to the chorus, with one line in particular striking a chord in my heart—*baby, something's tellin' me this ain't over yet*. Why did I have a feeling that the relationship between Peter and me was, in fact, not over yet?

After the DJ set, we shared a drink together at the Rhinestone Lounge before being pulled in opposite directions by our groups for Kane Brown's performance. Love song after love song sent a pain into my chest; my heart caught in an emotional tug-of-war, my throat tightening with unspoken feelings. I hid my tears under the dark shadow of my cowboy hat, with a fabricated smile as I danced with my friends. I'd developed a skill over the years of disguising what I was really feeling from others, often saving the tears for when I was alone in bed, or claiming "this song just hits, you know?" when caught wiping the water from under my eyes.

The song did hit as Kane Brown started singing "What Ifs." It was the "what-ifs" between Peter and me that lingered in my mind. What if I had told him how I really felt? What if I had told my bosses what really happened between us? What if we had given us a shot? What if, in the words of Kane Brown, Peter was made for me, and I was made for him?

All these suppressed feelings I had worked hard to remove were rushing through me again. I wanted to be with Peter, dancing in his arms. I was also missing Henry, wishing he were there with me, holding me tight so I could feel the warmth and safety of his love. I was madly in love with Peter. I was madly in love with Henry. How had it come to this? What was a girl to do?

People would often ask me about how real *The Bachelor* is, and how it was possible for contestants to fall in love with two people. I would always defend the show, as I had seen it happen firsthand. Now, here I was, in love with two people. Was it possible that I was living my own real-life version of *The Bachelorette*, with Peter and Henry as my final two men? There was a feeling of joy and agony at the thought.

I began to realize that, while I had left the show for my own pursuit of love, the show had never really left me. I had become so entangled with crafting love stories in real time, how could I not, if even subconsciously, do it for myself as well? A blurry line was now drawn in my mind between what was real and what was fantasy. Yet I couldn't deny what I was feeling. It felt more real than ever, as indicated by the visceral reaction throughout my body and deep into my heart.

I started reflecting on the past couple of years since my departure from the show. Was it possible that all my supporting characters, drama, villains, and the troupe of my very own "love producers" (ahem, therapists) had led me to this very moment? I had been working through what had held me back in the past from being vulnerable and expressing my truth in the name of love. Ironically, this was something I was a pro at getting others to do on national television yet lacked in my personal life.

In this moment, I knew I'd never be able to get past the *what-ifs* with Peter until I was fully vulnerable and shared my heart with him. Why was that so hard for me? Would I be able to finally do what I got so many contestants to do and express my love to Peter? How would I do this without hurting Henry? I was beginning to feel the pain and struggle the leads of the show would go through on a personal level.

As I was leaving Stagecoach, I received a text from Peter asking if I wanted to go to the house he was staying at with his friends. As tempted as

I was, I knew nothing good would happen at an after-party. A late-night, tipsy expression of my love, with a boyfriend back in England whose biggest fear was infidelity, was something I was rational enough to know was not a good idea.

I didn't get the hall pass of a fantasy suite and a producer to work through these feelings of the heart (for those who may not be privy to what fantasy suites are, this is the time on a Bachelor or Bachelorette's journey where they get to spend the night, off camera, with their final suitors). Instead, I sat alone with my feelings and questions. I got to decide how the story unfolded from here. Would I find the courage to admit my truth … to Peter, to Henry, and, most importantly, to myself? What did I really want—who did I really want?! Was I one step closer to my happily ever after, or was the clock about to strike midnight on my love story?

1

Fairy-Tale Dreams

Some might say I was destined to work on a show about love. I was boy crazy from a young age, dreaming about princes, faraway lands, and my happily ever after. I felt a part of Cinderella within me and was hopeful that my fairy godmother would arrive when the time was right and bibbidi-bobbidi-boo me into a princess ready for her prince.

Until then, "faraway lands" consisted of the endless acres of forest surrounding my family's house in Goshen, Connecticut, population 2,879—a feel-good place to raise a family. With no stoplights or gas stations and an abundance of land to let my imagination go wild, wild it went. Like all the princesses before me, as a child I'd sit by the stream and talk to the animals, watching critters scurry by, catching and kissing frogs and imagining they'd turn into my prince.

I was half glamorous and half hippie at heart, wearing a tutu and crown over my OshKosh B'gosh overalls and bare feet with dirt underneath my toenails. My big sister, Jen, and I had a "castle" in the woods. To enter the castle, there was a secret code. We had to shake a small tree until a leaf fell, and we caught it. Once in hand, the gates would magically open to our fairy-tale land, where each large rock was a different wing of the castle. I imagined bringing my crush there, dreaming of our future together where he'd declare his love for me, and we'd get married amongst the rocks and trees.

The Love Producer

My first crush was Billy. He had dreamy, molten chocolate brown eyes that matched his wavy brown hair. I thought he was the cutest thing ever when we first locked eyes during preschool in our church's basement. I shared my crush with my best friends, the J-Unit—Jane, Justine, and Jessie. Our teacher yelled at us when we drew a giant heart around J+B on the birch tree in the playground at school.

I quickly moved on from Billy, however, when my mom invited him over for a playdate. Instead of going to the castle, we opted for our hot tub (very *Bachelor* of us; we didn't have a pool, so it was the next best thing). Things took a rough turn when he tried to dunk me under the water. Young boys are so not prince-like.

Next there was Teddy, my first kiss. We shared a babysitter after school, whose daughter, Carly, had a gumball machine that dreams were made of. All I ever wanted was a darn gumball out of that machine. Carly and the other older kids told Teddy and me if we kissed on top of the monkey bars, she would give us one hundred gumballs each. This was a win-win for me. I was determined to get those gumballs, and Teddy was a cutie.

From opposite ends of the monkey bars, Teddy and I nervously climbed to the center. The group of kids cheered us on from the ground as we leaned in for a quick, awkward kiss. Eager to get our gumballs after climbing down, I quickly learned about false promises. We held up our end of the bargain, but Carly did not. To this day on my list of things people owe me is Carly Jones, ninety-nine gumballs.

There was a big gap between that first kiss and my first *real* kiss—you know, the kind with tongue. I was in middle school, and had been dating my first boyfriend, Robby, for a week. The kiss happened at my friend Rebecca's party. She lived in a giant log cabin that was only half finished, giving us the space to have a party without the adults lingering over us. We dolled up the unfinished side with streamers, balloons, bowls of Doritos, and a cooler of PG drinks—sodas and Capri-Suns. In the corner was our master creation, a sheet pinned up to make our very own kissing booth. That night, after a few rounds of spin the bottle with the group, Robby and I made our way to the booth for our "seven minutes in heaven." Cue "Kiss Me" by Sixpence None the Richer, which conveniently started playing from the burned CD in the boom box. It was pure, awkward, middle school bliss.

After Robby, I was shooting for the stars—the superstars. My bedroom walls were covered with all the tween heartthrobs from *Tiger Beat* magazine. I'd wake up staring into the eyes of Jonathan Taylor Thomas, Devon Sawa, Andrew Keegan, and *NSYNC. Justin Timberlake was my number one crush, and I was convinced we were destined to end up together. I was a manifester from a young age, and one day I got my shot. I convinced my mom to drive into New York City on 9/9/99 to catch a glimpse of *NSYNC from the crowds gathering around Lincoln Center for the MTV Video Music Awards. I pushed my way to the front of the crowd where ticket holders were entering. Eagerly I shouted, "Can I have your ticket?" to a bunch of stuck-up New Yorkers who ignored me. All except Jessica. Jessica pulled out an envelope from her purse and handed a ticket to the cop next to her, pointing at me.

He made his way over. "Well, young lady, you just won the golden ticket. That lady wanted me to give you this!" I nearly fainted. I ditched my mom and friend after making plans for where to meet after the show and ran straight to the red carpet. (This was pre–cell phone days for the youngsters out there.) I remember the moment so vividly. I looked into the distance and saw *NSYNC at the start of the red carpet. Joey had bright red hair, Lance was rocking a purple and green three-piece suit, Chris was in his crazy braid era, and JC was looking handsome despite his weird, furry vest. Most important was Justin, in true Justin perfection, with a black leather jacket, a diamond T necklace, and his curly, perfectly gelled blond-tip hair.

As they made their way toward me, I did everything I could to contain myself. Then Justin and I locked eyes. This was my moment. Somehow, I got the words out . . .

"Can I have a hug?" I asked eagerly. He smiled, leaned in, and wrapped his arms around me. I still remember the smell of his leather jacket as he pressed up against me, which may explain my love for men in leather jackets that still holds true today. I left my outfit hanging on my bedroom door, unwashed, for a year after that.

The whole night was a dream come true. If you find a clip of *NSYNC's performance with Britney Spears, listen closely and you'll hear a faint voice yell right before they started singing, "I love you, Justinnnn!!!" That was me, with my first confession of romantic love to a man. It was so easy back then. Why did it become so hard later on?

It probably had something to do with my first real love, Cody. Cody and I met the following year. He was the star basketball player at the rival high school and had piercing blue eyes just as dreamy as Justin's. Our first date was to McDonald's followed by the movie *Bring It On*. We were inseparable after that, with Friday nights spent going to his basketball games followed by late-night bites with our crew at Friendly's, where we always shared a cone head sundae. My parents had been high school sweethearts and were still happily together, so I was certain Cody and I would have the same trajectory, especially when he ended up transferring to my high school later that year. He gave me my first blue box from Tiffany's—the silver heart charm bracelet—which was basically the equivalent of an engagement ring at the time.

We locked in our love by losing our virginity to each other on our nine-month anniversary, on his family's black leather couch after his mom had gone to bed. It took a few condoms before we got it on right. I remember my back sweat sticking to the leather as he managed to get inside of me. It didn't hurt as bad as I thought it would, and it didn't bleed like I had heard it would. *Did we do it right?* I wondered. I certainly didn't come that night. I doubt I came at all while we were together. What do we know about pleasure in our bodies at sixteen? I later came to realize that my first orgasm was actually from the ab machine at the YMCA. I never seemed to understand why crunching my body in a certain position felt so good down there. It's called a coregasm—look it up. Talk about motivation to keep crunching.

My parents had had "the talk" with me a month before Cody and I started having sex, thinking we already were. By then, I had already gone to Planned Parenthood after convincing myself that I might be pregnant after feeling a bump in my stomach one night while lying on my back. We hadn't even had sex yet; we had gotten close though—there was definitely cum down in that area, so there was about a .0001 percent chance that sperm could've made its way up inside of me, right? Because, again, what do we know about our bodies at sixteen? I was so terrified of teen pregnancy thanks to those fear-driven sex education videos. I started on birth control and didn't stop taking it for twenty-three years after that. I sometimes wonder what effect that had on my body. Boobs—it definitely gave me boobs.

I already had a fraught relationship with my body. In true *Bring It On* fashion, I dreamed of joining the high school cheerleading team. But there was no chance I'd try out again after having been rejected in middle school. My sister inquired as to why I didn't make the team, and the staff told her it was due to my double-jointed arms. There was nothing I could do to improve that feature. I understand now how those early moments of rejection can seep into the subconscious, having an impact for years to come.

The biggest rejection I experienced during high school was from Cody. We had been dating for over a year and a half. I now had my very first cell phone, the Nokia 3310, with an electric blue case that matched my bright blue and silver bedroom I was in when it rang. I lay back on my sky-blue faux fur comforter of my twin bed to have what I thought would be normal girl talk with my friend Olivia.

"Hi, hun!" I answered, staring up at my blue paper lanterns hanging between posters of *NSYNC and glow-in-the-dark stars.

"Heyyy…" she said, her tone less perky than usual. "How's your day going?"

"Good. What's going on—are you okay?" I asked. "You sound off."

"Have you talked to Cody today?" she inquired.

"No, I called him a bit ago, but I haven't heard back yet … Why?" I felt a rock forming in my throat, the insides of my stomach twisting together, bracing for what I was about to hear. The same areas of my body where I'd later learn I stored all my shame.

"I just got off the phone with Tim," she began. "Last night, he and Cody and some of the boys hung out with the Litchfield girls. They all played strip Go Fish." My stomach dropped. Strip Go Fish? I'd never heard of such a thing. The Litchfield girls went to Cody's old school and always tried to flirt with our guy friends and were so cold to us.

"Did he say anything about Cody? Like … he stripped too?" I asked, fearful of the answer.

"He did. But that's not all …" I could hear her take a deep breath before she continued. "He and Alyssa were getting a little too close. Tim wouldn't tell me straight up, but I suspect by reading between the lines that they kissed."

I thought I might throw up.

"I'm sorry, Jules. You should talk to him about it," she said.

"Yeah … I definitely will … Thank you for telling me. I'll call you back later, okay? Love you." I hung up and cried.

I don't remember who did the official breaking up once Cody called me back. My dad had always ingrained in me: *Once a cheater, always a cheater*, so I had no intention of fighting for us to stay together. If he had fought for it, though, I would've stayed. But he didn't. All I really remember him saying is, "You have big dreams to move to California and New York. I don't want to hold you back." *Damn straight, Cody. You won't hold me back anymore!* He started dating Alyssa the very next day. They are now married with three kids and live in our small town. In hindsight, it was a blessing from the universe. In high school, though? It was soul crushing.

While it seems silly thinking back to young love with such merit, I now realize what a strong impact those first romantic relationships can have. Cody began instilling the belief in me that "men don't choose me." There were also the guys in high school who would call me a "homewrecker" in a flirtatious way because they had girlfriends but wanted to hook up with me. I didn't do anything to wreck their relationships. I just loved fashion and enjoyed dressing cute. But it left me wondering, *Why do these guys want to hook up with me but not date me?*

So, what did I do? I fully leaned into the strong, independent Aquarius woman I was, where a relationship was not my priority, and I held a little shield over my heart. I'm a millennial, after all. The Destiny's Child lyric *all the women who independent, throw your hands up at me* was my mantra. I knew I could have it all; with time, a man and kids would come. But for now? I was going to focus on conquering the world and achieving all my dreams.

What were those dreams, you ask? Great question.

2

Career Dreams

I always knew I was a creative . . . but I struggled with what my creative niche was. I'd see the talented artists in school and wish I could draw like them. I'd listen to the school band and regret quitting the violin, then piano, then clarinet. I took dance classes even though I had two left feet. I enjoyed acting but always felt like I was in the shadows of my sister Jen, the more talented one. She'd be the star of the musical, and I'd be in the chorus. *Maybe my thing could be modeling,* I thought. I flipped through the pages of the Delia's catalog and dreamed of being one of the girls.

As teenagers, Jen and I both ended up getting agents in New York and our sweet angel of a mother would take us on the two-hour train ride from rural Connecticut into the city for castings. After months of castings with no bookings, I finally booked a big job. I was asleep in my closet when my mom opened the door to tell me. (Yes, sometimes I slept in my closet, a long, narrow passage that connected to my parents' room and was full of my collection of trinkets.)

"Julie, are you up?" my mom whispered. "Your agent is on the phone." My eyes immediately shot open.

"I'm awake!" I said, sitting up quickly, looking into my mom's blue eyes with eager anticipation.

"You booked the Nickelodeon campaign!" she said with a proud smile on her face. The news hit me like a beam of sunshine in my dark closet. I looked down at my wrist and saw that my wish bead bracelet had fallen off overnight. Remember those—where you make a wish as you tie them on? They say when it falls off the wish comes true, and that was exactly what had just happened. I was overcome with joy, knowing magic was real and my modeling dreams were finally coming true.

My mom and Jen came with me to the city the day of the shoot. The braces on my teeth were fully exposed (clear on top, metal on the bottom) as I smiled ear to ear when stepping into the studio. Bright lights were shining on the seamless backdrop of the industrial space, racks of clothing lined up for me, makeup stations ready to go, and a photographer clicking to test the lighting. As a girl who grew up in a small town, this was the definition of having *made it*.

The creative director ended up taking a liking to Jen as well and offered for her to be a part of the campaign. I was truly happy my sister would be joining me. In many ways, she helped ease my nerves. Together, we got our hair and makeup done, wore lots of fun outfits, and did a real photo shoot as models, striking poses as they blasted our favorite pop hits.

The campaign was for Nickelodeon's Kids' Choice Awards. We would be on the posters and physical voting boxes in Burger Kings nationwide (online voting didn't exist yet). The day it came out, we hopped in the car and drove to the closest Burger King. A thrill ran through me as we walked in and I saw the giant voting box in the distance. That thrill quickly diminished as we got closer and I saw a giant version of myself on the box…

Of all the cute outfits and shots, they had chosen the one where I was dressed like a tomboy in oversized jeans and an oversized sweatshirt, distorted by a fish-eye lens that made me look wide. So much so that I didn't even make the cut for the poster that hung beside it. My sister was on both, though, with a big smile, cute braids, and a flattering outfit. I did not look like a model. I looked ugly. I thought modeling was going to be my thing since Jen was the talented singer/actress. But now, she was the star, again. I had been so excited to tell all my friends at school to go to Burger King, but instead, I wanted to hide the box so no one could see it.

Career Dreams

I wasn't mad at Jen—she was my best friend. But as a young teen trying to figure out my own identity, this experience only added to my insecurity and uncertainty of what dreams I could achieve. I had always looked up to my sister and admired her confidence. If it weren't for her, I wouldn't have dared to pursue modeling in the first place. As a young kid, I was super shy and would latch onto my mother when out in public, while Jen would march up to strangers and start belting Barbra Streisand. Our younger sister, Janelle, who was born when I was nine and Jen eleven, developed her own insecurities after seeing both her big sisters as the more "talented" ones. We all have our own perceived realities, don't we? Side note—Janelle being born was my biggest manifestation come true. Every time I blew out my candles or saw a shooting star, I wished for another sibling. When my parents told us the news that she was on the way, I truly believed I was the one who had made it happen.

As I got older, Jen's confidence rubbed off on me, to a degree. It was the type of confidence that would stand up to the principal when she told me my black-and-white retro skirt from Wet Seal was too short.

"Look, it's below my fingertips!" I said back, showing her as I slapped my hands along my sides.

"Julie, the rule is mid-thigh. Please go change," she declared. That night I went home and measured to mid-thigh. Know what was shorter? Mid-thigh. The next day I marched into the principal's office and proved my point. How dare she judge me for having long legs!

It was the type of confidence where, when the older bully in school said, "Hey, Julie, don't you think your pants are a little too short?" I spoke back with poise, "They are called capris, and they are supposed to be like this." I had gotten them on Canal Street during a trip to New York, and you bet everyone else was wearing them that following spring. I prided myself on being ahead of the trends.

It was also the type of confidence that had my choir teacher, Mr. Pratt, label me the "leader of the pack" when he spied on a group of us girls flirting with boys during a choir trip to the Bahamas in the middle of spring break. We were literally just talking to them, but the next day he punished me, just me, by taping my hotel door shut so I couldn't leave (how wildly inappropriate!). There were plenty of kids doing things they shouldn't, drinking and smoking weed, but I wasn't a partier in high school. I just liked talking to boys. What did he expect, taking us to the Bahamas on spring break?!

Yes, I was confident in standing up for myself and challenging authority when needed, but I lacked confidence in knowing who I was creatively—or what I was supposed to "be" when I grew up. It's crazy how much pressure we put on ourselves as teens, like we are supposed to know! I wish I'd known then that creativity doesn't need to be defined by a certain talent or hobby, and that living life with a curious spirit is creativity in and of itself. But in high school, I hated that I didn't thrive with a talent.

Sometimes I regretted not pursuing acting further, but at the same time, I wondered if I actually liked acting or just liked the idea of being famous at a time when celebrity obsession was peaking. I loved everything pop culture. I'd come home every day to watch *TRL* as I flipped through *Teen People* and *Seventeen* magazine. I was glued to the screen for the early seasons of *The Bachelor* and then *The Bachelorette*. The fairy-tale dreamer in me imagined one day being on the show. I didn't know at the time there were job options behind the camera…like being a producer. I didn't know what a "producer" was. The home economics class at my school (known for its Future Farmers of America program) didn't teach us about those things.

When it came time to decide where I'd go to college, I weighed my options. I knew I wanted to get out of my small town and do something big with my life. I always had a vision of moving to Los Angeles, but had never actually been there, so New York felt like the next best place to launch my move away from home. Jen was going to school there, so I was comfortable with the city, having visited her often.

While my parents were always supportive of our dreams, my dad is a bit old school when it comes to work. He would always say, "You don't have to love what you do. You do what you do so you can do what you love."

My parents came from humble beginnings. Soon after he graduated high school, my dad started working as a recreation counselor at a school for juvenile delinquent boys. When my mom finished college, she got a job teaching there. They became campus "house parents" to the students and lived rent free for the first seven years of their marriage, allowing them to save their money. That led my dad to take a risk by investing in an oil truck. During their off time from school duties, my mom and dad were shoving flyers into the mailboxes around town to launch their new venture. Over the years, my parents built a successful blue-collar business— LaPlaca Oil & Propane.

My dad's decision to go into the heating business was because he loved golfing. He'd work hard during the winters and have summers off to play golf. And hard he worked. He was the guy that would get a call at midnight on Christmas Eve with someone out of oil, and trek through the snow to heat their home. I saw how hard both my parents worked, and I was determined to work just as hard to be successful at whatever it was I was going to do.

My dad tried to convince me to join the army. "Think about it, Julie. You'd be set for life, education paid for, full benefits . . ." Me, in the army? I pondered the idea for a minute, just to get a killer body so I could drop out and be a model. But if there was one thing I knew I didn't want to do, it was join the army.

I thought about all the creative jobs that were business oriented enough to come with a guaranteed paycheck, emphasized by my father. I had fallen in love with Times Square the first time I stepped foot in the concrete jungle as a young kid when our parents took us to see our first Broadway show, *Les Misérables*. All the flashing lights and big billboards caught my attention instantly. If I couldn't be the model on the billboard, perhaps I could be the creative behind the ads? That was what made me decide I would go to school for advertising.

I was intuitively drawn to the Fashion Institute of Technology. Not because I wanted to work in fashion necessarily, but because the Advertising & Marketing Communications program sounded fun and creative, and had a hands-on approach to its teaching. Plus, the campus was in the heart of Manhattan, walking distance to the hottest nightclubs in the city!

I was excited to get out of Goshen and revel in all the opportunities big city life would offer. My biggest fear was who I might be matched with as a roommate. Luckily, Leah and I instantly became best friends. She was from a small town in upstate New York, and less independent in nature. I gladly helped her navigate subway rides and getting around the city. She would always say, "Before I met Julie, I wouldn't even call and order a pizza on my own."

Our first subway ride was to Times Square after moving our things into the dorm room on the second floor of Nagler Hall. Our families went to Carmine's, my parents' favorite Italian restaurant, to grab a bite to eat together. My sister Jen was dating an actor, Josh, at the time, and they joined us for lunch. Jen had told me that Josh had worked the MTV Video Music Awards the previous year, and I couldn't wait to ask him about it.

"Josh! I want to work the MTV Awards!" I exclaimed, after a bite of penne alla vodka. "That would be, like, the dream! Can you hook us up with a gig?!" The awards were at the end of the week.

"I'm not sure. Let me reach out to my contact," he replied casually, like it wasn't a big deal that he might get me the coolest job ever.

"Yay, thank you! What was it you did for them again?" I asked.

"I work with the seat-filler company," he began. "If there are empty seats in the audience, like when an artist grabs their award and goes backstage, we have people on standby to run and fill the seats so it doesn't look empty on camera. We also handle the audience for special performances where they need a designated crowd of people."

"That's so cool! Who knew that was a job!" I said with awe, hopeful it would be my job soon.

And sure enough, it was. Jen called the next day. "Josh talked to his contact. He was able to get you, me, and Leah a day gig at the VMAs!"

"Oh my God, SHUT UP! How cool!" I exclaimed, hopeful I'd be able to play it cool once there working instead of screaming, *I love you Justin!* like I had only four years prior. These were the prime years of MTV, with Christina Aguilera, Britney Spears, Madonna, and Beyoncé all set to perform.

Four days later, Jen, Leah, and I showed up bright-eyed and bushy-tailed at Radio City Music Hall. I was handed an official lanyard at check-in. I had never felt so cool as the moment I put that around my neck. We met our boss, Elizabeth, in the production office backstage. All around us was organized chaos—people running with clipboards talking into flip phones, color-coded papers covering the walls.

"50 Cent and Snoop Dogg just arrived for rehearsal," I heard someone say. How was this real life?

Elizabeth gathered the group of about ten of us to go through the plan for the day. We would be with the outside crew, handling the crowd for the pre-show performances.

"All right, everyone. Grab your crew T-shirts and get your walkies," she said as the meeting wrapped. We put on matching bright purple T-shirts with the MTV Video Music Awards logo on the front, and CREW written across the back. Then we grabbed our walkies and put on our headsets. Okay, now I felt even cooler.

"Um, can you show us how to use this?" I embarrassingly asked Nate, one of the guys we were working with.

"Yeah, of course. When you turn it on, make sure you hear the beep," he began. "On the back of your lanyard there is a channel list. Our team is on five." I moved the knob to channel five.

"Then push that side button there, pause a second, and talk into your headset. Like this." He demonstrated on his. "Walkie check?"

I nodded, confirming I heard him.

"Reply by pressing down and saying, 'Good check,'" he said.

"Oh! Right . . . good check?" He nodded.

After Jen and Leah walkie-checked theirs as well, he warned us to be careful not to "key" our walkies. This happens when someone either accidentally pushes down the TALK button too long while sitting on it, or if the headset cord isn't fully pushed in, blocking the channel and causing everyone to hear your every move. Thus began my fear of being keyed every time I went to the bathroom for years to come.

Our job entailed checking in the casted audience members for the pre-show taking place around the corner in the plaza of Rockefeller Center. We put on their wristbands, escorted them to the bathroom when needed, answered any questions they had (as if I knew the answers), got them hyped up, and made sure the most energetic ones were front and center. The job wasn't brain surgery, but I was still a part of creating a live television show. And not just any live show, but one everyone I knew was about to be glued to their screen watching.

Through the walkie I heard, "All right, we're going live in 10 . . . 9 . . . 8 . . ." A wave of exhilaration surged through me as the adrenaline kicked in. I matched the excitement of the full crowd in front of me as I heard, "And we're live! Have a great show, everyone!"

In a matter of seconds, the whole audience was *shaking dat thing* as Sean Paul, followed by the Black Eyed Peas, performed. I took in the collective energy and joy of the audience, the beaming lights and cameras all around me, and the iconic 30 Rock building as our backdrop. I couldn't believe I was getting paid to be there.

After we were done wrapping up outside, we made our way back into the theater. Elizabeth grabbed us. "You three, take off the purple shirts and go be seat-fillers the rest of the show!" she said as she motioned to us. "Hurry! Quick. The commercial break is ending soon. Run!"

We quickly switched our tops and dashed down the center aisle of Radio City Music Hall to the closest seats in front. We got there just in time, as the lights went out and a spotlight shined on Beyoncé. She descended from the rafters for her very first performance as a solo artist. We danced our hearts out as Beyoncé belted "Crazy in Love." In that moment, I knew I was crazy in love with wherever this job could take me. I was hooked on the rush and excitement of working in television and bringing entertainment to homes across the country. I wanted to be a part of something big. I would do whatever it took to succeed in the wild world of creating TV. If there was such thing as love at first sight, I experienced it that night.

3

If You Can Make It Here, You Can Make It Anywhere

I dove into every production opportunity I could get my hands on after working the VMA Awards. Luckily, Elizabeth liked us and continued to offer work. My freshman year of college, I traveled to Houston to work the Super Bowl halftime show, running a crowd of thousands of kids onto the field to see my man Justin Timberlake and Janet Jackson perform (yes, the infamous nip slip year). I went to Cancún to work *MTV Spring Break*, staying out all hours of the night recruiting spring breakers to come to the shows we were taping. (That's right, Mr. Pratt—I got paid to flirt with guys on spring break.)

Over the next few years, I worked just about every live award show or TV special done in New York. I even paid my own way to Las Vegas and Los Angeles to work shows there, not wanting to miss out on the excitement and opportunity. When I wasn't working with an audience, I was a talent liaison, escorting celebrities to where they needed to be backstage.

I geared my school internships toward production, spending a semester working at *Extra*, the entertainment news show. I got a job as an audience page at the *Hope & Faith* show with Kelly Ripa and Faith Ford. Every Friday, I took the subway to Silvercup Studios in Queens to check in the audience, escort them to the bathroom, and pass out pizza and cookies.

That's where I learned to tie a tie, my required wardrobe, along with a white button-down shirt and black slacks.

I was excited when I finally got to dress cute with coworkers for the holiday work party at a popular nightclub in the meatpacking district. As pages, we were only there once a week and didn't know the rest of the staff well. I was looking forward to socializing with them. While ordering champagne at the bar, I started chatting with a cutie I'd noticed earlier on set, who worked with talent.

"Hey, I'm Mark," he said, leaning casually against the bar. I took in his tall physique, dark wavy hair, and the cute dimples that formed when he smiled.

"I'm Julie. Nice to meet you," I replied.

"You look great. I love your dress," he commented, stepping back to admire it.

"Thank you!" I smiled with a little curtsy. "You know, believe it or not, a tie and button-down isn't all that's in my closet," I joked.

We talked for a while, getting to know each other. He then put his hand out and asked, "May I have this dance?"

"Certainly," I said, letting him guide me to the dance floor.

We joined the others and danced the night away. Near the end of the night, he leaned in for the kiss. We had a passionate make-out session on the dance floor before closing the place down.

The next day, the show was filming. As I arrived to the set, Mark quickly found me. He looked anxious.

"Hey, can we talk real quick?" he asked, motioning for me to step aside, out of eyesight from the others. I followed him to a corner of the sound stage.

"I just want you to know I can't talk to you," he began. "I got ridiculed this morning by everyone for making out with you. Like, completely ripped apart."

"Oh . . ." I said, taken aback. "Uhh, okay . . . all good. Whatever." Not okay, whatever. The ache shot from my stomach to my throat, the signal of hurt I tried to brush off with indifference, my MO with men. What I really was thinking was, *What is wrong with me?! What's the big deal?! Fuck you and the rest of the stuck-up staff who think they are better than me!*

"Okay … cool, thanks," he said, awkwardly. "Sorry … I gotta get back to work now." And off he went.

Now, I'm very aware that making out at a holiday work party probably wasn't the smoothest move on my part. Was I expecting to fall in love with Mark? No. I was fully embracing being single in the city those days and loved all the perks that came with it—going out with the girls for VIP access to the hottest nightclubs and meeting all sorts of interesting people. But did it hurt to be laughed at as the little audience page at the bottom of the totem pole? It sure did. He was Kelly's right-hand man, so I imagined that she—someone I had always admired and looked up to—had been part of the mockery. I felt like I could sense everyone whispering as I handed out slices of pizza on paper plates to the audience. You can pass a slice of shame to me.

I share this story because it was in that moment I vowed to never mix work and pleasure again. Showmances, as they're called in production, are very common. Crew members hook up, especially when traveling together for months at a time, like on *The Bachelor.* Some have ended with marriages (shout-out to *The Bachelor* behind-the-scenes success stories!), while others end awkwardly watching the guy you hooked up with move on to the next new staff member. I stayed true to my vow for a long time after Mark … that is, until I didn't. But more on that later.

In what felt like a karmic moment, a couple years later I ran into Mark at a fitting. I was cast as one of "Charlie's Angels" for a Toshiba commercial set to air in Japan with Yankees player Hideki Matsui. I flaunted my cute little pinstripe baseball style dress to the team as he sat in the background doing whatever day player job he had. *That's right, Mark. Look at me now … I'm a star!*

In actuality, that was one of the biggest modeling/acting jobs I booked my whole career. I wasn't exactly thriving in that world, but I did have an agent during college and tried my best to model on the side. Sometimes I got booked as a fit model at trade shows, wearing the sample-size clothes to attract buyers. I was a size four, and most samples fit well. But the memory that sticks in my mind the most? When a pair of jeans barely snapped, causing my love handles to flop over. I quickly adjusted my shirt to hide the evidence, but it didn't get past the creative director, who gave me a disgusted look and muttered, "I see what you're doing there."

I wished I could starve myself and be skinny-skinny like a "real" model. But I grew up Italian, eating pasta and cannolis. My roommate, Leah, thought I was bulimic our first year in the dorms because I always went to the bathroom to brush my teeth after meals. I just loved having fresh breath after eating (hence my receding gum lines now). I did try once to see if I could throw my food up, though. Maybe it wasn't a big deal to do now and then after a big meal? I knelt by the toilet, put up the seat, and tied back my hair. I stuck a finger down my throat and starting coughing. After a few burps and gags, I gave up. *No, Julie, this isn't you. Just go use the ab machine at New York Sports Club. You love an ab machine!*

It's crazy to think that a size four was considered big in the industry. I was shocked when I got cast for an Axe bodywash launch event at Marquee nightclub, where I had to wear a bikini. I was so insecure about my not-flat-enough stomach. I don't think there has ever been a time when I wasn't sucking my stomach in. My job at the event? I stood on a platform in my bikini next to a male model, and we took turns rubbing Axe bodywash onto each other while people lined up to spray it off with water guns. Clever marketing, but talk about degrading . . . I cringe writing this now. The things we did in the early 2000s! On the plus side, I did make six thousand dollars that night, which at the time felt like winning the lottery. Especially compared to the flat rate of $100 per day for production gigs.

I'm glad to see there has been some change and more inclusivity in modeling today, but with social media, I can only imagine the pressure young girls feel to live up to unrealistic beauty standards curated as they scroll. I remember overthinking what to write in my AIM profile. Now, girls document their every move and feel the pressure to look perfect doing it. My heart is with the younger generation. Likes on a picture don't compare to how beautiful they are as their true, authentic selves. Sometimes, I still need to remind myself of this, as I pinch my love handles wishing they would go away.

While I didn't expect my side hustle as a model to lead to a big career, I was looking forward to moving to Los Angeles after graduating to chase the sunshine, work in entertainment, and live my *The O.C.* dreams (that show influenced my desire to be a Cali girl). Jen had moved out a year earlier for a job at *The Ellen DeGeneres Show* and I thought I'd soon join her, but after graduation I got an unexpected offer. An apparel company offered me a hybrid job: marketing associate, brand ambassador, and occasional model. I never imagined myself working in apparel, but when the owner, David, promised to feature me in their print campaign and send me on work trips to Asia, I couldn't resist. I always had a desire to explore the world, and now I'd get paid to do it.

He kept his promise. Soon I was in Japan with a full glam team, shooting a campaign. It was a dream come true when I saw myself in *Marie Claire* magazine. But that dream didn't come without a price. David always made me feel insecure, sporadically pinching my arm fat and saying, "Too much." I wish I'd said back, "How dare you degrade me and my body! I quit." Instead, I thought to myself, *Ugh, I know. I wish I could lose ten pounds, tone my arms, and be a skinny model. Maybe you should stop taking me to lavish dinners where it's considered rude to not eat everything placed in front of me, huh? Have you thought about that?* Instead, I swallowed my shame and buried it deep inside me.

There was another woman who worked for David whose relationship with him always struck me as . . . layered. Whatever was going on between them made me uneasy enough to steer clear and stay buried in my own work. Still, I couldn't shake the feeling that his enthusiasm for hiring young women wasn't purely about talent. And yes—he was very much married. My suspicions were validated when he crossed the line one night in Hong Kong while at the karaoke bar. He took my hand and started making out with it, trying to make his way up my arm. I pulled back in disgust. I thought my arm was too fat for him, anyway? But there it was again . . . that feeling that men just wanted to hook up with me. I couldn't even be taken seriously in the workplace.

Is this what older men in business did? Did they think they could get away with it? I guess it is what they did, and they did (and do) get away with it. Even in an era when women are encouraged to succeed on their own, it feels like men hold the power. It sickened me, yet also fueled my determination to be the one in power one day. I'm glad I was confident enough to know I deserved better. I never wanted to work for an apparel company, anyway.

When I returned to New York, I put in my notice. I moved to Los Angeles a month later, jobless and determined to succeed.

4

City of Dreams

"Cheers, girls! To following our dreams!" I exclaimed, clinking glasses of Two Buck Chuck with my roomies, Leah and Kelly. We sat on pillows in the empty living room of our new three-bedroom, one-bathroom place in a fourplex off Melrose Ave. I couldn't believe I could see palm trees out my window, something I always associated with vacation. I had found the place on Craigslist a couple weeks prior and knew it was the prime location to be in as newbies to Los Angeles (thanks to a short-lived long-distance relationship with a guy from LA who, shocker, cheated on me). The Fairfax District is like a rite of passage when moving to the city. We were walking distance to Erewhon before Erewhon was cool, could end the night at the local dive bar, The Dime, and stroll to the Fairfax Flea Market on Sundays.

Our building was the ugliest on the block—a faded pea green color with bars on the windows. But it still had some of that old Hollywood charm on the inside, most notably in the bathroom, with the quintessential mid-century mint green and black trim tiles. The scene in *La La Land* of Mia and her roommates getting ready for a night out while singing "Someone in the Crowd" perfectly sums up my early years in LA. To add to the Hollywood cliché, I immediately started waitressing, thanks to our new neighbor hooking Leah and me up with jobs at La Cantina, where he worked.

Coming off my *Sex and the City* years in New York, I had no intention of seeking a relationship. I was enjoying being single and going out with the girls. But I still kept my eyes open for "someone in the crowd." One night at a club, Bardot, I couldn't take my eyes off the DJ spinning tracks. He was tall and slender, rocking a fedora and black leather jacket as he spun a vinyl set. He had bad boy written all over him—my favorite type in my early twenties.

He must have caught my stare, because as my girls and I were heading out, he stepped down from the booth and intercepted me.

"Why are you leaving?" he asked. As I gazed up into his baby blue eyes, I wondered the same thing. It was nice to look up at a guy. Being 5'8" and in four-inch heels, that was a rarity in a town full of short men.

"I don't want to!" I shouted over the music. "I've been loving your set, but we told our friends we'd meet up with them. I can't abandon the group."

"I respect that. Can I get your number?" he asked, pulling out his Sidekick. "I'd love to take you out sometime."

"Of course," I said with a smile.

As he leaned in to hear my number, his skin brushed against mine, sending an electric pulse through my body that matched the electric beats pulsating around us. His scent intoxicated me long after I walked away.

Turns out, Dominic was far from the bad boy demeanor he exuded. I was impressed when he got car service for our first date, pre-Uber days. That night, and the months that followed, I got to know the sweet, sensitive soul beneath the edgy exterior. Dominic was from *The O.C.*, and I may have manifested my very own Ryan Atwood. Like many young, good-looking guys in the city, he was a model / DJ / actor / pro skimboarder. We love a hyphenated job title in our twenties in Los Angeles.

With us being new to LA, he took my girls and me under his wing. Days were spent at the beach with him and his friends, learning how to surf. As the sun set, we danced the night away at his DJ gigs.

Dominic was committed to me early on. I, however, told him I didn't want a boyfriend so soon after moving to LA, even after we had said "I love you." I'd take breaks, go on dates with others, yet always find my way back to him. It wasn't until our conversations took a serious turn that I knew I had to be honest—with him, and myself. One night, we were sitting on his couch having acai bowls, his little Pomeranian, Sophie, curled up on my lap, when he said, "You know, I've been thinking a lot about the future, and what that looks like for us."

My throat tightened. "Oh yeah?"

"You're someone I see myself starting a family with," he began. "I'd like that in the near future. I was thinking it'd be great to take that next step and move in together."

I was silent. What he was saying made perfect sense. We had been together, on and off, for nearly two years. But it was far from what I wanted at the time. I was just starting my career. Moving in meant commitment, and that I could see marriage and kids in our future. Committing to one person was hard for me. Maybe it was my ADHD; maybe it was my shielded heart. Or maybe it was because, deep down, I knew Dominic wasn't my person. His love was unconditional, and he deserved someone who could give him what he desired. I knew that person wasn't me. I was a classic avoidant at that time, and I had avoided the conversation far too long. But now, as he spoke of the future, I had to be honest.

"I'm sorry, Dom," I said, as a tear slid down my cheek. "I wish I could say I want that too. But it's not my priority right now. You deserve someone who can give you a family and that future. My heart just doesn't see that person as me."

He was gracious and loving as we embraced.

"I'm so grateful for our time together," he said. "I'll always love you, Julie."

"I love you, too, and I'm sorry our timing isn't aligned," I said. "I'll always be there for you as a friend."

How do people do it? Get married so young and live happily ever after? I used to think that's what I wanted. My parents married at twenty and twenty-two and were still happy. But I felt like I still had so much to learn about myself. I always felt torn between the hopeless romantic in me and the free spirit that didn't want to lose her independence. I still fantasized about having a love story as romantic as I saw in the rom-coms and fairy tales I grew up watching. But I didn't want to settle until I got that. Until then, I wanted to focus on my career.

When I first moved to LA, I got a part-time gig working for On-Camera Audiences, doing similar audience work as in college. I loved bouncing around to different shows—*American Idol, Dancing with the Stars, Family Feud*—but I craved something with the potential to grow. Jen had started working at *The Doctors*, a talk show co-hosted by former *Bachelor* star Dr. Travis Stork. Five months after I moved to LA, she helped get me a job interview for a production assistant role.

At the interview, my soon-to-be boss warned me, "You should think about whether talk shows are what you want to work on long term. Once you become a 'talk show producer,' that's what you're known for. It's hard to switch to other types of shows."

"Oh, I love talk shows!" I said. "I grew up watching *The Rosie O'Donnell Show, Oprah*, and *Live with Regis and Kathie Lee* and then *Kelly*. I always dreamed of working on a show like that." It was partly true; I did love those shows growing up.

I later learned she wasn't wrong—but I still think it's terrible advice! How are we supposed to know what type of show we want to work on? Isn't that what work in our twenties—heck, throughout our life—is about? Exploring different avenues and seeing what excites us the most; switching paths when we hit a dead end and are bored? I hated the idea of being put inside a box, stuck at one job for the rest of my life.

She did add, "Talk shows are intense and require the most work, so it definitely prepares you to be able to do just about any job." That, I soon realized, was definitely true. Especially on a talk show that wasn't primarily driven by celebrity interviews. *The Doctors* was a daily show hosted by four doctors, covering a wide range of health and medical topics. While I loved working on the Paramount lot, swooning when the men from *Glee* would stroll by in their letterman jackets, the job itself was far from glamorous. I quickly learned the rules of working in entertainment—arrive at the office before your boss and leave after them; lunch breaks don't exist; unless you're on your deathbed, neither do sick days.

As a production assistant, I was doing a lot more than a typical PA. Each week, our team of four produced an hour-long episode. I had to research every topic and come up with the talking points for our hosts. Every Thursday afternoon I had to hand in twelve thick binders with all my research to the executives and hosts. I still have PTSD from jammed printers an hour before deadline. I also helped brainstorm creative ideas and ways to present them—be it through onstage demonstrations, graphic animations, or field shoots. I practically earned an MD my first couple years of the show. Who knew that's what working in entertainment would entail?

I eventually got promoted to an associate producer position, and began working alongside Jen, now a producer. Along with developing the creative show ideas and handling logistics, my main job was booking all the guests to come on the show: pre-interviewing them to find the best candidate, hearing their backstory, planning field shoots, preparing questions for the hosts to ask them, and prepping them for show day.

Some bookings were easy, like when we were offering a free smile makeover with a celebrity dentist. Others felt impossible, like finding someone to talk on national television about their crooked penis. The more outrageous the booking, the better, according to our bosses. Some weeks, I was booking up to twenty guests for just a one-hour-long show. I'd have nightmares before show day, terrified a guest would back out. Most weekends were spent in the office working, due to the demands of the job.

My favorite episodes to produce? The ones about love, sex, and dating! I admired the strong female experts we'd book, like Dr. Wendy Walsh and Emily Morse. Jen and I would crush the Valentine's Day episodes. If you search online, you may find a clip of the effects a breakup has on the body, featuring yours truly. Another favorite was when we produced the "Hottest Doctors of America" episode. Jen and I convinced our bosses to let us create a "hot doctors" calendar for charity. It was a great excuse for a great cause to scout, cast, and flirt with handsome MDs.

Even though the big bosses were men, we had a strong female presence of badass producers at the show. That meant there were a lot of *The Bachelor* fans. During late nights at the office, I'd watch the show with coworkers. We'd play games and make bets, each pretending to be a contestant for the season. During pilot Jake Pavelka's journey, my coworker Alexis got the brilliant idea that I should go on the show. She filled out the online application for me right there and then. Soon after, a casting director reached out, and I found myself at the in-person casting call in Orange County (slightly embarrassing to admit now, but then again, this book is full of embarrassing confessions).

While waiting in the giant hotel ballroom with other hopeful singles, I took advantage of the complimentary makeup booth. Another confession: I was technically still with Dominic at the time, but we were in one of my *I don't want a title* phases. As I sat in the makeup chair, I realized one of Dom's friends from *The O.C.*, who I had just met the week before, was seated directly in front of me, also there for the casting. *Shit!* I thought to myself. I froze and avoided eye contact as I sat in the chair for a long twenty minutes. She definitely saw me.

Guilt sat with me as I was called into the casting room. In hindsight, it would've been a great story to tell the producer during our meeting—they love anything messy. But as the producer sat there with a camera asking me questions about myself, I just feared they'd find out I was seeing someone. I also feared that if she knew I worked in production I would automatically be disqualified, so I stayed vague with my work description, saying I was a researcher. How boring! After about ten minutes of questions about love and why I wanted to go on the show, I was done.

Needless to say, it wasn't written in the stars for me to be on *The Bachelor* for Brad Womack's round two as the lead. Instead, I kept grinding away at work. I didn't love the job, but I was scared to leave a steady gig in production.

I still had my fair share of fun outside of work, going out with the girls, dating, and having casual flings that never turned serious. I even found myself going on a date with a former *The Bachelorette* contestant who spent the whole time talking about being on *The Bachelorette*. There was no second date.

The best perk of working on a talk show? The three-month summer hiatus, a great rollover after college. During the summer of 2012, I took a solo trip to Europe followed by a stop on the East Coast to visit family and attend the wedding of my high school friend Megan. Megan and Matt were getting married at a summer camp I had grown up going to, and their wedding went with adult summer camp vibes. My inner child was thriving, as pre-wedding activities included the ropes course, canoeing, s'mores, and capture the flag.

The wedding ceremony, held at the camp's chapel in the woods, had been transformed into a fairy-tale setting, reminiscent of my childhood castle-in-the-forest dreams. The bride and groom stood at the altar as sunlight glistened through the trees, casting a glow upon their faces. The birds and crickets sang in the background as the pastor began.

During the ceremony, my gaze wandered through the crowd, taking in the expressions of those around me. I smiled at familiar faces and got emotional when I saw others crying. And then...

My eyes stopped in their tracks.

Across the chapel was someone I had not seen the night before. A man. A very handsome man. I swooned from afar, admiring his chiseled jawline that nicely complemented his perfectly tailored suit and sun-kissed brown hair. His light eyes sparkled in the sunlight, as I felt a sparkle within me, knowing I needed to know him.

While I was witnessing Megan and Matt's happily ever after, I began to wonder if this could be the moment my own love story was beginning.

5

Dream Man

There was one tiny problem. The night before I laid eyes on dream man, after a few too many Pinot Grigios, I had made out with the bride's cousin from Rancho Cucamonga. The make-out session went a little too far and I woke up in the morning to a hickey on my neck. A hickey! Who gets those anymore?! I think the last time I had one was probably at summer camp. I prayed that my makeup had done a good enough job covering up the evidence so that the man across the chapel I now had my eyes on wouldn't notice.

I was already over the cousin after he tried a little too hard to come back to my cabin the night before. All day he was like this lingering bug that wouldn't leave me alone, waiting for me outside my cabin as soon as I woke up. Admittedly, I've always known how to lure a man in with some eye fucking and flirtatious banter. That part was fun for me. So was an innocent make-out here and there. But when they think that's all it's going to take to get me in bed, it pisses me off. I mean, at least take me to dinner first …

Jokes aside, I was over casual hookups. Even after waiting my standard three-date rule, it still felt like sex was all men wanted from me. Looking back, I get why casual flings were all I was attracting. I prided myself on being the cool, chill, aloof girl who wasn't needy, clingy, or demanding commitment. Subconsciously, I guess I wasn't ready for

41

commitment, either. Or I hadn't figured out how to express my needs yet, always aiming to please a man and be the cool girl in a man's world. But maybe, just maybe, things would be different with dream man across the way … I just needed to figure out how to ditch the cousin who was sitting next to me now.

As the ceremony commenced and the cousin turned to leave out of the aisle closest to the exit, I quickly pivoted in the opposite direction to get closer to my dream man and hopefully catch his eye. Once we made our way up to cocktail hour, I wasted no time. I grabbed a glass of wine, made my cheese plate, and walked toward him.

"Is this seat taken?" I asked.

"No, all yours," he said with a smirk, motioning to the empty seat next to him.

"Hi, I'm Julie."

"James," he replied.

My heart raced. His name was James! I'd always known my soulmate's name would start with a *J*. My dad is Jerry; my mom is Janice. My dad's siblings are Jeff, Jay, and Ginny (okay, it's a *G* but let's just say Jinny because it still sounds like a *J*). My mom's siblings are Jim, Joanne, Jeanie, and Judy. Jerry and Janice got married and had Jennifer, Julie, and Janelle. My sisters and I have always joked that a prerequisite to dating us is that your name must start with a *J*. Jen almost kept the tradition going with Josh, and then with Justin. However, she was now getting ready to marry Blake this summer. It was up to me to make sure the J tradition carried on. James automatically went into potential husband material.

"You weren't here last night, were you?" I asked.

"No, I just got in from LA. I flew to my parents' house in New York yesterday and drove here today," he said.

My heart grew with excitement.

"Oh, I live in LA too!" I exclaimed. Had I just met an East Coast man who clearly loved his family, lived in LA, and had a name that started with a *J*? This seemed too good to be true. To add to my excitement, I remembered that my parents had met years ago at a summer camp as well, just thirty minutes down the street from where we were now. I mean, what were the odds? Surely, I was staring into the eyes of my future husband. I played it cool.

"Do you know the bride or groom?" I asked, after our living-in-LA small talk.

"Megan and I were good friends in college. We went to Yale together."

And he went to Yale! James was checking all the boxes of my dream man.

I told him I'd flown in from Italy earlier in the week—small flex. I discovered James was Italian as well and shared an equal joy for pasta and wine. Check, check! He proceeded to tell me that his parents had just closed on a villa in Lake Como, big flex. Lake Como? Like George Clooney Lake Como? Could this man get any more perfect? I started to wonder why Megan had tried setting me up with her cousin from Rancho Cucamonga instead of James. Did he have a girlfriend? His interactions didn't give me girlfriend vibes.

James mentioned he was going to drive back to New York that night after the wedding so he could spend more time with his parents before returning to LA. He asked for my number in case the night got away from us and our paths didn't cross again. I loved his initiative, admired his dedication to family, and was in some ways relieved since, had he stayed, I may have become the girl known to make out with two guys during the weekend extravaganza.

James and I went out on our first date the following week when I returned to Los Angeles, followed by another, and another. Being new to LA, he initially said he wasn't looking for anything serious. I played it cool, as I always did. My response? "Okay, then put a condom on it." But of course, it stung.

After a few months of dating, he eventually called me the best girlfriend ever. Did it take him being injected with a bunch of painkillers after I drove him to Cedars-Sinai due to a mysterious pain to finally call me his girlfriend? It sure did, but I was elated. Nothing like caring for a man in pain to lock him in.

Our two worlds soon merged, as my friends became his and his became mine. In between my long hours at the office, we were going to fabulous dinners, spending weekends at the beach, or going on quick getaways. We got along easily and effortlessly, and it wasn't long before we were expressing our love for each other.

I felt like Annie Warbucks when I first went to visit his parents in New York. I was in awe as the gates opened to their beautifully manicured estate straight out of a movie. The tour included the art gallery, tennis courts, movie theater, and my personal favorite—the wine cellar. After his dad showed me the section of "untouchables," we shared a bottle of Barolo that was the first of many glasses of the finest wines we'd share together.

As intimidated as I was by their wealth, James's parents were kind and humble, having come from nothing and achieved the epitome of the American dream. I soon was immersed in their life, pinching myself as I received Gucci purses for Christmas and flew private for family vacations.

James and I were in love and our future seemed so clear. I was in no rush, remaining in the present and enjoying what we had. A marriage and family would come in due time. We were both focused on growing our careers, me in television and him in film.

While I was happily in love with James, I was no longer in love with my job at *The Doctors*. I felt I had learned all I could there and was eager to spread my wings and find something I was passionate about. When it was time to renegotiate my contract, I decided to resign.

At the wrap party, Travis Stork tried to convince me to stay. He went on to tell me how impressed he was with the producers at *The Doctors* and all the hard work and meaningful content we created, saying what a contrast it was to the producers he dealt with at *The Bachelor*, who didn't come close in comparison.

Little did he know, that was exactly the show I had my eyes on.

6

Dream Job

All my life I've been told I am lucky. Living in New York and Los Angeles opened doors to all sorts of extravagant events and magical opportunities. I've always felt grateful for life's blessings, given my simple roots. But the older I get, the more I realize the truth to what my father has always told me: *There is no such thing as luck. You create your own luck.* From a young age I've had the ability to manifest things into existence. Some might call it luck, but I now understand the greater power at play—how I energetically aligned myself with what I wanted, believed it would happen, took action, and released attachment to how it would come to be.

After quitting *The Doctors*, I was determined to work for *The Bachelor* franchise. Happily in love myself, how great would it be to travel the world and help others find love? It was my dream job, and I set out to make my dream a reality. I first reached out to the director of the show, who I'd briefly worked with on *Family Feud* when I first moved to LA. He told me he would send producers my résumé, to which I never heard back. A friend of mine knew someone that used to work there who I met with for coffee. She offered to pass on my résumé, about which I never heard back.

During my work hiatus, I caught up on all my doctors' appointments I never had time for while working at *The Doctors* (the irony). During a visit with my dermatologist, who I had a great rapport with after booking him on *The Doctors,* I mentioned I left the show and was ready to try something new.

"Would you ever want to work on that show *The Bachelor*?" he asked out of the blue.

"Um, yes! That's where I want to work," I exclaimed, taken aback.

"One of the producers came to the office just last week," he said. "I'll do an email intro!"

The next day, he connected me with the co-executive producer of the show. They had just staffed up for the season, and I had just booked a gig on CeeLo Green's new reality show. He said to follow up in a few months when the season wrapped. I made sure to do so, and after Thanksgiving I went in for my interview.

During the interview, they asked me if I had any date ideas. I had heard they might ask this, so I came prepared.

"Yes! One idea I love is a surf to snow date, where they start on the beach and then take a helicopter to a snow-covered mountain," I said. "It's the real beauty of living in Southern California and would be so cool to experience and visually see on the screen."

The two co-executive producers (EPs for short) gave each other a look.

"That's literally on the date board for this season," co-EP 1 said. (I'm just going to reference all my big bosses as EP 1, EP 2, EP 3, and so on going forward … because most went from co-executive producer to executive producer within my first year or two on the show, and there are a lot of them.)

"Oh wow, amazing! I mean, I'd want to go on that date," I replied, excited I was nailing the interview. I was showing them that I was creative and could conceptualize ideas that were fitting for the series, important qualities for the role.

A few days later, they asked if I could come in for a second interview to meet the other EPs. I then landed the job, my dream job. I would be starting as a segment producer on Andi Dorfman's season of *The Bachelorette.* All thanks to my dermatologist. Isn't it fun how the universe works?

Dream Job

The role of a producer can mean a lot of different things depending on the show or movie. In the case of a dating show (I've now worked on a handful of them over the years), at the top are the executive producers. They oversee everything and have the final say on who gets cast, the creative of the episodes, where to travel for the episodes, budget, and so on. Some travel with the cast and crew, calling the shots and acting as the liaisons between the production and the executives at the network (in *The Bachelor*'s case, ABC and Warner Bros.). Some stay in the office and oversee the post department, where there are a team of story producers and editors stringing together the footage that comes in and building out the story that's unfolding.

Then there is a casting department or a casting company that is hired to find potential contestants for the show. They do this through open casting calls, online submissions, scouting, sliding into DMs, and so on. Once they narrow it down to the top contenders, they meet with the team of producers that would be with them throughout filming. In the case of *The Bachelor*, they are flown to Los Angeles so the producers can get a feel for their personality and how they think they would be on camera. This is also when the team runs a physical, medical, and psychological exam to make sure they meet network and studio vetting requirements, along with a background check if it's decided they want to move forward with them.

The casting team then hands the contestants over to the team of cast producers. (The general hierarchy of producers is executive producer, co-executive producer, supervising producer, producer, segment producer . . . with some seniors added here and there in between. Each promotion offers a little more responsibility and final say in the creative.) The cast producers are the ones who work directly with contestants all season. They are with them all the time, conducting their interviews, prepping them for dates, and helping guide them on their entire journey. They are basically their therapists, with no boundaries.

Then there is the date/field team. This was the team I got hired to be on. Our job? Plan all the creative date concepts for the show and find filming locations. What a dream, right?! The truth: While in theory it was my dream job, I was miserable my first season and almost quit. I had heard the show could be cliquey, and I soon found myself feeling like an outcast. No one befriended me, which was hard as someone who usually got along easily with others. And no one really explained to me how things operated, leaving me to figure it out as I went.

It was mostly men on the team, which seemed so strange to me for a show about love and romance predominately watched by women. All the EPs were men, with the exception of one, but she mostly oversaw the logistical side of things and left the creative to the guys. So here I was pitching date ideas to a bunch of men. I did look up to them, however; I admired their insight and feedback and aimed to please and impress. One of the greatest compliments I received was when one of the EPs said, "I wish everyone would pitch dates like Julie does! It would make these meetings much more fun."

I like to think I brought my sparkle and shine to things, making pitch meetings a song and dance performance where, even if the idea was shit, I still entertained them. The most annoying part, though? When they would say no to an idea . . . until it would reemerge a few weeks later as their own. Then, it was brilliant. I can't tell you how many times that happened! (I see the girlies from the office nodding their heads in agreement.)

But my sparkle and shine really did not flourish my first season, as it was dimmed by one of the only women on the team who I worked directly under. Let's call her Negative Nancy. She was so pessimistic, micromanaged every detail, and seemed more concerned with protecting her image than developing her team.

Ironically, we were going to travel to my home state of Connecticut for an episode, partnering with Mohegan Sun casino. Because it was Connecticut, they sent me on the scouting trip with Negative Nancy, co-EP 2, and one of the production coordinators. On scouts, we would meet with our hotel/tourism contacts, see various filming options, and piece together all the elements that would go into that episode. While at dinner one night on the scout, I learned that my first boss's advice may ring true, where "talk show producers" get labeled talk show producers.

"I'm so stressed. I have so much work to do…" Negative Nancy began.

"Well, that's why you have a team to help you, like Julie here," co-EP 2 replied.

Nancy dismissed the suggestion, making it clear she didn't think I had the right kind of experience. She went on about how she wished she had Jack on her team instead—he'd worked on another reality show with her, so she knew he could handle the work. She spoke like I wasn't sitting right there next to her.

What a bitch! I thought to myself.

Jack was the other new employee on the date team that season. While my reality TV experience was limited, I had been working in it the past five months post *The Doctors*, for Lionsgate's unscripted department, and they were so sad to lose me when I got the job at *The Bachelor*. There, I was appreciated, valued, and given real responsibility. Here, I was starting to wonder if I should've listened to Travis's advice and stayed at *The Doctors*, as I felt like I had dumbed myself down for this new job. For my last season at *The Doctors*, I had gotten producer credit, wrote scripts for the show, oversaw and came up with the creative, negotiated trade-outs, booked and prepped guests, and handled all the in-between logistical and creative needs, for an hour-long show … once a week! At *The Bachelor*, it felt like we were talking about the same creative for months leading up to when we finally started filming. Negative Nancy was hoarding all her contacts for dates, giving me basic tasks like making a B-roll and prop lists.

Once the season finally started filming, things got busier. We were at the shoots, making sure everything ran smoothly. We also got no days off. I remember when we were in Italy filming. I checked the call sheet the night before a rose ceremony and saw O/C next to my name (on call). They didn't always make the date team go to rose ceremonies since there were plenty of cast producers there to handle things. I asked Negative Nancy if that meant I was able to have the day off.

"We don't get any days off," she said back to me.

"Oh, okay," I replied.

So, what did I do the next day? I brought my computer to the empty production office and sat there alone all day. That night, I found the nicest Italian restaurant in the town of Abano Terme, where we were staying, and treated myself to a solo dinner and bottle of wine. I later found out Negative Nancy and others on the team went out and explored all day. I felt like the girl who ate alone in high school. Why was she so mean to me? I vowed that when I one day oversaw a team, I would make sure everyone felt seen, heard, and that things were clearly explained to them.

Luckily, by the next season, Negative Nancy had moved on to other projects. With her energy no longer dictating my assignments, I eventually found my groove, was actually given responsibilities, and soon grew to love my job. I was in heaven during *Bachelor in Paradise* season one in Tulum, where I got to test out all the woo-woo activities to see if they would work as dates for the cast. I received shaman blessings, went to temazcal ceremonies, rappelled into cenotes, went horseback riding, and got paid to do it all. I wanted to pinch myself as I watched the waves crashing over the Yucatán, the view from my office.

I was officially a part of the big dysfunctional *Bachelor* family, and I was loving it. I had finally stepped away from the shadows of my sister and made a name for myself. I had figured out a way to be creative and earn a good paycheck doing so.

I worked hard to prove myself over the next couple of years, and eventually I was overseeing episodes and had my own team under me. We were determining the locations and creative from beginning to end of the show, including where each of the dates would film, what the date creative would be, and what was needed to make it come to life. We worked closely with the art and production departments to make sure everything we needed was there, booked and prepped any celebrity/guest experts, and wrote important talking points and beats of the date. We worked closely with location contacts and negotiated trade-out deals with various vendors, from full trades with hotels and tourism boards to feature their destination on the episode, to wheeling and dealing to be able to film at iconic sites around the world. I would delegate specific dates to segment producers on my team and empower them to run with it. We worked collaboratively, and I'm honored that they still call me to this day for advice.

We were traveling for months at a time and working seven days a week. Reality TV doesn't stop for the weekends. I didn't mind it, though, addicted to the adrenaline and chaos of creating the biggest reality show out there.

It seemed like anytime I was back in Los Angeles after filming, I was soon on a plane again scouting our next location. The job security was there, with one show after another between *The Bachelor*, *The Bachelorette*, and *Bachelor in Paradise*. But work was my life.

Somehow this worked for my relationship with James; we are both Aquarians and independent in nature. We agreed that my travels were probably healthy for our relationship, keeping things exciting when we reunited. We made the most of our time together, and occasionally he'd come visit me on location.

As much as I loved my job, I knew it wouldn't be forever. I desired a family of my own someday, and this lifestyle was not sustainable for that. I knew eventually James and I would get married and have kids. I would become a full-time mom who would dabble in creative projects as I so desired. We would live a marvelous life together, with a beautiful home, summers in Italy, and travels around the world, as a family. I daydreamed about this next chapter of my life with joy and excitement. I was putting in the hard work now like the strong, independent woman I was. Yet, having been blessed to have a full-time mom raise me, I had a deep appreciation and admiration for what I believe is the greatest, yet most underrated, job on earth: being a mother. I was grateful to know I'd have the means to be this for our kids one day as well.

The Love Producer

Something I always admired about *The Bachelor* franchise was how we got cast members to quickly open up to one another. Being in a pressure cooker setting, where an engagement after two months is the end goal, it was important to have deep, meaningful, and vulnerable conversations much sooner than you would if you were out dating in the real world. I would witness these vulnerable conversations from behind the cameras and wonder when James would speak to me the way the men on the show were speaking about their lives—excited about an engagement, forever, and starting a family.

James had a bit of what you would call Peter Pan syndrome. While he said he knew I was the person he wanted to spend his life with, he didn't think it would all happen at "such a young age" (we met at twenty-seven). He was still figuring out his career, wanting to succeed in that before the whole marriage and kids thing. I never was one to pressure someone to propose to me. I was patient, focusing on my own thing, yet knew subconsciously if it didn't happen by a certain point, I would leave. Five years was the number that always stuck in my head. Surely, he'd figure his shit out by then, right?

At nearly the five-year mark, I was in Sayulita for *Bachelor in Paradise* with several of the girls from Nick's season, hanging out waiting for a storm to pass so we could continue filming the rose ceremony. We were gossiping about men and love, as we always did. After filming, I would be going to Lake Como with James and his family for our annual summer trip. The difference was that, this year, my parents would be joining us. Everyone was convinced that James would propose to me on the trip.

"It is finally your time, Julie!"

"What a dream it'll be to get engaged in Lake Como!"

"I hope I'm invited to the wedding! Please get married in Como as well!"

These lines echoed from the cast and crew's mouths and into my mind, building up the idea of the proposal. Danielle Maltby, one of the contestants, even said it was written in the cards, as she pulled out her tarot deck and did a reading. The producer in me began to imagine how it would all go down.

We would be at Villa d'Este, our favorite hotel. He and I would go for a stroll through the beautiful gardens before arriving at the lake's edge. It would be magic hour, with pink and orange skies casting a sweet glow onto the lake. Our parents would watch from a distance as James got down on one knee and confessed his love to me, ending with the phrase I'd desired for so long... "Julie, will you marry me?"

The Villa d'Este singers would serenade us with Frank Sinatra as we'd dance the night away, celebrating with our family and capping the night off with fireworks over the lake. It would be as picture perfect as any *Bachelor* proposal I had produced.

How lucky would I be to have the perfect engagement? It was finally my time, as the cast exclaimed. Surely, I was about to manifest my biggest dream yet.

Or was I?

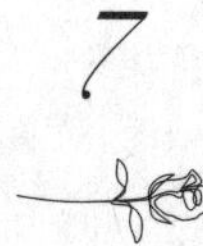

7

The Breakup

While there were garden strolls and fireworks at Villa d'Este in Lake Como, they were not accompanied by a proposal. It was disappointing, but not surprising. At least James and I were finally going to be moving in together in a month's time (yup, it took five years). After our return from Como, I had boxes ready to start packing up my apartment and had already given away my couch.

First, I had a quick trip to Montreal for my friend Lina's bachelorette party. While there, I shared a room with two of my closest friends, Leah and Taylor. As we were getting ready to head out for the night, I casually said, "I feel like James has this whole other life and group of friends I don't even know about since I'm away all the time."

The two of them gave each other a look that made me brace myself.

"What?" I asked with concern. There was a pause. "Just tell me!" I emphasized, feeling my body tense, a familiar lump rising in my throat.

"I mean, it was probably nothing…" Taylor began, deflecting. "There was just this girl at Drew's birthday party that none of us knew. She and James seemed very flirty…"

Leah chimed in now. "The girl was there with another friend who made a comment to me like James and her were dating. I went up and pinned him against the wall and started yelling at him! I said Julie is my best friend—don't you dare do anything to hurt her! He said he wouldn't, but it made us all uncomfortable. They kept going back to his room."

A wave of nausea surged through me. Drew was our friend who became James's once we started dating. While I was in Mexico for *Bachelor in Paradise*, he had thrown his birthday party at James's beach pad.

"Why are you just telling me this now?" I asked, wondering if they would have even said anything if I hadn't made that comment. (Note to ladies: Say something to your friends!)

"We didn't want to ruin your trip to Italy," Taylor admitted. "And honestly, we didn't actually see anything happen, so we didn't want to make it a bigger deal than it might have been. But you should definitely talk to him about it."

"Oh, I will," I replied, as the hurt sank in.

I waited until I returned from Montreal to confront James. He was in New York for the week, so it began as a phone conversation.

"So, we need to talk about something," I said, nervously, lying on my bed hugging my pillow.

"What's up?" he asked. I took a deep breath.

"I heard there was a girl at Drew's birthday, and things were flirty and suspicious between you two …"

"Oh my God, I can't believe they brought that up," James said, defensively. "Your friends are ridiculous. Nothing happened. We were just partying …" He went into full defense mode, bashing my friends for making a big deal over nothing.

"If it was nothing, why didn't you mention it to me before they did?" I asked.

"Because there was nothing to talk about," he said, before ultimately admitting that he sometimes missed the chase, flirting, and being single. He was starting to panic now that I was moving in, knowing he should propose soon.

We decided to put the conversation on hold until he came back to LA. All week I was a restless, emotional mess, knowing what needed to be done. When he returned, he came over to my place. We hugged, quietly walked past the couch-less living room, and into my bedroom to talk. I actually believed him when he said nothing had happened. I was always overly trusting and chill in our relationship. Whether anything happened or not, it didn't fix the deeper issues at hand. The Peter Pan symptoms weren't going away, and I knew he'd never be ready to "settle" until he achieved some level of success in his career.

He suggested we delay moving in together. I laughed. He then suggested we take a month break.

"I know a lot of friends happily married now that took a break and it was beneficial for their relationship in the long run," he said.

Oh, so you can go fuck a bunch of girls and then come back? No thank you . . . I thought to myself, instead saying, "I think you're going to need a lot more than a month to figure yourself out, James." We both started crying, knowing it was over. I had so much empathy for him in that moment. In the midst of my sadness, I felt sad for him. He was lost, and while I wished I could help him, it wasn't my job to do so.

"I guess I didn't realize how much you being away all the time affected me," he said, admitting that flirting with other girls was his way of seeking validation, to fill the void while I was away.

"All I ever wanted was for you to ask me to stay," I said, looking into his eyes as the tears coursed down my cheeks. I wanted to set roots and grow our life together. Why had he not desired that? Would any man ever desire that?

I walked him to the door and we embraced in a hug, neither of us wanting to let go. Once he was gone, I curled up in bed and cried until I fell sleep.

Less than a week later, I was on a plane to scout our next destination for work. Can you guess where we were heading? As we would tease at the end of an episode: *Ladies, it is time to grab your passports and say au revoir to America, as we are heading to the most romantic city in the world, the city of love, Paris!*

That's right, right after the biggest heartbreak of my life, I was on a plane to Paris to scout for Ari's season. The poetic misery, to be in Paris with a broken heart. I longed for my Carrie Bradshaw moment on the Pont des Arts bridge. James would fly to Paris and find me there. "Julie, you're the one," he'd exclaim, just as Big did. But James never came.

Instead, I found myself at the Gucci duty-free store at the Paris airport. Inspired by Carrie Bradshaw herself, I coped through retail therapy. It was an empowering moment as I made the first designer splurge of my life. James's family had introduced me to the finer things in life, and I was determined to be able to provide that lifestyle for myself going forward.

When I returned to Los Angeles, I had a week to pack up my apartment and be out. Thank God for my sisters and friends; otherwise, I might still be surrounded by boxes and pots and pans, crying on the kitchen floor. Somehow it all got packed and put in a storage unit, and I was officially homeless.

Not really, thankfully; I temporarily moved into my sister Jen's house with her family. I was only there a short while before leaving for two months for work, which ended up being a good distraction from the pain. When I returned, I was commuting nearly two hours each day from Glendale to the west side for work. In hindsight, I'm not sure what was worse, the breakup or this new commute, knowing that had James and I moved in together, I would've been living on the beach just ten minutes from the office.

I was intentionally torturing myself during the long commute, listening to love songs and crying. Ed Sheeran's "Perfect" had just been released. Can you name a more perfect song to ball your eyes out to on long drives to the office after heartbreak?

Then something miraculous happened. I tried hypnotherapy. My sister Jen had started going to school to be a hypnotherapist since being a television producer wasn't an ideal career as a mother. She first discovered hypnotherapy as a last resort for her TMJ pain. Shocked when the pain vanished after three sessions, she decided to share this magic as a new career. Jen asked if she could practice on me. I agreed, though I insisted I wasn't hypnotizable.

"It's impossible to quiet my rambling mind," I declared.

"Everyone is hypnotizable," she assured me, talking through common misconceptions. We decided to focus on helping me get over James.

After my second session, the shift happened. I found myself singing out loud in the car as I stumbled upon the early 2000s Sirius station the next morning. At work, my friend Hillary asked if I'd move in with her. She was twenty-seven, the age I'd been when I met James. I reminisced about how much I loved my life pre-James, feeling a new spark of excitement to return to single Julie in the city.

On the car ride home that night, "Perfect" came on the radio, again. It felt different this time, as I sang the lyrics aloud with a new sense of hope. One line in particular struck a chord in my heart, and that's when it clicked. James and I never danced barefoot in the grass. He wasn't really one to get his feet dirty, if you know what I mean. I grew up with my feet in the dirt. And, while I say this more as a metaphor, I realized that, while with James, I suppressed parts of my free-spirited, quirky self, trying to blend in with his lifestyle. You know where my release was for that side of me? Work. I was fortunate I had a job that embraced my weird, creative, curious ways. Maybe I had been living two different lives as well? I mean, did I even like Gucci? I've always been more of a vintage girlie. It all seemed so obvious now. I would not settle until I met a man who would grab me and dance barefoot in the grass. And if it was raining, even better.

Almost back to Glendale, a text from my sister popped up.

Jen: Julie, did you sing in the car today?

Me: Uh yeah, why?

Jen: Oh good, the hypnosis worked :)

Me: What are you talking about?

Jen: Last night in hypnosis I told you that you would sing joyously in the car and remember how much you love your single life.

I read the text in disbelief. I had no recollection of these suggestions, thinking I had fallen asleep during the session. That's when I became a true believer in hypnosis and was ready to embark on this new "single" chapter. Oh, and you know what else helped me move on quickly? Finding out that the girl at the party, the one James was "just partying with," had stayed the night with him. Ouch.

While I was embracing being a strong single woman, on a deeper level the belief that men don't choose me built up inside. I guarded my heart, repeating the mantra from my youth: *All the women who independent.* I moved into a new place in West Hollywood, jumped on Raya, and had fleeting flings in between my travels for work, ignoring that deep desire for something meaningful. Between work and casual dating, I didn't have time to heal so that I could open myself up to love again. Instead, I lived out of a suitcase and put all my time and energy into helping others open themselves up to love, on TV. Work was my focus, and I was going to keep climbing that producing ladder.

But in the back of my mind, my age was starting to linger over me. James and I broke up when I was thirty-two. I was never in a rush to have kids, but I assumed by my mid-thirties it would happen. Yet, each season of the show, the contestants were getting younger and younger as I was getting older and older.

I've never been one who needed a man to be happy. I've always had a pretty full cup of love with family and friends. While it was hard being away from them all the time, I found meaningful connection with co-workers who had become family and with all the new friends I'd make during our travels around the world. Connecting with others always came naturally to me, often sparking deep and meaningful conversations with strangers in the streets. I like to think I've always led my life from a place of love and curiosity, making it easy for others to open up to me.

Maybe that's why it hurt so bad when I got a new role at work and suddenly everything felt ... disconnected. It all began with Ms. God Bless This Mess, Hannah Brown.

8

Bless the Distress

I sat on the floor of my hotel room, gazing out the window at the New England winter coastline—the empty harbor with boats packed away for the season, an American flag waving in the distance, and the slight crashing of waves against the rocky shoreline as the sun was beginning to set. I was in Newport, Rhode Island, scouting for an episode that would be filmed there in a couple of months. Pamphlets and notes from the day were spread across the floor as my phone rang. It was my boss.

"Hello!" I said.

"Julie! You have all of us on the phone," EP 1 said, followed by hellos and heys from EPs 2, 3, and 4.

"Oh. Hi, everyone! How's it going?" I asked, wondering why they were all on the call.

"Good. We've been thinking a lot about what you said to us," they began. The previous month I'd had my usual postmortem meeting after we finished filming Colton's season of *The Bachelor*. I expressed that I was feeling a bit stuck in my current position. There were two supervising producers above me on the date team who were never leaving, giving me little room to grow. I was starting to get that five-year itch like I had at *The Doctors*, ready to spread my wings and try something new.

"We see your talents extending beyond planning dates and getting trade-outs," they continued. "You're someone we can see running the show one day."

"Thank you for saying that. It means a lot," I responded, flattered by what I was hearing. I also wondered what the punch line was.

"We were thinking, this season we'd love for you to be the Bachelorette's producer." Ah, there it was! Me? The lead's producer?! I was shocked.

They continued, "The team would be you and Derek, co-producing together, as equals, and Brittany as your handler."

Typically, this was a role someone from the cast team would get promoted to, not from the date team. Derek was coming from the cast side, but me … that sure was a plot twist. While both teams got along and were friends, there was always a hint of competitiveness. As date producers, we were handling a lot of logistics and long-term prep; there were times during the offseason I was getting up at 2 AM to have calls with Asia trying to find a hotel partner. We were the ones who planned fun dates! They were the ones who created drama!

But, in reality, I was always a little envious of the cast side of things, especially the team with the lead. As a storyteller, I loved seeing how their journeys unfolded and the pivotal role their producers had in it. The hopeless romantic in me will never die, and I legitimately got excited seeing their feelings grow and watching them fall in love. As someone who values authentic connection, I felt a quiet longing as I'd watch producers become close with the cast member they were working with. I was excited for this opportunity I never saw coming.

"Oh, wow! I was not expecting you to say that. But yes, I'd be honored! How fun!" I responded.

"Things have been getting a little stagnant on the show, and we really like how weird and quirky you are," they said. "We want you to just be exactly who you are with whoever the lead ends up being. Less rules, more weird!"

"Well, that I can certainly do," I said with confidence. I always got excited about the little, silly things in life. On scouts, I might randomly start running through a field with a flock of birds, hug a beautiful tree the cast could sit under, bust out into dance down cobblestone streets, or do cartwheels along the mountaintops. I liked to see the wonder in everything around me.

The timing of this news wasn't ideal, as I was currently scouting with the date team. But I made sure to wrap everything up and pass on my contacts to the rest of the team once we returned to LA.

Being with the lead meant I would be with them all the time, prepping them for dates, doing their interviews, and guiding them on their entire journey for love. I was excited to start this role on a *Bachelorette* season. I'm a girl's girl. If there is one thing I'm good at, it's chatting with my girls about boys and dating. I didn't plan to go into filming with any method or strategy. They just wanted me to be me, and I was hopeful to form a real bond with the Bachelorette so I could help her navigate falling in love like I would a friend.

Hannah Brown had been the seventh runner-up on the previous season of *The Bachelor*. Usually, they pick a Bachelorette who was second or third runner-up, as fans see their heartbreak and are really rooting for them. But my bosses saw something in Hannah and decided to move forward with her.

We did things a little differently when sharing the news, wanting to capture it on camera so fans could see her genuine reaction. Derek and I flew to Alabama for what she thought was just a meeting. Chris Harrison then FaceTimed her, a camera busted through the front door, and we filmed her finding out she was the lead. She cried tears of joy when he told her, as did I from behind the camera.

Hannah had started to break through her picture-perfect "pageantry" ways during Colton Underwood's season, admittedly calling herself a hot mess express. I was excited to see her come into her own as the lead of our show. After the shoot, we sat on her bed, talked about boys, looked through old photo albums, and came up with ideas about where we could shoot when we returned to Alabama to film her intro package.

I wish I could say that day was the start of a fun season together. Unfortunately, it was not. Hannah and I had a bit of a love-hate relationship over the couple months that followed. I didn't actually hate her. If anything, I so desperately wanted her to like me. Instead, I was often left feeling dismissed. I say this not to bash Hannah. I didn't have the pressure she was going through during filming. We all are the way we are based on our own trauma, upbringing, and conditioning. But I have to be honest—that season was really hard for me.

I've since discovered that I am an empath. So, not only did I carry the weight of my own emotions while working on the show, but I absorbed all of Hannah's emotions as well. I didn't know the tools to protect my energy. Add the fact that I was getting an average of four hours of sleep a night, and it was a recipe for disaster.

My breaking point came just a few weeks into filming, when we traveled back to Rhode Island for the fourth episode. Luckily, my parents had driven from Connecticut with their friends to attend the concert Hannah and her date would be going to after their dinner. Derek and I decided to finally give each other a break, and I took the night off to meet my parents for dinner. As I walked into the restaurant and embraced them with a hug, the tears streamed down my face.

"I'm so glad you're here," I said, getting choked up. "I've missed you both so much."

"We missed you, too, honey," my mom said. "I don't like seeing you so upset. What's going on?"

"I just don't know what to do," I said through the tears. "I'm so unhappy. I don't know why she doesn't like me. I'm trying so hard and have been nothing but kind to her. I'm so tired—all I want to do is sleep. My left eye hasn't stopped twitching for the past two weeks . . . Is that normal? I feel like I'm falling apart."

My parents would have fully supported me if I wanted to quit. The thought crossed my mind that week. But I'm not a quitter. I always need to see things through. Work was my life, and I could never let my bosses down. But was it worth it?

They listened with compassion as I finally unleashed all my bottled-up emotions. I usually held everything inside as I helped others work through their emotions. This wasn't something I just did at work. This was a characteristic of mine overall, helping everyone else, offering them advice, being a shoulder to cry on. But if I needed support myself, I felt like an inconvenience.

My dinner was cut short when I received a text from Brittany:

Hey, do you have Hannah's hairbrush?

Oh no, I thought to myself, feeling a ping of anxiety. I slowly unzipped my backpack and there it was . . . her favorite hairbrush.

I texted back:

I sure do, oops. I'll head back soon

knowing that suggesting she use another hairbrush wasn't an option.

I had a moment alone with Hannah during that episode. I took the daytime portion of a date, and it was just her and me in the SUV while driving to the dock where she would meet Tyler. I wasn't feeling great after overhearing her complain to the EPs about me.

"You know, you and I are a lot more alike than you realize," I said. "It'd be nice if you would just give me a chance." She seemed to be listening as I spoke but just stared out the window. I didn't understand why she would go to the male executives for things over me, a girl that could actually relate to what she was going through.

Things did get better after Rhode Island. When Hannah was pleasant, I really enjoyed my time with her, and we had a lot of fun. There was a part of her that reminded me of my younger self. She could be equally as quirky and weird, and some of my favorite times were when we were totally ridiculous together, skipping through the airport, doing silly dances, or communicating through just "meows" for an hour straight leading up to a cocktail party in the Netherlands. That's right—we fully embraced our inner felines that night, crawling around on all fours.

There were other perks to working with the lead as well. This mostly included flying business class, being able to order room service instead of crew meal, an SUV over a fifteen-passenger van, getting massages and mani/pedis with her, and having everyone be at your beck and call for things. I appreciated that part of the job! But trust me, it was well earned.

When coworkers would comment, "Are you holding up okay, Julie? You look like you've aged ten years," that didn't feel great. Was I still pretty? I didn't feel pretty. My pants were starting to get tighter from stress eating and snacking to keep me awake during late-night shoots. Workouts were nonexistent. I was making sure Hannah had no boogers in her nose or food in her teeth, spritzing her with Listerine spray so that she looked and felt great during dates. I stood in the shadows, listening to their vulnerable conversations with one ear, and my bosses' voices in the other, as one man after another confessed their love to Hannah. It still got me every time, with a gentle tear of admiration rolling down my cheek.

Yes, they really did fall in love (not all, but some!). No, the show is not scripted. Think about it for a moment. Imagine removing all your outside distractions—phone, work, social media, barhopping, nagging parents. You're put in an environment where oxytocin is released on a regular basis as you travel the world going on extravagant dates with a desirable leading lady or man. You spend hours on end in the interview-turned-therapist chair, talking about love and heartache. You are pushed to be vulnerable, wear your heart on your sleeve, and have the serious discussions about your wants in a partner, early on. You're having conversations it may take a year to have when dating in the real world. And sure, the bubble often pops when you have to take the real-world things into account, like geographic location for starters. But even when that happens, the journey the show takes you on, the falling in love, the person you become, is often still worth it, in my humble opinion.

That bubble sure did pop, though, after I witnessed Hannah get engaged to Jed on the rolling hills of Crete, as I sat on sheep shit scattered across the ground while behind the camera. For those that didn't watch, the engagement ended soon after when she discovered he had a girlfriend when he first came on the show. For the record, I was always team Tyler Cameron (Hannah's second runner-up and forever a Bachelor Nation favorite). While that love story didn't age well, I do believe the journey Hannah went on as the Bachelorette changed her as a person. She evolved out of her "need to be perfect" ways and into her true, authentic self, learning a lot in the process. Somehow, a religious girl from Alabama came out of her season a sex positive, strong feminist representing women all around the country.

I'd like to think I helped play a role in her growth. When someone from the post department told me my personality really shined through her on the screen, I was proud. But it also had me wondering: When would it be my time to shine? When would a man choose me as my authentic self? Would I fall in love again before I aged another ten years?

As the season wrapped and I flew from Greece back to LA, I really did feel like I had knocked a decade off my life. As I returned to my apartment, that feeling hit home in ways I couldn't have imagined.

9

Bachelorettes, Proposals, Wrinkles, and Catching Bouquets

I wheeled my two large, coastal blue suitcases down the corridor of my motel-style apartment, overlooking a lonely little pool in the center of the courtyard. I flicked on the lights as I entered my unit and made my way to the kitchen for two glasses of water—one for myself, and one for my plants, in an attempt to save the ones that had clearly died while I was away.

I went to the bathroom to brush my teeth. As I was brushing, something caught my eye in the mirror. *No, it can't be,* I thought to myself, leaning in for a closer look. *Oh my God, it is!* Panic ran through me. I quickly spit out the toothpaste, put my brush down, and took my hands along the part line of my hair. There, toward the front of my scalp, was my very first gray.

"No, no, nooo…" I started to cry as I stared into the mirror. "Whyyy?!" Despair was kicking in.

"You are beautiful, Julie. It's just one gray. You will be okay," I said, trying to trick my mind with positive affirmations. I then started analyzing my face more closely. I burrowed my eyebrows together and apart, noticing lines forming in between. I pufffed my cheeks out to try to erase my smile lines.

Dammit, why have I smiled so much in my life? I thought to myself. *I'm way too expressive in my face. I need to have less expression going forward if I don't want these wrinkles to thicken!*

I had held off on getting Botox or fillers thus far in my life, even when I got multiple free offers during my *The Doctors* days. "It's preventive," they would say. I was in my mid-twenties and thought they were absolutely crazy. What is with this Hollywood bullshit? I wanted to age naturally, gracefully, although it was getting hard to resist as I saw contestants in their twenties and coworkers younger than me, with their "preventive" injections. But I hated needles. The thought of Botox, egg freezing … it all terrified me.

I stripped down to take a shower. As I glanced at my naked body in the mirror, all I could think was, *I wish my stomach was flat like Hannah's.*

"You are beautiful, Julie!" I said one more time to my mirror reflection.

As I stepped under the running hot water, I felt like I was washing away all the toxic energy from the season. I took a deep breath and allowed myself to enjoy this moment, this cleansing, a coming back to my soul. I was finally home, and able to care for myself for a bit.

I lathered my hair with my good shampoo, which I'd forgotten to pack for my travels, giving my scalp and temples a gentle massage to ease away the tension. The suds built up in my hands, and as I put them out in front, something else had built up as well. I took the wet, large clump of hair in my palms and pressed it against the shower wall. I had gotten used to it at this point, with every rinse sacrificing chunks of my dirty blonde locks. It still caused a tightness in my chest, as I tried to wash away the ways my body was speaking to me. *Hopefully my gray will fall out with the next round*, I thought.

Maybe it was time I took dating more seriously. No man was going to want me once I was gray, thin haired, and wrinkly. While I was content with my single life, I feared waking up one day old and alone. As I lay down in my bed that night, I opened dating apps and started swiping.

Bachelorettes, Proposals, Wrinkles, and Catching Bouquets

It always felt strange returning home after months on the road. It's hard to explain to friends what I just went through. Part of me wanted to see everyone, squeeze in dates while I could, and take full advantage of the time I had in LA before getting on another plane. Another part of me wanted to retreat to my bed and enjoy my time alone.

I had a packed schedule before taking off again in two weeks to film *Bachelor in Paradise*. I still had to go into the office, attend my sister's engagement, and get on top of planning my best friend's bachelorette party. I was going to roll over from one maid of honor duty to the next. But I owned those duties with pride and enjoyed them. I mean, I did work on a dating show, after all. Love is my middle name.

The following week I witnessed my younger sister get proposed to on a hot air balloon in Temecula. When they landed, our whole family was waiting at the bottom to celebrate.

"I'm so happy for you, Janelle!" I said, squeezing her tight and admiring her ring. She and her fiancé had a beautiful one-year-old daughter together, and I was so glad to see her family dreams coming true.

Right after my sister's celebration, I was on a plane to Mexico for the next month. (The post-Stagecoach love triangle drama ensued that summer.) I hung out with cast on the beach and talked for hours on end in the interview chair about love, dating, and fuck boys. Even with all the fuck boys that appeared on the beach, we had seven happy couples walk away from paradise hand in hand, two of which are happily married today. Pretty good odds for a reality show, if you ask me.

Right from paradise, I returned to Rhode Island, this time for my best friend's bachelorette party. We played pin the kiss on the dick, drank out of penis straws, and I rocked my Bae of Honor swimsuit. I loved celebrating the love of the closest people in my life. I really did. It made me happy and warmed my heart to see them finding their happily ever after.

I stayed on the East Coast for a couple weeks after that, hopping on a ferry from Connecticut to Montauk to celebrate the Fourth of July weekend with my girl Natasha. Natasha and I had met while working at *The*

Doctors together years ago, but she sadly had moved to New York a few years back. I was glad to reunite with her for a weekend of fun in the sun with East Coast men. She had just quit her job and was figuring out what was next for her. One day we were lying out at the pool on her friend's beautiful estate, with its perfectly manicured green grass, when I decided I knew what was next for her.

"Natasha, you should really be on *The Bachelor*. You would crush it," I declared.

"Girl, you know I don't watch those shows—no offense," she said.

"No, seriously, like, why not?!" I began. "And if things pan out the way I think they are going to, you would totally vibe with our upcoming Bachelor."

She turned to me and lowered her shades, raising her eyebrows. "Didn't you say this to me last year, too, Ms. LaPlaca?"

Okay, I confess. I had planted the seed that she should be on before Colton's season, but clearly no girl was right for him (he came out as gay).

"Yeah, yeah, that was a lapse in judgment. But the next Bachelor is, like, so cute, and really fun," I said. "Your energies together would be contagious!"

She laughed. "Eh . . . I'll think about it."

When I returned to LA the following week, I welcomed the city's newest resident, Hannah Brown. After all we'd gone through, she was like a younger sister to me. I helped get her set up with a publicist and an agent, get professional photos done, and settle into her new place. Outside of the chaos of filming her season, I rather enjoyed hanging out with her. I appreciated that she was self-aware of how mean she had been and acknowledged her shortcomings.

As summer was coming to an end, I returned to Connecticut for my best friend's wedding, where I crushed the maid of honor speech and caught yet another bouquet. The whole idea that the woman who catches the bouquet will be the next to marry was really starting to lose its merit.

The next week, it was time to meet with our new Bachelor, Peter Weber. My life since then, well, hasn't quite been the same.

Part Two

THE DRAMA

10

Pilot Pete

Peter Weber was the third runner-up on Hannah Brown's season, leaving Greece heartbroken and emerging as a fan favorite who deserved love. He also became a bit of a sex icon amongst Bachelor Nation after Hannah confessed that they'd had sex four times in a windmill during fantasy suites.

When Peter was chosen as the Bachelor, we met at a café in Studio City to talk about the adventure to come. I had met him during Hannah's season but we hadn't spent much one-on-one time together, as I usually was watching him and Hannah make out from behind the camera.

As soon as Peter and I sat down for lunch, we immediately clicked on a personal level. He felt like an old friend I'd known for years. His favorite book was *The Secret*, and he was a big believer in the power to manifest dreams into existence. He said he manifested being the Bachelor on the show, and I believed it wholeheartedly, sharing my own stories of manifesting over the years.

Peter had a genuine, pure heart that struck me. I sensed that he really did want to find love, get married, and start a family. There was an innocence about him, and his optimism reminded me of myself before my heart had been hurt. His glimmer of excitement was like that of a kid about to enter the candy store, cute and a bit naive. He wanted to have the most beautiful love story the world would ever see and I really hoped we could deliver that for him.

Our first shoot together was for his intro package, or backstory. Peter grew up fifteen minutes from *The Bachelor* mansion and was practically neighbors with Chris Harrison. We did a fun shoot where Peter and Chris drove around the neighborhood, highlighting spots from Peter's upbringing that were meaningful. The tour finished at the Webers' family house where Peter grew up, and still lived, because Peter still lived at home with his parents…

Walking into the Webers' house, I understood why he never left. I instantly felt at home. The warmth and love reminded me of my own upbringing. Family photos and motivational art from HomeGoods lined the walls, just like at my parents' house. The aroma of a home-cooked meal filled the air, with my Italian family's macaroni dish replaced with a taste of their Cuban roots: ropa vieja with rice and beans. The love shared over a home-cooked meal with lots of laughing and dancing brought a warm familiarity to my heart. Peter's mother, Barb, and I were instantly best friends. They immediately made me feel like I was family.

When Peter and I stepped outside to do our first interview together, we both shed a tear as he spoke of his hopes and desires for love. "I have a feeling we are going to get along well, Jules," he said.

"I agree," I replied, smiling through the tears of joy, truly excited for the adventure to come with him.

As the lead's producer, I was with Peter almost every waking hour. Derek had gone back to the cast team, so I was no longer co-producing, but the head producer with a team beneath me. Brittany was now my segment producer, there to assist and jump in for interviews as needed, and Michael was our handler, dealing with logistics, meals, and making sure Peter was ready on time.

Part of my job was making sure Peter was comfortable opening up, being vulnerable, and sharing his heart and feelings with me. While this can be challenging if you don't naturally connect with the person you're producing, with Peter, it was effortless. I found myself opening up to him equally, as we'd sit in the interview chair for hours, talking about our hopes, dreams, love, heartache, and desires for the future. He showed a genuine interest in getting to know me, sometimes turning the questions in my direction.

"Would you ever get back with your ex, James?" he asked. "I have a feeling you'll end up together again."

"No, I think that ship has sailed," I replied as I sat in the chair next to the camera rolling beside me, pointing in Peter's direction.

"Why so?"

"I believe when a relationship ends, it's usually for a good reason," I responded. "I'm grateful for my time with him; I really am. But I have a stronger understanding of myself and what I deserve now. He was pretty selfish in the relationship. And I think, when I was with him, I lost a bit of my sparkle." I gave a little wink.

"Well, you deserve someone who makes you shine," he said.

"Thank you. I'm hopeful he's out there." I smiled. "I would like to get married and have a family one day. When I'm done helping all of you guys find love!"

"Do you see yourself staying in California?" The questions continued.

"Yeah, I think so. Both of my sisters are out here and have kids, so they aren't going anywhere," I reflected. "But ideally, I'll be bicoastal, with a spot on the East Coast near my parents for summer vacations."

"Yeah, same. I can't wait for you to come to our family's cabin on the lake in upstate New York. You're gonna love it!"

"And you're going to love Connecticut!" I responded. "The stars on a clear summer night are unbelievable. We'll have a bonfire in the yard, and my dad will make his homemade pizza and wine. You guys are going to love each other."

"I can't wait to meet him!" he said with a smile.

When the cameras weren't rolling, it still felt like I was hanging out with my best friend. Upon reflection, I realized I was more vulnerable and open with Peter than I had been when I was with James for five years. I was comfortable being my authentic self, without the shield and filter I put up in romantic relationships. I sincerely cared about Peter, and he cared about me.

Peter even started campaigning for me to be the next Bachelorette. While I knew the likelihood of having a producer be the star of the show was slim to none, especially at the 'ripe' age of thirty-four, having the lead thinking about *me* in the middle of their chaotic journey really touched me.

During our time filming, I didn't look at Peter romantically. I took my job seriously and focused on delivering the best possible season. I would tell him he looked hot before a date, but it was more in an older-sister-hyping-up-her-younger-brother way. I was six years Peter's senior. Most of the girls on the show were in their early twenties. Their being six years younger than him seemed normal, but when it comes to younger men dating older women, that's less the norm. The only contestant older than Peter was my girl Natasha, who I was able to convince to come on the show just a couple weeks before filming. (No, she was not a producer plant as some online sleuthers declared. Did I downplay how good of friends we were to my bosses? Sure did! But hey, producers' friends deserve love too!)

In a world where women seem to be waiting longer and longer to get married, it seemed crazy to me that these contestants were getting younger and younger. But as I was quickly approaching the official mid-thirties mark, my age was really starting to hit me. I wondered if the narrative I'd been fed of being a girl boss who can have it all was bullshit. Maybe these young southern belles looking for a husband were onto something?

I mean, sure, I had a decent savings in my bank account, but I didn't have a house with a yard. I didn't have a man, kids, a 401(k), or Roth IRA. All that stuff would come when I was an adult. Shit, when did I become an adult? Did I forget to plan for my future as my future hit me in the face? I was never a planner. I was a live-in-the-moment kind of girl! But I was starting to fear my moment, my prime, was far behind me—especially in Hollywood, where over the hill seems to be once you hit thirty.

Pilot Pete

Even though my age was getting to me, something about Peter brought me back to my youth. Maybe it was his small-town, down-to-earth demeanor. Together, we were fun and playful, our free-spirited energies bouncing off of each other. But for every light, heartfelt moment, there were several others where I challenged him to look at things from new perspectives.

Peter challenged me as well. One night, we were sitting outside his suite at the Westlake Village Inn, looking at the stars and sharing a glass of red wine while waiting for his night date to begin. He turned to me and asked, "Do you think God exists, Jules?"

I paused. I wasn't sure how to answer that. I grew up in a Christian household, but relaxed Christians. We were baptized Catholic and then switched to the Protestant Church, which was more chill and fun, where we didn't have to stand up and sit down every few minutes. We eventually stopped going besides holidays, until, as a young teen, my sister Jen decided she wanted to get more involved. I kicked and screamed when she dragged me to Pilgrim Fellowship (PF), the church's youth group, but it ended up being one of the best parts of my adolescence. I had my confirmation and eventually became president of the group. We went on mission trips, did volunteer work, and I had a weeklong excursion in the wilderness to connect with God and the Bible.

My involvement in the church helped shaped who I am today. I am grateful for that experience in my life and the community it offered. Our church welcomed everyone with open arms, including my dance teacher, who was the only openly gay man in my small town.

When I moved to LA and started working in Hollywood, I seemed to be surrounded by atheists. People would laugh when contestants came into casting and claimed that being on the show was "God's plan." I started to laugh with them. I'd pop into Oasis Church here and there in LA, until I stopped going altogether. Over the years, my relationship with God diminished. I started to question "his" existence in the same way all those around me did.

"I don't really know," I replied, honestly. "I'd like to say I do. But with the amount of judgment, hate, and war that seems to be prompted by religion, I find it hard to believe in. Some of the stuff in the Bible just doesn't make sense to me."

"Yeah … I get that," Peter responded. I could see the thoughts rippling behind his gaze. That night as I was lying in bed, I thought about what Peter asked me. While my closest connection to God those days was via the *Jesus Calling* prompts that popped up on my phone (an app Hannah made me download to read to her), I realized I probably didn't answer his question right. He was the Bachelor, after all. His top contenders were God-loving women from the South. Of course we needed him to believe in God. The next day, I corrected my answer.

"I thought more about what you asked—you know, about God," I began. "I believe. I mean, how can God not exist? Just look at this massive, magical universe!"

He smiled. "Yeah, I think so too."

I really wanted to believe what I was saying. I hoped God existed … but I was skeptical and so disconnected from what that even meant at the time.

The thought of a higher power continued to run through my mind as I stared out the airplane window, watching clouds pass by, en route to our first international destination, Costa Rica. After landing in San José, we drove for hours on winding roads through the lush rainforest before arriving to our hillside hotel, The Springs Resort & Spa. I could hear howler monkeys echoing in the distance, with sweeping views of the Arenal Volcano towering above the jungle's canopy. We each had our own little villa and a golf cart to zip around the property. The first day was dedicated to interviews and B-roll of Peter arriving at the resort. Days like this were the closest we got to "days off" and were nice because we could take our time and enjoy the setting.

When we were done filming Peter strolling through the hotel lobby with his suitcase, we grabbed drinks to take back to the bungalow.

Brittany sat in the front seat of the golf cart, while Peter and I took the backward-facing seats. Peter placed his suitcase under my legs and ducked down to fit under the overhang. As he sat up, the back of his head banged into the metal frame. The beer in his hand propelled into his face, glass shattering everywhere.

"Ahhh, fuck…" Peter mumbled in pain.

"Oh my God!" I screamed. "Are you okay?" The ground was covered in blood now. Peter's head was tilted down, his hand covering his eye and forehead.

He must have stabbed himself in the eye and is going to be blind, I thought to myself. *The season is ruined.*

I felt nauseous. I couldn't bear the sight; blood and I don't go well together. I quickly ran inside the hotel to find help, leaving Brittany to handle the horror scene.

Luckily, he didn't hit his eye, but he had a big gash across his forehead that would soon become a replica of Harry Potter's scar. We went to a local clinic to get it cleaned up, but they suggested going to San José for stitches to make sure it was done right. The company arranged a charter to get us there ASAP so we wouldn't have to drive six hours. Unfortunately, the weather had different plans, and it was eventually deemed too risky to fly. Already queasy from all the blood, I sent Brittany and Peter off on the winding road to recovery while I went back to the hotel for a glass of wine and a good cry.

I felt horrible and couldn't help but feel responsible, replaying the sequence of events in my head and what I could've done to prevent it. I didn't like seeing Peter in pain. He had gotten jab after jab thrown at him already during filming with all the drama, and now he was literally jabbed with a mark that would be there forever.

I found my bosses at the hotel bar. After they calmed me down and the tears stopped, one of them said something that took me aback.

"You know," he began. "One of our biggest fears before starting the season was that Peter would fall in love with you."

"Oh yeah?" I replied with laughter. "Or what if I fell in love with him?" I joked.

"Well, we know you aren't dumb enough to fall for Peter."

"Ha, yeah, totally," I responded.

Of course I wasn't dumb enough to fall for Peter. I was a professional at the peak of my career and took my job very seriously. I had sworn off showmances more than fifteen years earlier after that holiday party make-out gone wrong. Besides, Peter wasn't my usual type. I swooned over complex, artsy, non-commital men with interesting backstory. And yet, for some reason, that statement stayed with me, swirling through my mind…

Costa Rica was the first time Peter got frustrated with me. Maybe I had gotten too close to him; I could be a bit too honest about my opinions on some of his ladies. After sharing what I thought during one of his dates, he wanted alone time after filming. I should've been glad to have a free moment. Instead, I was sad that he was upset with me. I wasn't dumb enough to fall for Peter, was I?

After Costa Rica, we ventured to South America. When we landed in Chile, Peter insisted our team go out on the town. It would be our only chance since we had back-to-back dates the following days. While I would normally choose sleep over partying, something about Peter's persuasion worked on me. And boy, did we have fun! There is nothing like drinking through jet lag and sleep deprivation; the delirium put me in an odd state of bliss, the music bringing me back to the days of dancing on the tables of nightclubs.

There was a moment that night where I fully surrendered my producer hat, lost myself to the music, and was just a girl dancing with a boy I had spent the past month getting to know. *The Bachelor* glow-up was real, as I was no longer looking at Peter like a younger brother but as a hottie. Or maybe it was the bandage across his forehead, giving him a bit more edge like I'm normally drawn to. We were moving in unison to the music, in flow with one another. If my life were a rom-com this would be the moment our gaze was held a little too long and we leaned in for a kiss. Wait, should we lean in for a kiss? Or was that just my wine-buzzing, fairy-tale imagination getting the best of me?

Peter then spilled his glass of wine on the floor, snapping me back to reality. I quickly rebounded into producer mode and exclaimed, "Time for bed. You have a big date tomorrow!"

After helping clean up the wine, I said good night and went back to my room. My head and mind were spinning. I chugged a large glass of water so the hangover wouldn't be too horrendous when morning came in a few short hours. I wasn't dumb enough to fall for Peter. Was I?

Some of the best times of Peter's season were the in-between moments, not captured on camera. We'd blast country music on the way to filming, singing, and dancing along. Late nights were spent stargazing as we swung on swings on the ocean's edge, looking up at the starry night sky. The reality is, he spent a lot more time with me than any of his suitors. When the cameras weren't rolling, we kept them apart, or hung as a group, to make sure conversations weren't had that should be saved for on camera. Our own relationship was forming, different than those with the contestants, and, some may say, deeper. The contrast between my relationship with him versus my relationship with Hannah was evident from the start. It felt like Peter wanted me to be a part of his journey, that I was included in the experience, versus just the producer in the background.

As we traveled, we took full advantage of the perks of our business-class seats while Peter entertained me with fun facts about airplanes. I loved how passionate he was about flying. On the way to Australia, we put on matching Qantas pajamas and enjoyed the finest dining experience either of us could wish for, 36,000 feet high in the sky. The flight attendant handed us glasses of champagne, and we raised them for a toast.

"I'm so grateful to have you on this journey with me," he began. "How lucky are we to be flying in style, to the other side of the world, on an adventure for love? I couldn't imagine doing this with anyone but you. I love you, Jules."

"I love you too," I said, feeling a warmth in my heart. "Thank you for always being the best sport, keeping a positive attitude, and appreciating the beauty of it all. You've made my job fun and memorable in the best way possible. Cheers to love."

Our eyes locked as we clinked our glasses and took a sip of our bubbly.

"Here, let's take a selfie! I'll send it to the fam," I said, pulling out my phone. I sent the picture to his parents and mine, separately. Heart emojis were sent back, and a response from my dad that read

That's a good-looking couple!

I texted back

Oh dad, LOL! I'm working!

I wasn't dumb enough to fall for Peter. Was I?

I couldn't fall for Peter . . . My dear friend Natasha was falling for him. While a lot of their moments together weren't shown on TV, the two of them got along really well, and had some of the most genuine and mature conversations. Ultimately, for Peter, it felt more like a friendship, and he sent her home right before hometowns. I was saddened for my friend, and left wondering—who the heck from these final four women did Peter have a chance with in the long run? It was down to Madison, Hannah Ann, Victoria, and Kelsey.

I'll spare you all the ins and outs of the final weeks of filming after the hometown dates, as it was a clusterfuck. But in summary, for those that didn't watch, one of his top contenders, Madison, revealed before fantasy suites that she wouldn't be happy if he slept with other women. Peter went on to sleep with the other two contestants remaining, causing Madison to leave on her own and break Peter's heart. This left Peter with one remaining girl, and somehow, he got down on a knee and proposed to sweet, sweet Hannah Ann, who seemed equally as surprised by the proposal.

The cameras stopped rolling, the season wrapped, and the couple got a house together for a few days alone, supervised by Brittany. I, on the other hand, hopped on a plane to the Great Barrier Reef with a friend from work. My job was done, and I was ready for my own vacation after the turmoil of the season. After snorkeling in the reef, we spent a few days in Sydney, where I wasted no time opening Raya and matching with a hot Aussie. Something I did love about the apps is that it connected me to interesting men all around the world I would never have otherwise met. Hot Aussie took my friend and me out for a fun night with the locals, and he and I made out on the streets of Sydney before I hopped in our Uber and bid farewell.

After Sydney, I flew to New York for a few days to catch up with friends before spending Thanksgiving with my family in Connecticut. The last guy I'd been talking to before work consumed me was someone I'd met over the summer through mutual friends. Zach lived in New York and worked in sales. While we had a fun weekend and kept in touch, I didn't see any real potential—he lived on the opposite coast and was a bit too pessimistic for me. But I was in New York, he was persistent, and the truth? I hadn't been laid in almost a year. Maybe that would change my opinion of him? Unlike Madison from Peter's season, who was saving herself for marriage, I found sex to be an important element to see if there was a connection with someone.

Zach conveniently did what men tend to do and had me come to him. We had a drink at his place, grabbed dinner nearby, then went back to his place to hookup, on the couch, might I add. And nope, it didn't change my opinion. Afterward, we made our way to the bedroom, where there was a little cuddling before he quickly fell asleep, snoring loudly with his arm wrapped around me. Shit.

I was wide awake on Australia time. I'm not a cuddler. I'm OCD about my brushing, flossing, and gargling with gold Listerine nighttime routine. All I kept thinking about was how I had booked myself a room at the Soho Grand Hotel, and here I was, trapped under the arm of a guy I wasn't even into anymore. I wanted the plush comfort of a bed all to myself, where I could sprawl out in my white bathrobe and get coffee delivered to me in the morning as I took in the view from my window.

I was listening to his snoring and wondering how long I had to wait before I could sneak out. The arm was starting to make me feel claustrophobic, and the more I thought about it the more trapped I felt. I needed to leave. I slowly shimmied my body out from under him, praying he wouldn't wake up. Thanks to his deep snore, he didn't.

When I left his place, it was 3:45 A M. Still wide awake, I decided to take the long walk back to the hotel to clear my head and take in the city that never sleeps. I had done my fair share of walks of shame in my New York years. It was part of the energetic debauchery of the work-hard, party-hard mentality. Back then, the late-night winter walks were in four-inch stilettos, a miniskirt, and no jacket. At least I'd learned something in my mid-thirties, now wearing comfortable booties and a warm jacket.

Being in New York always filled me with excitement and energy. Yet, I was feeling something heavier. The city that never sleeps was fast asleep and the streets were empty. I also felt . . . empty. I thought to myself, *Peter would be having so much more fun in New York with me than he's having with Hannah Ann in Australia. And I'd be having so much more fun if Peter were here.*

I had just wrapped one of the most successful seasons of my career, but I was craving so much more. A quiet longing had been building up inside of me and it was hard to continue ignoring it. It was a longing for love. I wanted the love story I was creating for others. Instead, I was getting a make-out session in Sydney and a couch fuck in New York, followed by a lonely walk home.

My mind drifted back to Peru, where Peter had had a date with Kelsey in the countryside. They rode ATVs to a picturesque picnic setup, with the Cordillera Blanca mountains as their backdrop. After their picnic, Peter had an urge to run up the hill behind them, with Kelsey reluctantly following. What wasn't shown in that moment was me running ahead of them, behind the camera, being their cheerleader. "The higher you get, the better the view!" I exclaimed.

As they lay down to take in the view, I lay back in the grass as well. What had started as a misty, overcast day had now cleared to blue skies. I watched the white clouds slowly drifting above me and took in the beauty of Mother Earth's creation.

As Peter and Kelsey cuddled, he said, "This is what I want to do for the rest of my life with the person I love."

"Me too," I whispered softly to myself.

Twilight was upon the city as I returned to the Soho Grand Hotel, taking note of the mistletoe hanging above me on my elevator ride back to my room. I showered and slipped into my robe just in time to see the city begin to wake up, with the sun sending a soft glow over the buildings below me. As I took in the view, I couldn't help but notice all the water towers on the rooftops for as far as the eye could see, something that had clearly been there since long before my New York days, yet I had never noticed them before. It's amazing how, from a new perspective, you can discover something that was there all along.

As I sat in the window seat admiring the city, I thought back to that time cheering on Peter and Kelsey up the hill. Would I ever find my cheerleader? Someone who would climb life's mountains with me? If so, would it be with someone new and yet to come or someone who'd been there all along?

I wasn't dumb enough to fall for Peter. Was I?

11

The Cinderella Story That Could Have Been

December was filled with press trips to promote the upcoming season of *The Bachelor*. As Peter's producer, I traveled with him to help prep for the segments and make sure the media didn't pressure him to say anything he wasn't allowed to. Journalists did whatever they could to trick him into revealing spoilers for the season, getting clever with their questions to throw him off. I listened in closely and intervened as needed.

I was thrilled when I learned I'd be joining Peter for his appearance in Times Square on New Year's Eve! During my New York days, locals avoided the area at all costs, but this time we'd have VIP access, the best and only way to do New Year's Eve in Times Square.

Peter's family got to be there for the celebration. We had been wanting our parents to meet, and since mine were a short car ride away in Connecticut, they joined us for lunch before our evening began. My dad booked us a table at Carmine's. The lunch was delicious, and our families got along beautifully. We were one big Italian-Cuban family!

One of Barb's friends, who joined us for lunch, couldn't help but notice Peter and me prancing and laughing down the streets of New York together. She teased, "I think I know how the season ends. You two are together, aren't you?"

That line became a theme as the night went on. We rang in the new year from the ABC studios, dancing in confetti as we sang Frank Sinatra's "New York, New York" alongside thousands of others, sharing the collective joy of the celebration (a memory that will forever radiate in my heart). New friends we made throughout the night commented on how fun we were, and made remarks such as, "Are you sure you two are not together?" We laughed, knowing Peter was still happily(ish) engaged to Hannah Ann, and that we were genuinely just good friends.

Peter, in fact, seized an opportunity to pimp me out as the ideal next Bachelorette. As we stood at the bar for the after-party, eating exuberant amounts of sushi, Rob Mills, the head of unscripted at Disney, joined us for drinks. That's when Peter went in for the sales pitch.

"You guys need to make Julie the next Bachelorette!" he declared. "She would be great! She's fun, outgoing, loves love, is hilarious . . ." Peter went on listing all my qualities while I played along, telling Rob it was time to shake things up at the franchise. While I knew it wouldn't happen, I enjoyed hearing Peter boost my ego.

We closed the party down that night, prancing out of Nobu with a bouquet of balloons, singing "Fly Me to the Moon" through the streets of New York, all the way back to the hotel. Times Square was now quiet, but the energetic vibration of the shared joy of that night pulsed through my body. It was a stark contrast from the lonely walk home a month prior.

"In other words, hold my hand!" I sang out, grasping the balloons, lifting my hands as Peter twirled me and sang the next line, "In other words, baby, kiss me . . ."

It wasn't long after ringing in the new year that Peter realized he and Hannah Ann were not meant to be. We arranged to film the breakup; while Hannah Ann thought she was coming to LA to spend the weekend with her fiancé, she soon left heartbroken and angry. Peter was sad, lost, and confused. This was not how he, or the producers, envisioned his season ending. As much as we love the drama, we also love a happy ending—a love story that gives the viewers hope too.

The show had started airing a few weeks prior, and Peter was now reliving the experience with all of America. Technically single again, he was still heartbroken about the breakup with his runner-up, Madison. While her producers explored whether there was any hope for reconciliation on Madison's end, I spent a lot of time with Peter. Since he lived nearby, Brittany and I would often go hang with him—it beat sitting in the office all day. If we got a home-cooked meal from Barb, even better! Watching the journey back with the rest of the country could be emotional, especially since he was now alone. We were there to support him and talk through things as needed.

Despite the heartache of a failed ending, Peter still had the best attitude. He was grateful for the experience and all he learned about himself, and love, though not everlasting. None of us knew how the season would ultimately end. In his mind, this was it; he'd come out of it single, yet stronger than ever. In the producers' minds, we wondered if there was any way yet to get him his happy ending. For the viewers, it was the first time ever that the notorious *Bachelor* franchise spoiler alerter, whose name I shall not mention or give credit to, hadn't figured out the ending of the show. The mystery led Bachelor Nation to do their own online sleuthing, leading them down a Reddit wormhole theory that pointed right to me.

As the alarm went off on my phone, I reached over to hit the SNOOZE button. I tend to set about five alarms, starting a good hour before I actually have to wake up, giving myself a false sense of joy that I get to sleep longer and continue my fantasy dreams in my subconscious mind. This habit isn't exactly enjoyed when I'm in a relationship and may explain why I'm still single.

The Love Producer

When I grabbed my phone to check the time, I saw an abnormal amount of text messages and Instagram alerts on my screen. *What is happening? Did someone die?* Tempted to keep sleeping but overcome by curiosity, I rubbed my eyes and opened my phone. I had texts from ex-lovers, friends I hadn't heard from in years, and a family group chat with all my aunts and cousins exclaiming,

JULIE AND PETER SITTING IN A TREE—K-I-S-S-I-N-G—PLEASE TELL US IT IS TRUE! YOU DESERVE LOVE!!!

I clicked on the links of various news articles with headlines that read:

- Do Peter Weber & a Producer on 'The Bachelor' End Up Together?
- A New 'Bachelor' Finale Conspiracy Theory Says Peter Weber Ends Up with One of His Producers, and There Is Some Evidence to Back It Up . . .
- About That 'Bachelor' Reddit Theory Claiming Peter Weber Ends Up with Producer Julie LaPlaca . . . I NEED ANSWERS.

One friend sent me a recording from *Good Morning America*. I hit PLAY, expecting a quick mention, yet instead watched a whole segment dedicated to the rumor of Peter and me ending up together. A slideshow of Instagram photos flashed in their studio. The evidence was silly, with Michael Strahan laughing while reporting it. Right before the premiere of Peter's season, there was a new company rule that we couldn't post pictures with the cast on social media until after the season ended. But how could I be in Times Square for New Year's and not share that special moment? Peter photobombed almost all my photos, but I managed to find one without him to post. Although, turns out he was in it . . . his back, that is.

"OMG—there Peter is in the background!" sleuths exclaimed.

During our family lunch, Peter's dad posted a picture since he didn't have to follow the silly rules. Another fan pointed that out.

The Cinderella Story That Could Have Been

"OMG—there is Peter and Julie and both their families!"

When the Seahawks were in the playoffs, Peter gave me some swag to wear to a party. Now, *Bachelor* fans were saying, "OMG! She is supporting HIS TEAM!" The one photo of the two of us that I posted before the rules changed had fans saying, "They look perfect together!!!" I couldn't argue with that one. We did look good together.

I opened Instagram. My following had more than quadrupled overnight! My inbox was flooded with messages, most in full support of the two of us together, with swarms of fans sending lovely, kind, and hopeful words.

Praying Peter and Julie end up together!

Hope it's you, this is the kind of story to tell your kids one day.

You're like the most beautiful hippie chick.

She's 35? HOW?

I sure hope he ends up with a grown badass woman!

She should be the next Bachelorette!

If I was the Bachelor I'd pick you!

This is such a RomCom moment.

I basked in all the supportive, sweet messages. They touched my heart and made me feel seen. I was no longer just the girl behind the camera, but someone worthy of love too. I couldn't reply to any of them, of course. But I soaked up every heartfelt DM and comment that came my way. If you're reading this and were one of my cheerleaders, thank you. I appreciate you more than you know.

But then there were the trolls. So many *Bachelor* alumni vented to me about this in the past. I was getting a mini taste of what they go through:

Fuck off, bitch, Peter isn't interested in you.

Obviously, you just want attention. How about you get cancer and die!

You fucked him and ruined the show hoe he had better options.

You should get fired for that.
Slut!
Too plain, Peters gonna hit it and quit it.
You're like a 4, just another lame chick.
Are you the stray little alley cat that pilot boy scooped up?
It's a clear case of sexual harassment. She's his superior.
Reminds me of Harvey Weinstein.

Wow, there are some cruel people in the world. Wishing cancer and death upon someone? Me in the same sentence as Harvey Weinstein, a convicted sex offender?? And four seems to be my number; I thought back to high school, when the boys passed a note around rating girls' asses. I got a four then too. Part of me was honored to have made the list—that meant they were looking at me. But a below-average rating stung.

Luckily, I have thick skin and laughed at most of the hate, with the positive comments outshining the insults. Besides, what they said couldn't be true, seeing that the rumors were simply rumors. I couldn't fall for Peter, right?

The comments that did get to me? The ones that exclaimed I was way too old for Peter and wouldn't be able to have kids. I wanted to say, "Fuck you, Karen from Wisconsin. People are waiting well into their thirties to have kids these days—get with the times!" But their words traveled deep into my womb, reminding me of the dark void within. When did thirty-five become geriatric? Why did this fear continue to echo inside my mind? And could I do anything about it?

Sometimes I'd do the math in my head. If I did meet a guy now, we'd date for at least a year before an engagement, seeing as I'd be gone for work half that time. Once engaged, people typically wait another year for a wedding. I always fantasized of the newlywed years without kids, but that was out the window. The ticking clock was really starting to catch up to me. If only I could be the next Bachelorette, like some commented I should be. That might speed up the process!

The Cinderella Story That Could Have Been

As I was scrolling through the comments, my dad called. A couple weeks prior, my parents had been in town, and with Peter's new love of golf, my dad took us to the driving range to give him a mini lesson (my dad could have gone pro in his heyday). Afterward, we went to dinner with our parents and sat there awkwardly as they all spoke candidly about how happy they'd be if Peter and I ended up together.

"Hi, Dad," I answered.

"Julie. I have a sneaking suspicion that these rumors are true. Is there something you want to tell me? I know you probably won't because I have a big mouth, but I'm your father—you can trust me!" He went on to tell me how he'd never seen me light up the way I did around Peter when we were together, how we got along so well, and it felt like there was something more there.

"I'm his producer, Dad!" I exclaimed. But a part of me couldn't help but wonder . . . Do parents know best? Were my mom and dad, and Mr. and Mrs. Weber, onto something? The truth is, I did light up around Peter.

One of my favorite edits came from the @realitysavvy Instagram account, where they cropped my face onto the maid character from our soap opera date in Chile. The maid, played by cast member MacKenzie, was always in the shadows of the leading man, played by Peter, while all the other characters threw themselves at him. The caption read, "Sometimes you don't need to look far to find love," as Peter ultimately ended up with the maid in the fictionalized soap opera. Never had I felt more seen. I was the maid—the girl in the background cleaning up the messes of others, both literally and figuratively. I really was Cinderella before she got her glass slippers. Would I finally get my glass slippers?

Over the next couple of weeks, I had over a million people visit my Instagram page. My following jumped from six thousand to over seventy-five thousand in a matter of days. I got Venmo requests from fans trying to get me to spill the tea. My landlord called the police after paparazzi trespassed on the property looking for me. I even had people recognizing me in public. Each day a new headline came out, with all the major entertainment news sources picking the story up. Friends in Europe reached out, having read about it. Howard Stern talked about me! And most importantly . . . I made Page Six, a true accomplishment for the inner Carrie Bradshaw in me.

I'll admit, I was enjoying the attention. How can I not marvel in the love, likes, and fifteen minutes of fame? While I've never been a big social media person, I can see how people get addicted to it, constantly refreshing to see the latest comments coming through. I even got a blue check mark next to my name, a big deal back then. I was officially a Public Figure. And it was all due to the illusion of a real-life Cinderella moment. A moment I had always longed for as a young girl.

While the rumors weren't exactly true, the theory did seem like the perfect way to make this THE MOST DRAMATIC SEASON IN *BACHELOR* HISTORY. I fantasized about how it would all play out on TV. It went something like this . . .

MY FANTASY *BACHELOR* FINALE

CHRIS: Good evening, Bachelor Nation! I'm your host Chris Harrison, coming to you LIVE from Los Angeles for what is sure to be the most dramatic finale anyone has ever seen, really! How will Peter's journey for love end? No one knows, not even Peter. Let's find out together. Take a look.

The audience watches as Peter gets engaged, and then breaks up with Hannah Ann, and is now . . . alone and single. After a segment where Hannah Ann and Peter reunite to discuss the breakup, we return from commercial break to . . .

CHRIS: I'm here live with our Bachelor Peter, who now is . . . single?

PETER: I am single, but I did, in fact, find love on this journey . . .

The Cinderella Story That Could Have Been

CHRIS: With whom?

Peter doesn't reply right away; he just offers a smug smile.

CHRIS: Is it someone from this season? Are they here tonight?

The camera pans across his season's ladies who are there for the taping.

PETER: She is from the season. She is someone who may not have stood out at first glance, someone who was more in the shadows. But someone I realize, looking back, I couldn't have done this journey without. And, looking forward, I don't want to do life without.

CHRIS: I'm sure America is curious to know who you are talking about. But before we do that, let's play a special clip with some of the highlights from your season.

As I watch on a monitor from backstage, I get confused, calling on the walkie-talkie to my bosses, "He is going rogue! I don't know what is happening. Should we cut to a commercial? Who is he talking about?! I didn't prep him for this clip. What is this clip?" My bosses ignore me.

I then notice that the clip has switched its point of view and is now playing a montage of behind-the-scenes moments as I see myself on the screen, watching and reliving all the honest, sincere, playful, silly, and emotional in-between moments that the camera had somehow captured of us. A tear drips down my face as I take it all in and the clip finishes.

PETER: I'll be right back!

A camera follows Peter as he gets up from his chair onstage and makes his way backstage. I now notice a camera pointing at me. The scenes collide as Peter approaches me backstage.

The Love Producer

PETER: Jules, come with me.

He reaches out and grabs my hand.

I'm still in shock as we slowly make our way to the stage. Peter takes off my walkie-talkie, slowly brushing my hair behind my ears with his fingers before taking hold of both my hands.

PETER: Jules, wow, what a journey we've had! The moment I met you there was an instant connection. I remember during our first interview when we both started crying, I knew we would get along well. Who would've thought that would be the first of many tears shed together? We are two sensitive souls, two people who believe in love and happily ever after. But for every tear shed, there were even more laughs, smiles, and fun adventures. Boy, did we have fun—from nights out dancing in the streets, to stargazing all around the world, talking about life, God, and love. Golf cart rides, both good and bad. Our 36,000-foot adventures high in the sky. As I reflect on my journey you helped guide me through, I realize the best part of the journey . . . was you. It was your bright energy behind the camera, cheering me on, believing in me, seeing me, and caring about me. It was those conversations in between filming, when the cameras stopped, yet you and I kept going. I'm so grateful for the experience this show has given me, and the confusing turmoil of highs and lows . . . because, during all of that, I had my rock right alongside me. And I want you to be my rock, my dance partner, and my copilot, for all of life's adventures to come. If we could've gotten through this shit show of a season together, I know we can conquer anything. I want to wake up each morning with you, my best friend. I love you, Julie.

Knowing there was no way producers would let Peter get down on one knee without me saying something first, I begin . . .

The Cinderella Story That Could Have Been

JULIE: As a young girl I would fantasize about a love story made for the big screen. I've always been a dreamer, a romantic, and hopeful that, one day, someday, my dreams of everlasting love would come true. Ironically, years spent in Hollywood creating these stories for others pulled me further and further away from the love I so desired, as I stayed in the background and began to lose hope that I may ever find my life partner. Then you came along, Peter. And you saw me, not just as a producer, but as a girl who had similar hopes, desires, and dreams for her life. Your vulnerability opened my heart to be vulnerable with you as well. You appreciated my quirky ways and brought out my youthful spirit. The more I got to know you, the more I began to realize how much our lives aligned. I was saddened when the season was coming to an end, because this wasn't just a job for me; it was a part of my journey as well. It's a journey I want to continue with you as we navigate life as each other's copilot, not just for the smooth skies, but for the unexpected turbulence that will come our way as well. I love you, Peter Weber.

Peter gets down on one knee and pulls a ring out of his pocket—my dream ring I had shared with him during his visit with Neil Lane in Australia (he paid attention).

PETER: Julie Emily LaPlaca, you are the final chapter of this journey. You make my love story the most beautiful the world has ever seen. Will you make me the happiest man alive? Will you marry me?

JULIE: Yes, yes! Oh my God, yes!

Out from backstage comes my entire family, and Peter's. A giant moon mastered by our art department lowers from the ceiling with some twinkly lights. Frank Sinatra's "Fly Me to the Moon" starts playing as Peter takes my hand, gives me a twirl, and kisses me.

The Love Producer

As if this weren't enough, he has one last surprise. Cameras follow as we walk outside where a biplane awaits. We get in and take off down the created runway of the studio lot, as clouds in the sky write out "And They Lived Happily Ever After." (Hey, this is Hollywood—a girl can dream!)

END FANTASY *BACHELOR* FINALE

There you have it! That is the delusional inner dialogue of a crazy producer's mind that lives in a world of writing love stories and making up fairy tales. That makes me a good producer for a dating show, right? Or does it make me a terrible producer and a totally ridiculous, crazy person? This is where the real mind fuckery started to heighten. This is where it got messy and confusing… Producers producing, humans feeling—what's right, what's wrong? What's real and what's reality TV?

While I didn't talk to anyone about what was going on inside of me, I was a jumbled mess of confusion. Did I have strong feelings for Peter, or was I falling for my own tricks? Was I sucked into the fantasy of the world I created for your viewing pleasure, or was I resisting something that was actually quite real? Could it be so real that the universe was conspiring to make it happen, with seemingly the whole world rooting for us? Or were the Bachelor Gods influencing me? I admit, producers can prey on contestants when their emotions are high. I had just turned thirty-five—my emotions were high!

I've seen the memes: *The devil works hard, but* The Bachelor *producers work harder.* But here's the thing: I was a Hopeless Romantic Producer, not a pot-stirring, drama-causing producer. As producers, we unofficially got put into categories depending on our specialty. A Hopeless Romantic Producer is good at connecting with the cast members on a human level, getting excited about the love story, crying with them, swooning over the Neil Lane diamond rings, the stories they'll tell their grandchildren one day, keeping the fantasy alive … because we believe in the fantasy. I thrive at it because I myself LIVE IN MY OWN FANTASY WORLD. I'm always writing potential rom-coms of my life in my head, craving main character energy.

But alas, perhaps I was destined to remain in the supporting character role for the rest of my life. Amidst all the chaos, I got called into my boss's office to congratulate me; I was getting promoted to supervising producer. It was the title I'd been working so long and hard for. My job wouldn't actually change; I would still be the main producer for the lead. I was just finally getting the title and pay raise I deserved. I should have been thrilled. But instead, I went into my office, shut the door, lay on the floor, and cried. They were not tears of joy like most people have when told they are getting promoted. These were tears of sorrow, tears of fear, tears due to the fact that I was now committed to living out of a suitcase, giving my life to other people's happiness again and again until I was old and gray and no longer fertile. I wish I were exaggerating, but I'm not.

Getting the promotion meant I was locked in for at least another year. I was burned out and exhausted. What was I doing with my life, and was it worth it? While I had fun as Peter's producer, the chaos, drama, and TV-making part of my job was getting to me on a personal level. I didn't know how to close off the emotional stress of the lead's emotional stress. On top of that, I now had my own emotional stress, trying to navigate whether I was actually falling for Peter or not. Where was my therapist to talk through my feelings? Oh yeah, nonexistent.

Just when I thought the pressure might break me, I was able to escape from the chaos for a few days in Florida to celebrate my papa's (my grandfather's) ninetieth birthday. I was grateful to be surrounded by the unconditional love of my family.

While there, I got the call that made me believe that maybe, just maybe, I wasn't so delusional after all. My fairy-tale dreams might actually come true!

12

Forever a Bachelorette

Florida has always held a special place in my heart. I live for the humid saltwater air, shuffleboard, and the LIFE'S A BEACH signs that hang on every wall, including the bathroom I was curling my hair in when I got the call.

"Julie, it's Kate. I have Mike on the line for you."

Before I could process what my coworker said, she was already transferring me. I quickly ran to the backyard of the vacation rental for some privacy.

"Julie, it's Mike Fleiss! How are you?"

My heart raced. Why was the creator of *The Bachelor* calling me? Mike was someone I had only exchanged small talk in the elevator with. While the rumors were still circulating in the press, they weren't true. Was I in trouble? I hadn't done anything wrong. Still, it could look like I had.

"I want you to know we're loving these rumors!" he said. A wave of relief ran through me.

"So fun, right?!" I exclaimed. Then it happened. He said the words the hopeless romantic in me dreamed of hearing.

"I wanted to know… Would you ever consider being the Bachelorette?"

OMG, OMG, OMG!

"Yes, absolutely!" I blurted out without hesitation, feeling an electric pulse of energy flow through me as I smiled from ear to ear.

Is that crazy? For a TV producer to want to be the lead of the craziness she devises? Probably, but I've always been a little crazy. And as a producer, I know crazy makes great TV. I'd make great television.

"The storyteller in me sees it as the modern-day Cinderella story . . ." Mike said with excitement.

"I couldn't agree more and would be lying if I said I hadn't dreamt of the idea myself!" I exclaimed.

We arranged to have a secret meeting when I returned to LA, because my immediate bosses, according to him, were against the idea and didn't think it would work. But he was the boss of the bosses and loved it.

After hanging up, I immediately ran inside through the sliding doors to share the news.

"Family! Come here!" I yelled, gathering them all around the sea-shell-themed living room filled with rattan furniture.

"Oh my God," I began, catching my breath. "You won't believe what just happened."

"What?!" my mom asked with eager anticipation.

"Mike Fleiss—like, the creator of *The Bachelor*—just called me," I emphasized with wide eyes. "He asked if I would consider being the Bachelorette!"

"Shut up!!!" my sister Jen gasped with excitement. My mom shared her thrill, with an explosion of joy and disbelief on her face.

"I mean, it's not for sure, but I'm going to meet with him and an executive at ABC next week!" I exclaimed.

"Oh, you're totally gonna get it. It's such a perfect Cinderella story," my brother-in-law said. He is an executive in unscripted television as well, so he knows what he's talking about.

"Right?! That's what we said!" I felt a sense of hope run through me. My dad didn't seem to share the same sentiment.

"You don't really want to do that, do you, Julie?" he said, expressing concern. "I can't imagine watching you go through all that and making out with all those guys."

"Don't worry, Father! It would be great—trust me," I assured him, wrapping my arm around him as we all walked out to the minivan to head to the party. I felt a warmth in my heart and basked in the possibility of it all. The universe had heard my desires, and soon my love story may begin.

We were greeted by our big Italian family as we arrived at the event space. The round tables were draped with blue plastic tablecloths, with HAPPY BIRTHDAY and YOU ROCK! balloons as the centerpieces. I was already eyeing the dessert table, with my aunt's homemade Italian cookies next to a box of Dunkin' Donuts.

Everyone is always excited when the California girls (my sisters and I) come back East, and they were especially thrilled now that I was the talk of the town.

"Oh my God, the flight attendant recognized me on the flight here!" I giggled with my Aunt Jeanie at the fun of it all.

Then the man of the hour arrived at his surprise party, my papa! When we locked eyes, he threw his hands in the air with excitement.

"JULIE!!! My Hollywood star!" my papa said, beaming with joy.

"Happy birthday, Papa!!" I exclaimed as we embraced in a big hug.

"You know, that Pilot Pete is a handsome man," he said with a tone of suggestion.

"Should we call him?" I asked.

I then pulled out my phone and FaceTimed Pete so he could join the party! Every aunt and cousin made sure to get some camera time to let him know what a great catch Julie was.

I then ducked outside to let him in on the secret.

"Peter, you're not gonna believe it," I began. "Mike Fleiss called me earlier. We are meeting next week about me possibly being the Bachelorette!"

"Oh my God, Jules! We totally manifested this!" he exclaimed. "You have this in the bag. I'm so pumped for you!"

"Eek, thank you!!!" I shrieked. "I have to get back to the party, but I'll call you later—love ya!"

Admittedly, after hanging up, a bit of sadness ran through me. As you know, I had already started writing the hypothetical love story in my head of Peter and me jetting off into the sunset together. Becoming the Bachelorette would mean this scenario couldn't happen. So, I began day-dreaming about another version . . . Peter showing up mid-season to profess his love and join the cast. My mind was writing all the versions of how our love story would unfold if there was a love story there. This is when I started to admit to myself that my feelings may be real. Of course, I kept them safely tucked away in my rambling mind.

The day before my meeting, I went to Nordstrom and bought five overpriced dresses, intending to return four. I needed to look the part of the leading lady, and the leading lady does not shop in the discount section. I opted for a floral Reiss dress. As I am notorious for being a terrible returner, the other four dresses are in my closet to this day, which still makes me cringe thinking about how much I paid for them.

I purchased SiO overnight wrinkle patches for my chest and entire face to wear the night before our meeting (the Instagram ads had found me). My biggest fear was that I was too old to be the Bachelorette. Most leads were in their twenties, and I was thirty-five, with an all-natural, injection-free face, heightening my insecurities. I looked like a silicone sea creature as I went to bed that night, praying I wouldn't have an adverse reaction to a product I had never used before. Luckily, they did a pretty good job. I then splurged on a blowout from Drybar and had my makeup done professionally for the first time since my sister's wedding. All dolled up and in an expensive dress, I felt and looked like the Bachelorette!

I met with Mike and Rob at a hole-in-the-wall Mexican restaurant I was way too overdressed for, but that's what the Bachelorette does, and I was owning it. The meeting went great. I knew what they wanted, and I charmed them with it all. I even let them in on a few secrets, like the fact that I had auditioned for the show thirteen years prior while I was seeing someone. Clearly, I wasn't ready then, but I was now! One hundred percent single!

"I know I would be the oldest Bachelorette," I said during the meeting.

"I've never had any work done on my face, but I'm happy to get Botox before the season starts so I look younger!"

"No, no, don't do that. You don't need it!" they both assured me, giving me a slight confidence boost.

We left the meeting with a plan to meet with the other network executives soon. As the possibility of being the Bachelorette became real, my biggest fear became… OMG, what if I have herpes?

I mean, I had no symptoms of herpes, but this is where my mind went. An STD is an automatic out for the show. I had my annual exam just about a month before and the gyno gave me a whole lecture about why they don't test for herpes anymore.

"Oh, darling, just about everyone has it now," she stated. "It's best to not know unless symptoms arrive; it could be dormant in there for years!" I stared at her, so confused. But she was the professional, so I followed her advice. I also learned it's standard medical practice to not test for it because of high false-positive rates.

Now, my mind went down a rabbit hole. God forbid they declare they want me to be the leading lady, I go through all the appointments, and it doesn't happen because I have herpes! I would be mortified as all my coworkers would find this out through the rumor mill. After my meeting with Mike and Rob, I ran right to a walk-in clinic.

"Please test me for everything!" I exclaimed to the doctor. Fortunately, I'd made it thirty-five years without herpes. A sense of relief ran through me as I turned my attention toward manifesting my Cinderella story.

It was hard to stay focused at work as I anxiously awaited next steps. Finally, I got a call into the head executive producer's office. He sat me down. After a long buildup of how they spent hours and hours deliberating, they ultimately determined that I wouldn't be the Bachelorette. No matter how real and vulnerable I was, no one would believe a producer's love story. She knows too much of the behind-the-scenes of the show to make it feel authentic.

I couldn't hold back the tears. I argued he was wrong and that producers deserve love, too, and I was now going to be single forever! When I left Head EP's office, I went back to my windowless office (after I got promoted in title, I got demoted in office space), shut the door, collapsed on the floor, and completely broke down. I had a full-on sob fest. I was left with racoon eyes from the mascara and dozens of snot-filled tissues surrounding me. I was so sad that I wasn't the Bachelorette and embarrassed that my bosses knew how sad I was about not being chosen.

Where would I go from here? I clearly wasn't happy at my job, and I clearly wasn't happy with my love life, or lack thereof. Now, I also resented my bosses who were obviously the villains of my love story, caring more about keeping a talented supervising producer than they did about my own personal happiness. How dare they!

I wanted to be the protagonist of my love story. If they weren't going to create the Bachelorette dream for me, maybe I could create it for myself?

Like all good seasons past, there was one very important element missing that could possibly give me the clarity I needed—my very own fantasy suite. With Peter Weber.

13

Fantasy Suite

Julie opens up her imaginary Fantasy Suite Card:

Peter & Julie,

Welcome back to Westlake Village, where your journey for love first began! I hope you're enjoying the local wine and on-screen entertainment.
Should you choose to forgo your individual rooms, please use this key
to stay as a couple in the fantasy suite . . . that is, Peter's room, in his
parents' house.

—Chris Harrison

It was the day after I found out I wasn't going to be the Bachelorette. I
was emotional, vulnerable, and fully in sad girl mode, not girl boss mode.
Brittany and I went to Peter's house to spend the day with him and watch
the next week's episode in preparation for "The Women Tell All" filming
later that week.

We decided to head to our old stomping grounds, Westlake Village
Inn (where we lived while filming in LA), to share some wine at Stone-
haus, the hotel's wine bar. We love wine, just like Bachelor Nation! Chris

Harrison and Lauren Zima joined us for dinner, with more wine (a very nice bottle, compliments of Chris).

After dinner, Brittany and I went back to the Webers' house to finally watch the episode with Peter and drink more wine. Peter was trying to set Brittany up with one of his friends, Jared, so he came over to join us. Brittany and Jared were on one corner of the wraparound couch, Peter and me on the other, and Barb was asleep upstairs (Peter's dad was flying that day). Peter and I weren't cuddling, just lying next to each other—not a big deal, since we had become besties over the past six months.

But then, something shifted. It felt like that moment in high school when, at the movies with your crush, your hands slowly find their way to each other. The only difference was we weren't watching *Titanic*; we were watching Peter and Madison's breakup. It was almost as dramatic and heart-wrenching, with Peter basically sinking to the bottom of the deep, dark ocean (aka the vast, dry, fly-infested outback).

Is this intentional? I thought to myself as his hand started rubbing against mine, warm and lingering. *Perhaps he is just sad and wants his friend's hand for comfort?* Still, I couldn't ignore the electric tingle that pulsated through every nerve of my body. What was happening?

When the episode ended, Jared said goodbye and we turned the TV off to head upstairs. Since we'd had too many glasses of wine, Barb offered Jack's room to Brittany and me. I went to the bathroom, put some toothpaste on my finger to "brush my teeth," splashed water on my face, and washed my hands.

As I was about to turn into Jack's room, where Brittany was already asleep, Peter came to the doorway. "Jules, come here," he said.

I walked into his room, not realizing what was about to happen. He shut the door behind me. We sat on the edge of his bed.

"We don't have to—this is bad," he said. "It's up to you."

Oh! This is what's happening. My heart pounded as all rational thinking went out the window. After a couple of *umms* and looking off in the distance, I said nothing more before looking up and locking eyes with Peter. My face said it all. He leaned in and we kissed.

Peter reached up and turned the lights off, just like in the fantasy suites. The rest is what happens when the cameras stop rolling, and stays between Peter and me.

Until the morning after, that is. I was not so gracefully woken by Barb busting open the door to declare, "Peter, it's time to go. We are going to miss our flight!"

I quickly ducked my head under the covers and said a little prayer. *Please, Lord, please don't let her have seen me.*

I waited for the coast to clear, then slowly crept my head out from under the duvet. Peter looked at me. "We good, Jules? Sleep as long as you want and help yourself to coffee in the kitchen."

"Uh, yeah, have a great flight . . ." I said, throwing a pillow over my face.

My head was pounding. *I might still be drunk*, I thought to myself. I fell back asleep. Peter called me from the airport. We both agreed to laugh it off—a drunk rendezvous between friends. No one would ever know.

"But your mom must know?" I asked.

"No, no, we're good," he replied. Lies. She definitely saw me in the bed.

"Fuck me!" I said out loud as I hung up the phone. As I lay in Peter's bed hugging one of his airplane pillows and looking at his airplane wall art, reality was kicking in about what had happened. Of course, there was a part of me that had secretly desired this. But now that it was my reality, fear spread throughout my body.

This isn't what my bosses had ordered. I never wanted to disappoint them. I was the good girl, the one who always followed the rules and pleased everyone. If they had said, "Julie, we want you and Peter together in the end!" I would have been okay with what just happened. But that's not the ending they were hoping would unfold. Peter was still in love with Madison, or so he thought. I knew this. I had just rewatched the scene of their breakup mere minutes before getting into bed with him. How fucked up was that?? I was technically his boss. I could get fired for this. Maybe I *was* a hoe.

I grabbed my phone and opened my email. A coworker had sent the newest clickbait article of Peter and me at the winery the day before.

"Hahaha, so funny," I replied, trying to sound breezy. The paranoia kicked in—what if everyone knew? What if the paparazzi were outside right now? I peeked out the window. The coast seemed to be clear. I checked Jack's room; Brittany was long gone. I quickly got myself together, dashed to my car, and got the fuck out of Westlake Village.

On the drive home, my phone rang. It was one of my bosses. My stomach dropped. *He knows*, I thought to myself, fearful as I answered. *Please, Lord, don't let him know.*

"Hey, Julie! I just sent over the script for 'Women Tell All.' Take a look when you get a chance to see if you have any notes."

A sense of relief ran through me. "Yes! Of course—will do that today!" I replied, trying to sound like I hadn't just slept with the star of the show.

I got home and took a long, hot shower. I wanted to lie back in bed and pretend that it all had been a dream. Did I really, though? I wasn't sure. Part of me was glad it happened. It validated what I had been feeling—chemistry I couldn't deny. It made me feel desired after worrying I was too old. But now what? Now . . . I had to do what I always do. Act like I don't care, be chill and cool about it, and continue with my work duties. I popped a couple Advil and headed into the office.

Brittany didn't make it to work that day, but she had pieced together what happened and was not happy about it. I went to meet her after work to talk. It wasn't a great talk. I tried to downplay what had happened; blamed the wine, brushed it off like it wasn't a big deal, and promised that it wouldn't change the team dynamic.

"Peter and I have already talked. We are laughing about it! Silly drunk kids doing silly things, that's all!" I said. "I swear, everything will go back to normal. Let's just pretend it never happened … okay? Promise you won't tell anyone, please? It would ruin my career … it would ruin everything."

I sensed she was conflicted, debating reporting it to my bosses. I couldn't face the humiliation and potential loss of my job … unless that meant they would find a way for Peter and me to end up together in the end. But I couldn't take the risk, not knowing the outcome.

Tears were streaming down my face.

"I won't say anything to anyone, and I never want to talk about it again," she declared. We never talked about it again.

Reality was sinking in. I fucked up. I fucked up big-time. The guilt, shame, embarrassment, and constant paranoia of someone finding out haunted me. While part of me was drowning in regret, there was something else happening too. Something undeniable. It's like I had cracked open a shell I hadn't realized I was stuck in. I was growing tiny magical wings . . . or perhaps devil horns? I was filled with a sense of rebellion, wanting to misbehave and break the rules. While I dreaded the thought of getting caught, another part of me *wanted* to get caught. If I was caught, maybe I'd finally fly free. Just maybe I could admit I was falling in love.

Fuck me.

14

The Grand Finale

Part of me wanted to tell Peter how I really felt; maybe then he would be able to wake up from his Madison spell and see why I was the person for him all along. But if he didn't feel the same way, how would I be able to continue producing him for the upcoming finale?

And who was I kidding—I'd never been one to spill my feelings and emotions before a guy does to me. I kept my heart protected, only opening up when I felt safe to do so. I didn't have a producer to guide me and force me to wear my heart on my sleeve.

Shame crept in. The mere thought of having to come clean with my bosses debilitated me. I would never. As the trolls on the internet had said, I was his producer—I should have known better. And they were right. How horrible of a producer could I be? I literally went and fucked the first male contestant I produced. That is wrong on so many levels. Of course, men in the industry do this all the time and get promoted. But I was a woman climbing the ladder in a man's world. I needed to be perfect.

Instead of telling my truth, I went fully into producer mode, suppressing what I was feeling and focusing on my job duties . . . for the most part. But something about Peter's persuasion could get the best of me. One night, things came close to going somewhere again. It was the night before an important shoot with Peter. He didn't know it, but we were going to throw a curveball at him.

Peter had just landed at LAX after being away for a week. He called and convinced me to meet him at his friend's yacht docked in Marina del Rey. So, at like 9 PM on a Wednesday before an important shoot, what did I do? I got an Uber from West Hollywood to Marina del Rey. I felt like a teenage girl sneaking out on a school night.

Now, this is where my inner producer takes over. If my life were a dating show, the night would read something like this:

DATE CARD:

I like you a yacht!

B-ROLL LIST:

- Establishing shot of the marina glowing under the moonlight
- Boats gently swaying in the water
- Docks lined with yachts and sailboats, softly lit at night
- Establishing shot of the yacht docked in the marina, close-up detail shots of the boat

ARRIVAL:

You see an SUV pull up to the marina. Julie steps out and walks along the dock. She stops and contemplates, looking out at the water. We see her pacing slowly, deep in thought.

VOICE-OVER:

Going into tonight, I'm looking forward to hanging with Peter, as friends. I know I need to protect my heart, so my guard is definitely up. I'm just going to use this time to see where his head is at, you know . . . as his producer.

MEET & GREET:

Peter is standing alongside the yacht slip. Julie walks down the lightly lit dock toward him, smiling.

"Jules! You made it," Peter exclaims. *Damn, why does he have to look so good?* Julie thinks to herself.

"Hi, Peter," Julie gives a sly smile. "Is this your new toy?"

"Yes! Welcome aboard," he says playfully, reaching out and grabbing Julie's hand to pull her up. Julie could feel the magnetic pull just as strongly on the inside.

DATE ACTIVITY:

A night on the yacht ... docked (because it's nighttime, after all). Peter gives Julie a tour of the luxurious hundred-foot yacht, introduces her to the owners—father and son—and they enjoy champagne as they look out at the glistening water lit by the moon and stars above them. There is dancing, laughing, and as the others step inside, a 1:1 conversation.

"How are you feeling about things with the finale airing soon?" Julie asks.

"Honestly, I'm feeling good, Jules," Peter begins. "Obviously it's not the ideal ending, but I don't have any regrets. I trust everything happened as it was supposed to and I'm coming out of it all stronger than ever."

"I think that's wonderful." Julie smiles softly, gazing down at the water gently moving below them.

"How about you? How are you doing?" Peter asks.

Julie looks up and their eyes lock. *How am I doing? How do I even begin to answer that question? I'm full of fear, shame, sadness, and hope ... hope that maybe you'll see in me what I see in you ... someone you could build a beautiful life with*, she thinks.

"I'm okay," Julie states. "Just busy getting things ready for Clare to be our next Bachelorette! I fly with her to New York in a few days to announce it."

"I still think it should've been you, Jules." Julie feels his arm brush against hers.

"Thanks. I guess it just wasn't meant to be." Julie doesn't trust herself to stay much longer. "It's getting late. I should probably call my Uber." She reaches for her phone.

"No, don't leave." Peter reaches to take the phone from her, grasping her hand. "You should stay." He gives her a look that needs no explanation.

"I can't stay—you have a big shoot tomorrow!" she declares, jumping up. "We both need to go to bed."

"C'mon, Jules. It's just a chat with Chris Harrison—no big deal," he says as he stands up alongside me.

Just Chris Harrison. That's what you think.

The next day I arrived at a rented home in Agoura Hills where we would be filming for the day. Peter and I did a quick interview, then went to the backyard to shoot B-roll.

Since Peter thought the shoot was going to be a chat with Chris Harrison following the breakup with Hannah Ann, he was stunned when he turned to see Madison walking toward him. I stood behind the camera watching as the two of them sat down to talk. While I can't give the ins and outs of the shoot, this was my moment to wash out my *I'm a bad producer* belief and make sure we got that happy ending. As the two of them kissed, I shed "tears of joy for the happy couple" to all those that walked by.

They agreed to take it day by day. The cameras stopped rolling. We were going to give them as much time as they needed off camera between now and the finale the following week so they could have the important conversations to determine their future.

I got them situated with a handler before grabbing my stuff and heading out. I got in my car, took my walkie-talkie out of my ear, and pulled out of the driveway. I cried the whole way home.

As people saw play out on TV, Peter's family was not a fan of Madison. When Peter returned home and asked them to please give her a chance as they were likely going to try to be together, they weren't happy. Feeling like he had to choose between his family and Madison was leaving Peter torn and confused.

We booked him a hotel in the days leading up to the finale so he could have time to process everything. I didn't push him one way or the other; I was done pushing for the show and wanted him to do whatever he felt like doing in his heart. I knew it wouldn't be me, and while I wasn't a fan of Madison, I kept that to myself. Peter's happiness was most important.

When the day of the live finale came along, I really wasn't sure what was going to happen. Peter had been restless, his family had been restless, and I had been restless. As they say in TV, "Fuck it, we're doing it live!"

I was with Peter in his dressing room when his family arrived. They were being kept separate before the taping, so I went to greet them. I'd like to believe it could have been anyone who walked in that felt Barb's wrath, but it was me that got it. Barb let out all her frustration, hurt, and anger. Just a week prior she was my biggest fan, praying Peter and I would end up together. Now it felt like I was public enemy number one. I apologized through the tears for their hurt. I told them the truth, that I didn't know what he was going to do, and that while I agreed with them that Madison wasn't a good fit, it was up to Peter.

All I remember her saying was, "No wonder people who come on this show commit suicide." Her words hit me like a brick thrown into my heart.

Before continuing I feel it's important to address this comment. Prior to my time at the show, a fan favorite, Gia, committed suicide. It broke my heart to read that headline. It was a few years after her appearance on the show and prompted by a fight with her boyfriend at the time. Along with Gia, it appears that three others, out of the approximate 1,500 contestants over the years, have sadly taken their lives. I'm not a mental health expert, but none appeared to be a direct result from their appearance on the show. I acknowledge that for some, however, being on a show like *The Bachelor* can have long-term effects on mental health. I'm glad reality shows have started taking this more seriously, offering therapy and mental health services to contestants that request it.

But in that moment, Barb's words left me questioning, *What have I done? Was this my fault?* I felt the weight and responsibility of all that had transpired with Peter, my body slowly sinking to the ground as his family left the room. The tears wouldn't stop flowing. I had never felt so defeated.

The finale continued to be just as dramatic as backstage in the dressing room. Peter and Madison said they were going to try it out, and Barb expressed exactly how she felt about that, not holding anything back. It was intense, dramatic, and real.

Two days later, Peter and Madison broke up.

Somewhere in between all the Peter finale drama, we were revving up to announce Clare as the Bachelorette. Since we would be starting her season three days after Peter's finale, I had to work on both simultaneously.

The week before the most dramatic finale in *Bachelor* history, I was in Sacramento filming Clare's backstory, followed by New York for her *Good Morning America* reveal. Then it was on to full prep mode in Los Angeles with wardrobe fittings, interviews, and B-roll.

As a reminder, this was *The Bachelorette* that, just a week and a half before, I thought might have been my season. I watched Clare try on stunning gowns, shoes, and jewelry any girl would swoon over. Even if she only got to keep a handful of them after the show, it was still a dream I envied. I put on a happy face, excited for Clare's journey that could've been mine, while also helping to craft Peter's happy ending that I had hoped could've been mine as well.

Clare and Peter were both staying at a hotel near my apartment (aka, no time off). First, I was with Clare, putting out fires, hoping she would still make her 5 A M call. Then, I was with Peter putting out fires, as he was starting to see other sides of Madison.

I walked home, slept a few hours, and prayed Clare would get in the car for the promo shoot. She did, and was a trooper for the long day, even when she broke her toe in heels.

That night at the hotel, a few of us were hanging with Peter, as his new girlfriend was nowhere to be found. I then got a call from my younger sister.

"Hi, Janelle, what's up?" I could barely make out her words through the tears.

"Brad just walked out on us," she said.

"What happened?" I asked, my worry setting in.

As Janelle told me about the circumstances leading to her fiancé leaving, all I wanted to do was be with her and her daughter, holding them tight. I knew she needed me, but there was no way I could get to Orange County that night.

The next morning, Clare would be moving to Westlake Village Inn, as would I, and I wouldn't return to my apartment for two months. I had not even begun to think about packing. Now the bigger concern on my mind was my sister and niece.

"If I order you an Uber, will you come up here? You shouldn't be alone," I said. She agreed, and I got her and her daughter a third hotel room down the hall from Clare and Peter. I felt like I was juggling emotions from all sides, dipping in and out of each room to comfort everyone in their own crises. What about my emotions?

I texted my boss, *I'm sorry, I'm going to be late tomorrow. I have some family stuff I need to deal with.* They were understanding.

The next morning, Janelle heard from Brad, who was home again. I got her an Uber back. I said goodbye to Peter, who was also heading home, and put Clare and her handler in an SUV to head up to Westlake Village Inn. I then walked back to my apartment to pack for the next two months on the road.

To put it simply, I was not okay. I was in no way mentally, emotionally, or physically ready to start another season of the show. On top of everything, Covid-19 was looming, and our travels had shifted from international to domestic. I collapsed onto my bed, surrounded by clothes I needed to pack, and cried.

Dear Lord, I whispered. *Please help me. I don't think I can do this right now. I just need a break from it all.*

As if the Lord had answered my prayers, the world shut down the very next day.

Friday, March 13, 2020, was the night we were supposed to start filming Clare's season. Instead, production was halted, and Clare flew back to Sacramento.

Now, Lord, that wasn't exactly what I had in mind! But before realizing how serious Covid-19 would become, I was grateful for what I thought would be a short pause and reset for me.

I had just settled in at Westlake Village Inn. Seeing as my apartment was in cyclone conditions from trying to pack, I decided to stay put for a couple nights and enjoy the hotel's plush white robes, room service, bathtub, and Netflix.

Peter and I texted. He was back home, broken up with Madison, and made up with his family.

JULIE: I'm heartbroken with how things were left with your parents and me at the finale.
PETER: We'd like to see you. Are you free to come over?
JULIE: Of course, I'll head over in a bit.

I went to their house where we talked, cried, hugged, and became one big happy family again.

Afterwards, I did a post on social media from Peter and me on New Year's Eve, with a caption that read:

The Grand Finale

It wasn't exactly a lie. We hadn't kissed that night, after all.

Since Clare's suite was now empty, Peter and I decided to have some friends there for a little get-together. We were both ready to let off some steam after an intense week. We all danced, played games, and laughed, just like the good old Peter and Julie days, as friends. One friend even looked at us and said, "You two are totally going to date in the next year."

That night, and again the following week, Peter and I had another fantasy suite. I knew he wasn't mentally in a place to jump into a relationship. Not after everything with Madison. But I couldn't help but think about the possibility of whatever was happening. Maybe he could quarantine with me; we could have fun and say fuck it to the world.

But then, I found myself shifting my dynamic with Peter. I stopped being my honest, silly, vulnerable self with my best friend, and started acting how I do when I have a crush on a guy. You know my M.O. by now—cool, aloof, and not communicating what I'm feeling. My heart was guarded as I waited and wondered when he might text again.

A few days after our Sunday fantasy suite, I woke up and did my usual morning scroll through Instagram. My heart dropped as I saw a photo on my explore page. I clicked it and zoomed in on a paparazzi shot of Peter and Kelley together in Chicago.

I was crushed. Humiliated, embarrassed, and heartbroken. I was so mad at myself for having been so dumb. How could I have been played by someone I knew better than arguably anybody else? The biggest hurt of all was that he didn't tell me. We had a strange relationship of bouncing between hooking up and me comforting him about Madison. If I could handle that as a friend, you'd think he'd at least have the decency to call or text with a heads-up that he was seeing someone else.

Now with pictures out in public, surely, he would reach out, right? He didn't. My body ached as all my past rejections came to the surface. I felt sick to my stomach. I couldn't sleep. My mind was racing with a million thoughts as I tried to process what I was feeling. I rehearsed the conversation I needed to have with him in my head yet was too scared to send a single text.

I noticed that Kelley and Madison, the first two cast members to have started following me on Instagram, had both unfollowed me in the past week. I never had enemies. What was happening? I knew they must both know the truth about Peter and me. This added to my paranoia that everyone would find out.

It took me almost two weeks before I got the courage to message Peter. It was only after he responded to something on my Instagram story that I replied with, *Can you call me when you get a chance, please?* He called right away. He admitted he had been scared to reach out and took full responsibility for handling it wrong. I told him how much it hurt, as a friend. I told him it was a confusing time for me, as I was trying to process what I was feeling.

Peter and I would always say *I love you* to each other. It was the type of casual *I love you* we'd share with a best friend or parent—unconditional love. While I was trying to understand the romantic side of this love, I knew Peter was not. I also knew Peter and Kelley wouldn't last, but that he was lost and searching for any type of comfort.

I told him I cared deeply for him as a friend and would always value that first and foremost. He agreed and wanted to remain friends as well. But it was clear to me that his new girlfriend, Kelley, did not want us to stay in touch. Peter disappeared from my life, besides work-related calls, which felt different—guarded. I found myself paranoid that Kelley might be listening in on them. For the past eight months, I had spent more time with Peter than any other human. Now, he was cut out of my life. My heart was shattered.

Why had I been dumb enough to fall for Peter?

15

Stillness of the Face, Mind, and World

During *The Bachelor*'s finale week, right before Covid-19 shut down the world, I got Botox and filler for the first time. I'd been wanting to age naturally, but societal pressure caught up to me. How could it not when I worked in Hollywood, surrounded by youth and beauty, where no one seems to age anymore? I got invites to Botox parties, saw ads on every corner to stay "forever young," and watched aging men only date twenty-something-year-olds.

Maybe it was because I had been rejected as the Bachelorette, or because I now had a crush on a guy over six years my junior. Honestly? It was mostly because my dermatologist made me an offer I couldn't refuse. Yes, the same dermatologist whose email intro led to my job at *The Bachelor*. I had helped his business over the years by booking him on *The Doctors* and referring clients to him. As a thank-you, he offered to keep my face looking naturally youthful for next to nothing in cost. I've always loved a bargain!

I had squeezed in the appointment before a field shoot in Malibu for Clare's intro package. Numbing cream was slathered all over my face to prep for the injections. As the doctor entered the room, needle in hand, lightheadedness kicked in as everything around me started to blur . . .

Next thing I knew, the doctor and nurses were standing over me, shaking me to wake up. I had passed out, from trying to get Botox! The horror. It brought me back to another time needles had caused my disappearance into darkness. I was at Erewhon for a field shoot for *The Doctors*, where a wellness event was happening. A booth was offering free acupuncture, and being a sucker for freebies, I decided to try it. I passed out, not once, but twice, for an extended period of time. Before I knew it, there were hot firefighters carrying me out to an ambulance. I fully leaned into damsel in distress mode.

Back in the Botox chair, my face was completely numb as I ate crackers and drank orange juice to try to raise my blood pressure. I had come this far; I wasn't backing out now! Eventually I felt okay, and the doctor did his thing. What a weird feeling, to have someone injecting things into my completely numb face. Although I was radiating with youth afterward, I'm sticking with face yoga, gua sha, and retinol moving forward (but don't quote me on this).

A week and a half later, I was quarantined with the rest of the world. The day I saw paparazzi photos of Peter and Kelley was the day I looked in the mirror and saw a face that no longer looked like mine. It was as though all the injections had migrated to my chin, which was plump and red, with a butt-cheek crease in the middle of it. I was horrified. *I've been cursed by the Botox gods! I should have taken my fainting as a sign. I'll never look the same again!* I thought to myself, crying in despair as I stared into the mirror.

It wasn't just my chin. My smile lines had weird bubbly bumps, and my crow's feet wrinkles were replaced with a red rash. What was happening?! Thank goodness I had my dermatologist's cell number, given everything was shut down from Covid-19. He assured me it was nothing to worry about, and that an antibiotic would do the trick. Since I had a foreign substance in my body, it could be reacting from the stress of the pandemic (um, and the stress of Peter), or even the fact that I was on my period.

God, the things we go through as women.

Once the antibiotics kicked in, I had a smooth, wrinkle-free face, just in time to be locked inside for months to come. What a waste.

While my face and the world were still, my mind was an active three-ring circus. I'd never had this much time to sit with my own thoughts. I was too embarrassed to talk out loud about any of it, so I lay in bed restless, unable to sleep. I replayed everything in my head over and over, trying to make sense of it all. I tried to deny what I was feeling and brush it off as no big deal.

On one hand, I was heartbroken over Peter. On the other hand, I was heartbroken over my failure as a producer. Shame came from all directions. I felt rejected from love and reminded that 'men don't choose me.' I felt like a fraud at my job, with a permanent scarlet letter on my heart. Every time Peter's name was mentioned on a Zoom call, my stomach clenched with dread, fearful they knew my secret.

I felt like a fraud as a friend too. Natasha called me, still heartbroken over Peter, as I comforted her and offered advice. Hannah Ann had just moved to Los Angeles, and on a walk together, I comforted her and offered advice. I had always thrived on being an honest, sincere person, and it pained me to have this secret. The thought of revealing it? Even worse.

I was desperate to quiet my mind before it drove me absolutely crazy. If I could stop thinking, maybe the pain would disappear. While I've always considered myself a yogi, I was never great at meditating. But what better time than Covid to try? Instead of starting with the basics, I dove into *Becoming Supernatural* by Joe Dispenza, recommended by Peter himself. Joe Dispenza's meditation techniques bring you to another dimension, into the quantum realm, where he says all things are possible and you can change your reality. The book breaks down how we can use the power of the mind to essentially escape time and space and manifest all our desires, heal, and grow. It was like *The Secret* on crack. I was sold.

I was in awe as I read stories of people healing themselves from illness, blindness, and trauma. I started playing his guided meditations every night in bed but got annoyed with myself as my mind wandered and I couldn't relax. But slowly, night after night, I noticed a shift. One night after nearly a month of practice, I fully surrendered. My heart started racing quickly, then slowed down. I felt a wave wash over me, followed by stillness; it was like I had entered a soundproof chamber, as my mind went silent.

Behind closed eyes, I saw colorful, vivid geometrical patterns and fractals repeating themselves indefinitely, like a kaleidoscope in my mind. I then saw various vignettes play out, as if time were bending. I saw myself lying in mud, engulfed in the earth's soil. I saw an older version of myself, looking out the window as a ray of sunlight reflected upon me. I was watching young children playing in the grass, laughing and smiling as their giggles echoed through the window glass and landed in my heart. It was beautiful.

I didn't want the scenes to end. But eventually my conscious mind kicked in, trying to analyze and understand what I was experiencing. The visions faded back to black, as I felt myself lying in my bed again. For a moment, I had felt peace and serenity as my analytical mind went still. For a moment, love had prevailed.

Being at the center of a world that often feels skin deep, the meditation reminded me of the most important things. Below the surface of our smooth, wrinkle-free skin, there is a world of possibilities within. I had been a part of a superficial world for so long while working in Hollywood, surrounded by egos and money-driven motives. We created drama among a bunch of beautiful people who then went on to become influencers, showcasing boxes of beauty products for likes.

I reflected on the world around me, the rat race of life. Everyone seemingly in a hypnotic state doing the same thing over and over again, driven by external success—flashy cars, designer purses, and store-bought, youthful faces. It felt like the whole world shutting down was a collective message from the universe—slow down, wake up, connect with yourself. All these years of go, go, go had caused me to sacrifice my soul. I had lost touch with who I was.

But now? Now that I had a moment of stillness to breathe, I wondered what else was deep within me, aching to be set free.

16

Return to Chaos

Alongside my newfound meditation practice, the production break gave me a rare gift: a healthy routine. I was working out regularly, eating clean, balanced meals, and getting eight hours of sleep each night. I also wasted no time jumping on the apps and getting creative with dating. I didn't get Botox for nothing, after all.

I was having FaceTime dates, six-feet-apart walking dates, and if the men were really lucky, they might get a masked hug on the third date. I connected with some amazing men during this time, some of whom I'm still friends with today. But just as restaurants began reopening and real dates became possible, the moneymaking gods of Bachelor Nation figured out a way to get us back on set.

Still in the midst of the pandemic, we traded jet-setting for the most romantic travel destination of all . . . Palm Springs, in the middle of summer. We would create our own giant quarantine bubble at the La Quinta Resort & Club, where the entire season would be filmed.

While our original travel plans would have brought us across the Atlantic to Iceland and beyond, I was hopeful the lack of travel would mean hours wouldn't be so brutal, and I could maintain a normal routine. Plus, instead of squeezing my life into two suitcases, I could fill my entire car.

I was determined to keep namaste-ing in the desert, which meant my yoga mat, crystals, palo santo, diffuser, Alexa, and self-help books were all coming with me. I wanted to make a home away from home that felt zen and peaceful, even if within the confines of my bungalow.

Like many people during Covid, I had splurged on a Peloton to work out at home. It was back-ordered and arrived only a week before I was driving out to the desert for two months. You know what that meant, right? The Peloton needed to come with me. I asked the delivery guy if it could fit in a sedan. He said it was tricky, but possible. The next week, my neighbor and quarantine friend, Adam, helped me get it down to my car. It took both of us, and eventually a couple of the gardeners, to maneuver it into the back seat. The screen rode shotgun and I packed the rest of the car to the brim. As much as I'd been growing spiritually, Buddhist minimalistic ways weren't, and still aren't, a specialty of mine.

I hit the open road, desert bound toward 120-degree heat. My producer brain never turns off, so I shot B-roll on the drive, knowing the crews wouldn't be able to leave the property. I captured the windmills, and WELCOME TO PALM SPRINGS sign, all while blasting country tunes and trying to stay optimistic about the season ahead. While I had loved the break, a part of me was excited to get back to production and film this unique, weird season in a bubble.

Kudos to our production team and the hotel staff, who figured out contactless check-in to our rooms, where we all quarantined for a week before entering the bubble. As I pulled up to my Spanish-style bungalow and started to unload the car, I was determined to get my Peloton inside. Sweat dripped from all crevasses of my body as I somehow maneuvered the bike out of my car, nearly denting the side of my BMW in the process. I rolled the bike into my casita and slid the screen into place.

Thank goodness for my Peloton; even squeezing in a fifteen-minute spin was a great escape from the chaos of filming. For those that didn't watch, it was the first time we had two Bachelorettes in one season. Clare was all in on Dale early on, having had time during the break to get the scoop on the men. Knowing it would be hard to finish an entire season with the obvious connection, Clare and Dale got engaged after just twelve days, and Tayshia came in as the new Bachelorette with the remaining men.

I obviously can't spill the ins and outs of the season. What I can say is that the only thing hot for me about a 'hot girl summer' was the 120-degree heat. Oh, and the night sweats in my cold room—another way my body was speaking to me. Imagine producing the leading lady when there was a moment in time when you thought that might be you. Then, when Clare bounced early, the hope of being asked to step into the role swirled through my mind again. I mean, I was already in the Covid-cleared bubble, about the same size as Clare, and this pod of men were older than usual since Clare had been the oldest Bachelorette, four years my senior. It just made sense, right?

When I met with the executives to discuss the plan forward, there was a pause before the reveal of who the next Bachelorette would be. My heart braced itself. I really thought they might say my name.

"Tayshia!" they exclaimed.

"Oh my God, yay!" I said, forcing a smile, sad once again that it wasn't me.

"She just arrived and is starting her quarantine—fingers crossed she doesn't have Covid!" they said.

Fingers crossed she does have Covid! I thought to myself. Sorry, Tayshia! It was nothing personal; I considered her a friend. I just, you know, was hoping someday I'd be the desire of a man's attention, go on romantic dates, and fall in love again.

Of course, being the Bachelorette isn't the only way to go on dates and fall in love. I know that. When I wasn't out of town, I went on dates. Just none of them stuck. I don't know if the reason was my busy work life, unrealistic standards, or the desire to live the fantasy I created. For now, let's go with the desire to live the fantasy I created . . .

That night, I lit my "manifest" candle from House of Intuition, cleansed my space with palo santo, and played Joe Dispenza's guided meditation to manifest my dreams. I visualized myself as the Bachelorette, walking into the cocktail mixer room, greeting all the men, and giving my speech. I thought about all the guys and who I might end up with. I imagined Peter returning after I confessed my love for him in an interview. The producers would call him, and he would dump Kelley and come join the cast. If that didn't happen, Zac was likely the next choice for me. I love East Coast men and have a history with guys from Jersey (like, the nice part, not the Shore). Zac was mature, had depth and swag, and was doing meaningful work with his rehab centers. Maybe I subconsciously guided Tayshia toward him when my witchy voodoo to be the Bachelorette failed.

I know as a self-proclaimed master manifester, I clearly failed when it came to making myself the lead. I realize now that when you're living in a state of shame, it is hard to manifest such desires. And I was swimming in it.

Back at work, surrounded by coworkers, I lived in a constant state of fear that someone would find out about me and Peter. I was paranoid that they already knew and were gossiping about it behind my back. The scarlet letter of my mind grew heavier, as I felt trapped by my own internal humiliation. When people asked how Peter was doing, I didn't know what to say. It seemed so out of character that we wouldn't have kept in touch. But like an ex-lover whose new girlfriend didn't like you, we didn't. I missed him, sometimes wishing we had never hooked up so we could have remained friends.

That summer, I watched two love stories unfold. I sat behind the camera and talked to both Clare and Tayshia about men, love, heartache, and their hopes for the future. I listened to them have deep, vulnerable, and meaningful conversations with a diverse group of men. I saw the sparkle in their eyes as they fell in love.

I'd often lie on the grass during dinner dates, looking up at the night sky illuminated in the desert. My mind would drift to thoughts of love and connection, until I was interrupted with a request for lip gloss, or a request from my boss. What I would have given to put on a cute dress and some lip gloss, and connect with a man like they were.

I cried tears of joy when Dale, then Zac, proposed to their leading ladies. On the outside, I was always bubbly, upbeat, and a positive bright light on set. Even through the lack of sleep and toxic sides of creating a reality show, I never complained and always smiled.

But on the inside? I wasn't so sure I was happy anymore. How much longer could I put on a smile and ignore what was going on within my soul?

Home Is Where the Heart Is

It was still dark out as I threw on my black Carhartt beanie and army green jacket, and turned on my walkie-talkie. A to-go cup of coffee in my hand, I hurried down the long, regal corridor of Nemacolin Resort, the marble flooring lit by the procession of crystal chandeliers above me. As I stepped outside, I took a moment to breathe in the fresh fall air and take a big sip of coffee before putting on my mask.

"Good morning, boys!" I said as I stepped into the SUV, way too much enthusiasm in my voice for a 6 AM shoot.

"Heyy..." Matt James, our new Bachelor, muttered, not quite matching my energy. We were filming sunrise B-roll for his intro package that would play at the beginning of his season. As we pulled up to the lake we were filming at, I knew the early call time was worth it. Mist was rising from the water, creating an ethereal, dreamlike setting. Before the sun began to rise, we captured Matt gazing over the lake at dawn, with the full harvest moon peeking out from the silhouetted trees behind him.

We were still under Covid restrictions, so everything for Matt's season would be filmed on the hotel property in rural Pennsylvania. It was a nice contrast from the desert, as the crisp air and colorful fall foliage was reminiscent of being home in Connecticut.

Speaking of home, we were in the middle of filming B-roll when my dad called. Since I was working, I let it go to voicemail. Then came the follow-up text. My body instantly tightened with fear.

Call me as soon as you can.

Ever since moving away from home, anytime my parents call at odd times, or send texts like this, my mind instantly goes to the worst-case scenario, dreading what I might hear when I call them back.

"I'll be right back. I have to make a call," I said to my segment producer, stepping away from the little stone chapel along the forest edge.

"Hi, hunny," my dad said as he answered. I could tell from his tone it wasn't good.

"Hi, what's going on, Dad?" I asked, bracing myself.

"Your grandma passed away," he said softly through tears. "She was rushed to the hospital this morning and didn't make it."

"Oh no . . . Dad, I'm so sorry . . ." I cried with him as he told me more about what happened. My grandma had led a long, strong, and resilient life. She'd survived deep loss and heartbreak. Her husband, Charlie, was the love of her life. He was Italian and she was English. At the time, marrying an Italian wasn't acceptable, so the two eloped at sixteen. They went on to have three boys and one daughter, my Aunt Ginny. Sadly, my grandpa passed away before I got to meet him, of a heart attack at age fifty-five. My Aunt Ginny also passed away at fifty-five from lung cancer, having never smoked a day in her life. It didn't seem fair.

Enduring all the loss, my grandma went on to beat breast cancer and lead a fairly healthy life before succumbing to Alzheimer's in her final years. While sad about her passing, I hoped she was finally reunited with her true love and their daughter.

When a grandparent passes away, most people drop whatever they are doing to go be with family. Both of my sisters flew from California to Connecticut for the funeral. I was a mere seven-hour drive away from home, yet, for some reason, I didn't leave work to go. We were just about to start filming, and with the Covid protocols of having to quarantine for a week if I left, I would have missed the first three episodes. This was a crucial time for me to establish rapport with Matt, get a feel for his leading ladies, and set the foundation for the entire season. My grandma couldn't have planned her passing for a worse time, workwise. Horrible to say, I know. I look back with regret for not having gone to her funeral. Instead, I Zoomed in from my hotel room. It was so out of character for me to not drop what I was doing for family. What had I become?

The extra time with Matt didn't help with establishing rapport, either. I often felt like I was doing my first job ever, babysitting. For the first time, we had a lead who had not been on the previous season, so he was new to the TV world. Who was I to tell him what to do? He was skeptical and closed off from the beginning, and unfortunately it didn't get better with time.

A couple of weeks after my grandma's funeral, I got another call. This time, it was from my mother. My papa, her father, had been rushed to the hospital. Things weren't looking good. To make matters worse, Matt and I had just gotten into an argument that left me bawling my eyes out on the ninth hole of Nemacolin's golf course. I walked out on the golf course for privacy, sprawled out under a tree, and looked up at the sky through the rustling fall leaves. Knowing I was likely about to lose another grandparent, I wondered if heaven was up there. What is this life all about, really? Where do we go from here? Why did I feel so far removed from my connection with God? Is there a God?

Was this all worth it, only to be dismissed? I tried to stay grounded, but it was hard when the lead was closed off to me. Maybe I was too empathetic for this job, getting entangled in the emotions of others and taking things too personally, always wanting to people please.

For the first time in seven years, I asked to skip the rose ceremony. I took a long bubble bath. I prayed for my papa to be okay. Earlier that day, I sent a video to my family chat of a little interview I'd done with him. My mom played it by his hospital bedside. By some miracle, he woke up out of his coma state with a big smile across his face as he watched himself say, "Marrying Millie is the best decision I ever made!"

While this moment gave us hope he might come back to us, the next day my mom called and said he likely wouldn't make it much longer. This time, I didn't hesitate. I told my bosses I needed to be with my family. They were incredibly understanding, even giving me a production rental van to drive. I packed up my things, loaded the van, and drove straight home. I didn't really say bye to anyone, leaving as quickly as I could with the hopes of making it back in time to say goodbye to my papa.

By the time I reached Connecticut, visiting hours were over, so I drove straight to my parents' house, the home I grew up in. A sense of ease ran through me as they greeted me with a loving hug. I had a bowl of Cracklin' Oat Bran before my mom tucked me in for the night.

It was her voice that woke me in the early morning, just as the sun peeked over the horizon. My papa had passed away overnight. Sadness swept through me, but also comfort, knowing I was exactly where I was supposed to be. I was home with those who loved me most. I knew I would never put work before family again.

My parents built the house I grew up in while my mom was pregnant with me. My father literally laid down the foundation of the home with help from friends and family. They bought the forty-five acres of forest and swampland for twenty thousand dollars; people thought they were crazy to build a home there. My mom, a city girl, also wondered if she was crazy, having fallen in love with a country boy. Yet, over the years, the property became their magical oasis. My dad made his dream a reality, creating a space where he could hunt, fish, and golf all on his own land. My mom adapted nicely to country life, finding joy reading on the porch as hummingbirds swirled around and taking long walks down their dirt road.

I grew up in a warm, loving home full of memories that fill my heart with joy. Our house was always full—holidays, bonfires, homemade pizza, and wine night. My parents and their parents demonstrated a beautiful example of love. To have had three grandparents all my life that lived to see ninety is a true rarity that has helped shape who I am today. Not a day goes by that I don't count my blessings for the love, health, and support of my family.

While at home, I immediately went to work helping my mom with the funeral arrangements. We wrote the obituary, gathered photos of Papa with family and friends, and visited my nana daily. On the day of his funeral, surrounded by all who loved him, I read the following:

Dear Papa,

Growing up I always wanted a big family with lots of children, because I couldn't imagine not having macaroni Sundays with a full house. Specifically, I wanted five kids, so I could be just like Nana and Papa. Sundays at your house brought so much joy to my childhood . . . helping you crush grapes in the garage and admiring the birds flying around your feeder. Also, confession: That was your grandchildren that would crawl under the dinner table and untie all the grown-ups' shoelaces. And those peaches soaked in your homemade wine . . . boy were those delicious. But a glass of wine a day kept the doctor away! That was the key to you and Nana seeming to get younger and younger each year! Talk about hot couple goals! You and Nana had more life energy, positivity, and happiness in your eyes than most people I meet my age. I've always admired that about you two.

I loved hearing stories about when you first started dating—calling the corner deli boy to have him run down the road and let Millie know Roland was on the phone! I admire the romanticism and chivalry you put into going after what you wanted, Nana. Seeing the love you two have for one another reminds me that true love does exist. Not just with the two of you, but with the beautiful family you've created, full of so much love, joy, and happiness. To say we are lucky is an understatement, but I'll quote my dad in saying there is no such thing as luck—you create your own luck. I applaud you, Papa, for the life you created, the family you created, and the love you've shown and shared with all those that are blessed to have known you. I'll think of you every sunset I watch on the beach and cardinal I see in the sky. Thank you for continuing to watch over our family. We'll miss you.

Love,
Julie

I stayed with my parents for a few more weeks. During the first snowfall, I walked into the woods to sit by the stream I played in as a kid. I sat on a rock watching the snow sprinkle onto the tree branches and melt into the water below. As a cold breeze swept through me, I was brought back to the last time I had come home for an extended period. It was one of the darkest times of my life, prompted by news I received while in the darkest place in the world, Finland's north pole at the start of winter.

I had been in Finland four years prior, filming Nick's final episodes of *The Bachelor*. The sun set around 3:30 PM, which meant, for once, our days wrapped at a reasonable hour. I was back in my hotel room when I received a video call from my dad. He'd recently discovered a heart valve defect and would soon be having surgery to replace it. The doctors assured him he'd be as good as new after that.

Unfortunately, that's not why he was calling. After a routine scan of the chest area before surgery, lesions were discovered on his ribs. That, along with some blood work, led a new doctor to walk into his hospital room, from the oncology department. He was diagnosed with multiple myeloma, a type of blood cancer that forms in the bone marrow and has no known cure.

I felt numb as my father told me the news, tears streaming down both our faces. How could this be happening again? I thought I had checked the "parent gets cancer box" after my mom had a double mastectomy to beat breast cancer years prior.

"I've lived a good life," he said gently. My dad was always positive and hopeful. I felt the weight of the diagnosis in his voice.

I did my best to avoid googling it, but eventually gave in. The average life expectancy? Five years. My mind went down a rabbit hole of dark thoughts. You expect your father to be there to walk you down the aisle, and to meet your future children. The new reality? He may not be. I slammed my computer shut, crawled up in a ball under my covers, and cried as the snow fell down from the dark Finland skies.

After filming wrapped, I flew straight home to help post-surgery and to go to doctor's appointments. My younger sister, Janelle, was still living at home at the time, and along with the stress of my dad's health, my parents were dealing with the stress of her mental health leading her down a dark path. I spent nights following her and playing detective before she ultimately surrendered and got on a plane with me to California to get professional help. The pain of seeing someone I love struggling is something I carry with me deeply.

As those dark memories came back while sitting at the water's edge, so did the reality that my father still had an incurable cancer, and my sister was still going through her share of highs and lows. I closed my eyes to meditate, pray, and ask for guidance. Through the stillness, I got my answer clearly . . . Love and family are what matters most.

As I opened my eyes, a beam of sunlight pierced through the trees, causing the snow to glisten as it fell from the sky. Then, just in front of me, a red cardinal flew by and landed on the branch. I stared at it, frozen in time. Cardinals have long been considered spiritual messengers, a sign from a loved one who has passed. Cardinals were also my papa's favorite bird. I'm not sure how I could deny God's existence in a moment like this. I was grateful to know another angel was watching over our family, to protect and guide us on our journeys.

Twenty years of working in the entertainment industry had pulled me away from my connection with God. Sitting by the stream, I felt on a soul level that the cardinal wasn't only a sign from Papa, but also a message from spirit. The message was clear: *Come back.*

Come back to God, to source, to the truth of who you are.

18

Final Goodbyes

I knew it was time to quit my job. But like a true procrastinator, I put off the inevitable for fear of leaving a job that was "too good to leave" and fear of the unknown. I told my bosses I would return after the winter hiatus and planned on doing so even though my intuition and heart said otherwise.

The question now was about what department I would move to after the hiatus to keep me happy. We scheduled a Zoom call for the week after New Year's, right before we'd return to the office. So, what did I do in the meantime? I went to Cuba, obviously! My friend Adam's friend Allyssa, one of the OG travel bloggers (shout-out @mylifeisatravelmovie), was hosting a group trip and had a couple extra spots. The rate was too good to turn down, so we joined.

It was nice to not be the one producing everything for once. Our local guide's daughter, Devon, was an aspiring actress, model, and artist, and a bit of a Havana socialite. She instantly bonded with Adam and me and took us to an underground art exhibit and a night out on the town. She introduced us to all her friends, local artists and creators, who were fighting to be able to express themselves freely. Hearing their stories and seeing the passion in their eyes was a humbling and beautiful experience. It was sad to see how little control they have, living under dictatorship, yet they still find ways to create, play, dance, and sing.

The Love Producer

One artist who caught my eye goes by the name 2+2=5?, symbolizing how nothing is as it seems. His work is splashed across the crumbling colonial walls of Old Havana. His signature character is seen wearing a balaclava, a symbol of fear of expression in a place where freedom of speech is dangerous. His art is a form of protest.

We expressed interest in buying his art, so our guide arranged for our group to visit his home. We crowded into his tiny room in the apartment he shared with all his relatives—bunk beds on one side, art supplies on the other, and a rainbow of graffiti art and masked figures painted on the walls. He unveiled his collection, explaining it in Spanish as our guide translated. I purchased a painting I was drawn to, done on an old record, of a naked girl wearing a balaclava, gripping a threshold to another realm. He said it represented a woman longing to explore another dimension. Little did I know how deeply that piece would come to resonate later.

On our final night we threw a rooftop party at a hostel for Allyssa's birthday. All the locals we met throughout the week came—salsa dancers, singers, and our new artist friends, including 2+2=5?.

The DJ blasted salsa music as we danced under the stars. At one point, I stepped away to use the restroom in one of the empty hostel rooms. After reapplying my red lips, I stepped out to see 2+2=5? sitting on the edge of the bed, waiting. We smiled at each other, as he gestured for me to sit beside him. I could feel the nerves build up inside me, our skin lightly touching as I sat. Lost in translation with my limited Spanish, we attempted to flirt. The universal language of sex appeal was apparent as we gazed at each other. He knew the words that mattered, as he pointed to his arm and said, "Kiss me here."

I leaned in and left a red lip mark on his tattooed skin.

"Kiss me here," he continued, guiding me up to his bicep.

"Kiss me here." His neck now. I glanced at the trail of red lips before looking up into his molten brown gaze. He touched his lips.

"Kiss me here."

A spark rushed through me as I leaned in and we kissed. The make-out was sexy and a bit mischievous. As our lips separated, he smiled and whispered, "I love sex," pulling me in closer.

"Okay! Time to get back to the party!" I said, giving him a quick kiss before pulling away. Was I tempted? Of course. He was sexy and soulful. But I wasn't about to have a one-night stand. Instead, I pulled him back to the dance floor to keep the sexual tension, and mojitos, flowing through the night.

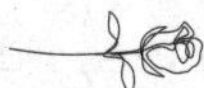

The next day we flew from Cuba to Miami, where we'd stay for a couple of nights. It brought me back to a time when I was on a flight from Miami to Los Angeles. I had kept to myself in my unfortunate middle seat, until mid-flight when the lady next to me tapped my shoulder. I turned to her and smiled.

"I hope you don't mind, but I just have to tell you something," she began. "Your lips, they are very honest. Make sure you always speak your truth."

The timing of this message was interesting. I was feeling guilty because I had run into a *Bachelor* contestant at the airport who had been sent home the night before. We were hanging out before our respective flights when she asked, "Did you know it was coming?"

"No, I had no idea," I declared. "You two seemed to be having a great time all day." I had sensed she would be sent home, but thought it would be best if she didn't know that.

"Thank you for sharing that," I responded to the lady next to me. "It's a good reminder."

"My kids think I'm crazy, but sometimes messages just come through me."

"Wow, fascinating." I was intrigued.

"Your work is a crazy three-ring circus!" she exclaimed, without having been told what I do. "Do not let it stop you from speaking your truth.

If I could advise, I'd tell you to get out of there! It is not aligned with who you are."

That conversation stuck with me. Four years later, here it was popping up again. I wasn't speaking my truth. I hadn't been for a long time. The truth is, I didn't even know what my truth was anymore. Maybe it was time to figure that out?

I got up early on the day of my meeting and went to Soho Beach House to sip my tea and gather my thoughts. I really didn't know what I was going to say on the Zoom call. I figured I'd talk through the various routes I could go next with producing, then decide what to do based on our conversation. But as I logged into the call and saw all nine executive producers' squares staring at me, I could barely get a word out; tears wouldn't stop running down my face. *Get it together, Julie!*

The tears brought me back to childhood when I'd seemingly cry for no reason. My teacher would say, "Great job, you got an A-," and I would cry. Why wasn't it an A? When someone asked me how I felt about something, I'd cry. If someone looked at me just slightly the wrong way, I'd cry. My sensitivity was a blessing and a curse. I recognized that the tears were often a defense mechanism when I didn't know how to properly communicate what I was feeling or wanted, and that was happening now. What was I feeling? What did I want?

I should be excited, I thought. The producers could see me running the show in the near future! That should have been a dream come true for a small-town girl who moved to Hollywood to make it in the entertainment industry (cue country music song). All the hard work and years of grinding away at various jobs, climbing the production ladder, were finally paying off. My roles had gone from production assistant, casting associate, associate producer, senior associate producer, segment producer, field producer, producer, senior producer, silly producer (wink, wink) to supervising producer, and I was now on the brink of co-executive producer, which would then lead to executive producer. The hustle, the grind, and the politics from this show and shows past were close to really paying off.

Final Goodbyes

But I wasn't excited about it. Instead, I found myself thinking, *All nine of you are on this Zoom call. Isn't that a bit excessive?* I did care about these people; they were the ones with whom I had spent the last seven years of my life, day in and day out. We were one big dysfunctional family that traveled the world together. Season after season, proposal after proposal, year after year.

Our adventures had taken us to over thirty countries; there had been moments when I truly pinched myself with disbelief and gratitude. I'd stood on top of glaciers in Switzerland, rode helicopters over volcanoes in Costa Rica, chased the northern lights in Finland, played with monkeys in Thailand, bungee jumped in Mexico and Macao, held baby kangaroos in the outback, and watched the most beautiful sunsets across the globe. How could I leave a job that allowed me to do all that?

Yet, as I stared into each of my bosses' Zoom square faces, seeing the future ahead of me, it didn't feel so rosy (pun intended). One guy had what felt like a permanent sty in his eye that I swear grew bigger as each season progressed. The men with families barely saw their kids. The women were in their forties and single. Is that what I wanted? Styes and no guy to call my own? They were successful, sure, but was the personal sacrifice and stress worth it?

As I stared at each of them, tears continuing to run down my face, I realized I was working toward something I had no desire of becoming. I had fallen out of love with my job. On top of that, I was two weeks shy of my thirty-sixth birthday. The two-year plan we were discussing would leave me two weeks shy of my thirty-eighth birthday. For the past seven years, I had been living out of a suitcase for half the year with no days off, wrinkles getting thicker and grays popping up like wildflowers. All that was going through my mind now was, *How will I ever find love before my biological clock strikes midnight?* If I ever wanted to find my prince, it was time to take matters into my own hands. After giving my all to everyone else's love and happiness, what would it take to bring me love and happiness?

We ended the Zoom with no conclusion. They told me to sleep on it and let them know what I decided. The next day, I emailed all nine EPs . . .

Hello,

After a lot of thinking, I don't think it's possible for me to come back this season. I know you want a long-term commitment and as I reflect on my priorities in life I don't think it's feasible for me to commit to being away half the year, for years to come. I need to be honest with myself and all of you. I'm sorry for not deciding sooner, this obviously is a very difficult decision for me that I hope I don't regret. I love you all and am grateful for your understanding, support, guidance & friendship.

With love,
Julie

And just like that, it was over. They all responded with kind emails and expressed that the door was always open if I wanted to return.
Shit. Now what?

Part Three

THE HEALING JOURNEY

19

The Supporting Characters

Now what? The journey, of course! It's finally time for me to emerge from the shadows and step into the leading lady role of my life.

I couldn't rent a giant mansion, line up twenty-five men, and put together my own rose ceremonies. I didn't have a production team and glam squad to get me ready for dates. And I couldn't recruit a producer from the show to dig into the questions of my heart. I did, however, find my own troupe of love producers to help along the way. This included therapists, hypnotherapists, life coaches, energy healers, gurus, intuitive guides, and more. You name it, I tried it.

Along with wanting to date and fall in love, I had to figure out what I was doing with my life! I had a million different creative ideas circling in my head. But as someone with undiagnosed ADHD left to fend for herself, focusing on one project for more than ten minutes didn't happen. I realize now why someone with ADHD thrives as a producer; producers work in a fast-paced environment where things happen in the moment. They have to think on their feet, be creative, and take risks. But now? The overwhelm of where to even begin kept me walking in circles.

My body went into complete fight/flight/freeze mode. I didn't realize it until I finally got a therapist, but leaving something that was my identity sent my nervous system into a state of dysregulation. And because we're no longer cavemen fighting off saber-tooth tigers, this translates in modern society to anxiety, depression, and procrastination. I had lost my tribe, my safety in this world. Leaving *The Bachelor* wasn't like leaving any old job; it was this weird family unit that consumed my life.

The show went on without me, of course. A lot of my coworkers didn't even reach out. Did they care? Was I like a cast member, who came and went? I could have reached out to them, but I had too much shame to do that. It's not like I cleanly bowed out after buttoning up a beautiful season. Nope, I left right at the climax of it all, after a fight with the lead (okay, and the death of two grandparents).

As lost as I felt, I realized I wasn't any different from the cast members I had guided for years, often arriving on the show at a crossroads in their lives—hopeful for love, connection, and growth. I stepped into the unknown with that same hope: that the universe, my showrunner, would send a cast of supporting characters into the portal of my heart, helping me grow and find everlasting love.

So with that, let the journey begin!

Night One Send-Homes

Like all great reality shows, not every scene in my real life makes it to the screen (or in this case, the pages of this book). But just for fun, below is a list of men that I met who didn't make it past the cutting room floor.

Owen

The Movie Star I Discovered Was Seeing Someone Else Through Deuxmoi

Chris

Asked to Pay My Rent on the First Date (In Hindsight . . .)

Cade

Commented On How Much I Ate During Dinner

The Supporting Characters

Tyler

The WYD Late Night Texter

Craig

Age: 65

A Zaddy the Same Age As My Daddy

Alejandro

Age: 24

Not Here For the Right Reasons

Matthew

Cried About His Ex-Girlfriend On the First Date

Marcus

Ex-Lover Who Asked for a Threesome with Him and His Girlfriend (So Not Leading Lady Energy)

Kyle

Out of This World Producer

The waves crashed along the California coastline as a cluster of seagulls took flight. The long stretch of sand was empty besides one couple sprawled out on a picnic blanket in the distance. The homes, one after another, stood on wooden stilts for protection from the tide that would soon be crashing against them. It was the beginning of golden hour, with the sun making its way toward the horizon. I breathed in the fresh saltwater air as I made my way down the wooden stairs, slid off my sandals, and stepped onto the soft sand.

Kyle had invited me to Malibu for a sunset beach walk. He was cute in the nontraditional sense, like a lovable teddy bear. He had salt and pepper curly locks and a warm, welcoming smile. He was a producer as well, but for movies.

As we walked along the water's edge, he said, "You know, my mom and sister were very excited about our date. They're huge fans of *The Bachelor* and knew exactly who you were."

I laughed. "I bet they want the inside scoop, don't they?"

"I told them I'd do my best to get it out of you," he said with a chuckle. "They were especially curious about the rumors of you and the Bachelor." I felt a quiet tightening in my gut, though my face showed joy and humor.

"Ha, that was fun, wasn't it? But no, those were just rumors," I said with a wave of my hand. "We were together all the time because that was my job."

"Of course. You were his producer—you'd never do something like that," he responded. You know, from one producer to another . . .

Despite the discomfort of that conversation, I found Kyle super interesting to talk to. We were playful with each other, writing our names in the sand and skipping along the shoreline. We eventually made our way to his balcony to take in the sunset, watching the sky transition from blue to shades of orange, red, and pink.

Our date then took an interesting turn. Kyle told me that, a month earlier, while watching the sunset, he took a picture of a helicopter flying over the horizon. As he snapped the photo, he captured something else— an object that shot up from the ocean into the sky.

"Woah! What do you think it was?" I said as he showed me the photo.

"I showed my friend who did a documentary on UFOs, and he confirmed that's probably what I captured," he said with excitement.

I had always been open to the idea of aliens. We certainly can't be the only species in this universe. But outside of the occasional *what else is out there* thought, I hadn't given much attention to the idea.

Kyle had recently downloaded an app by Dr. Steven Greer, the go-to alien guy, which guides listeners in meditation to connect consciously with extraterrestrials. Then, it plays tones to try to get them to emerge in the night sky.

"Let's do it!" I said with excitement. Before I knew it, we were meditating and gazing up at the night sky, looking for UFOs. After a few minutes of wondering how completely ridiculous we were, I saw something move in the sky.

"Look, up there!" I exclaimed, pointing to a star-like object that shot straight up, followed by another that moved right alongside it. Suddenly, we were like two young kids, looking up at the universe with awe and curiosity, convinced every moving object could be extraterrestrials communicating to us from galaxies far, far away. I was mesmerized, watching the magical universe above.

"Hello, friends!" I shouted, as the crashing waves below us were illuminated by the stars, moon, and supposed UFOs in the sky. I felt connected to the universe in a way I hadn't since I was a young girl looking through my telescope, wondering if I'd ever go to the moon. I had loved classic alien movies like *E.T.* and *Mac and Me*. (Where my *Mac and Me* fans at?!)

In hindsight, is it possible that what we saw were satellites? Sure, but what fun is that? This date sure beat a night out at the bar, and we were totally sober. As we wrapped on alien-gazing, Kyle and I shared a sweet kiss good night before I drove down the Pacific Coast Highway with a newfound fascination for the cosmos above.

While a romantic connection with Kyle wasn't written in the stars, I was grateful for the date, as he helped reactivate my inner child. Remember that time when we believed in magic, unicorns, aliens, fairies, and that all was possible? It was a time before our minds were conditioned with what is right and wrong, real vs. fantasy, and there was a whole universe of possibilities to explore.

When I had brainstormed dates for *The Bachelor*, I would think back to things I enjoyed doing as a kid for inspiration. Some of my favorite dates included summer camp–themed games like tug-of-war, zombie paintball, giant pillow fights, and trampoline dodgeball. We don't need to be on a dating show to go on fun, creative, childlike dates. That child still lives within us, craving to burst out. The poet Charles Bukowski said it best:

"The problem is, we look for someone to grow old with, while the secret is to find someone to stay a child with."

While I've always had a curious, childlike wonder, when it came to dating, I would suppress that side of me, trying to play it cool. But I'm not cool. I'm a dorky weirdo! No wonder I was attracting the wrong kind of men. Going forward, I decided, I would allow this authentic, curious, playful side of me to come out. Perhaps, if as adults we all activated that inner child within us, curious about the unknown, the portals of our imagination would unlock out-of-this-world possibilities.

Noah
Rom-Com Loving Movie Director

That inner child whispered when I connected with the next man that entered my portal—Noah, a movie director. I casually mentioned to him that I had a rom-com movie idea. (Hint: It was the story of what could have been if Peter and I ended up together in the end.) He thought it was brilliant and, before I knew it, we were pitching the movie to studios around town. While we got great feedback—with one executive even saying it was better than *How to Lose a Guy in 10 Days*!—we were told to come back when the script was written. Noah was booked up for the next year and didn't have time to write it, but his words of encouragement after reading some of my writing gave me the confidence to give it a go myself.

I loved writing as a kid. Then, in college, after a teacher in my writing class declared we would all get A's on our paper, and I got a B, I lost all confidence. I even stopped journaling. But thanks to Noah, I tapped back into what brought my younger self joy. I decided to write the story as a novel first, à la *The Devil Wears Prada*. I pulled out my laptop and began what was then titled *Forever a Bachelorette*, the fictional rom-com of the love story between Peter and me that could have been.

Simultaneously during this time, Peter was single again, and after over a year without speaking to each other, he reached out to invite my family and me to the launch of a book he had written, *The Adventures of Pilot Pete.* This would be the first time I would see Peter since our last night together a year and a half earlier. And just like that, my mind began to wonder if our love story was still being written.

Peter

Children's Book Author

"I mean, what are the odds that we're both in our author era? Crazy, right? Surely that's a sign," I said to my friend Alexandra when we met up in New York. She was helping me shop for a dress to wear to the event after being a true friend and telling me the dress I had packed was not sexy enough.

We were in the Bloomingdale's dressing room with a pile of dresses that cost way more than I should have been spending, seeing as I was currently unemployed. But tonight, I needed to feel hot, sexy, and confident.

"Is this too much?" I asked, putting on a silky short red dress (Peter's favorite color). "I don't want to look like I'm trying too hard," I said, looking at myself in the mirror.

"That's it! HOT. Julie, you're back in NYC—there's no such thing as too much," Alexandra assured me.

"You're right. We are bringing it back to my NYC clubbing days, but classier," I said with confidence.

I'd flown into New York the night before. My parents were driving in from Connecticut to meet me at the hotel in a few hours, before heading to the book launch together. Alexandra came back to the hotel with me and helped me get ready. We paired the red dress with my vintage Gucci knee-high boots and a classy vintage peacoat.

My parents arrived soon after and we all hopped in a cab. I've always had a very honest relationship with them, yet I'd held back on sharing what had happened with Peter and me the previous year. I feared if I told them, they would think differently about Peter, and I didn't want that to happen just in case we ended up together. I was trying to protect him while suppressing my inner pain . . . it's crazy the tricks our mind plays on us.

My parents were still hopeful the two of us would find our way to each other. Just like the good old days circa New Year's 2020, my dad made a big reservation at Carmine's for after the event, for our families and a few friends.

Nerves were running through me leading up to our arrival. I felt foolish being nervous to see Peter. I mean, come on, Julie, it's *Peter*. We rode the elevator up to the rooftop bar; the doors opened to a crowded room, with the twinkling skyline of Midtown as the backdrop. Through the sea of people, I spotted him immediately. As he looked up and we locked eyes, time stopped for a moment. It felt like it was just him and me, as big smiles came across our faces. He looked impressed. *This producer cleans up well*, I imagined him thinking. We made our way to each other and embraced in a warm hug. My nerves instantly vanished, as it felt like I was back with my best friend.

Peter introduced me to all his friends and colleagues. I assessed the girls in the crowd, wondering if any of them were his new fling. If so, they didn't make the dinner cut, as the party wound down and our select group made our way to Carmine's.

Our families enjoyed a feast of Italian food and wine, with our parents making not so sly comments about how great Peter and I looked together. After dinner we bid farewell to them and hopped in a cab to the Lower East Side's The Duck bar, where we joined everyone who had been at the book launch earlier. In my New York days I was a clubber, not a dive bar girl, so when Peter grabbed me to dip and head to DJ Zedd's set back in Midtown (we had met him while having dinner and he invited us!), I was all about it. Inside, memories came flooding back.

"I definitely had sex in this club back in college," I yelled into Peter's ear as we were waiting for our drinks. My freshman year of college the club was called Show. We spent every Friday night there with a group of guys from Brooklyn, including Jacob, who I was casually seeing. One night, he and I hooked up behind the stage; then, when I went to use the bathroom afterward and came back out, I saw him making out with another girl. I slapped him across the face. God, I really knew how to pick them.

Also, why was I telling Peter this? Why couldn't I just be a normal girl and flirt with him instead of going into full buddy mode telling funny, yet tragic, sex stories? I was also really aging myself with my *back in my college days* stories. It was hard to shift my dynamic with him outside of *The Bachelor* world; I stayed in my masculine producer energy. Not only had I coordinated getting us on the list for the show; I bet I hailed the cab and insisted on paying for drinks too. Why couldn't I just allow my feminine side to shine for once?

I realized this wasn't something I just did with Peter, but with so many men I dated. I've always felt the need to make it clear that I don't need a man and can do it all on my own. Fine, great—this may be a fact. This isn't inherently a bad thing. But it's important to have balance between the masculine and feminine, and I was so out of balance.

After leaving my job, I was having a hard time dating because I couldn't let men see me without my life all together. I refused to ever need help from anyone. *I'm fine. I can do everything on my own.* The truth? It was exhausting having to handle everything on my own and act like everything was okay. What was it going take for me to finally surrender, nurture the hurt inside of me, and express my needs, desires, and truth? My defenses were still up, especially with Peter.

As the night was winding down and Zedd's set came to an end, we grabbed a late-night slice, not wanting the night to end. We then hopped in a cab back to Peter's. One friend was passed out by the door waiting for our return, another was asleep on the couch, and Peter's parents were in his room. It wasn't exactly the setting to rekindle the flame.

We had a nightcap on the balcony before finding space in the living room to sleep. As I lay on the couch cushions, contemplating getting a cab back to my hotel, I felt Peter's hand touch my leg, gently caressing it. Was he testing the waters? He was lying on the floor next to me; the positioning was awkward. I didn't know what to do, so I just lay there. Then he stopped.

I wasn't about to hook up in a crowded room with onlookers. This time around, I knew it'd be best to have a conversation instead of just going at it. But instead of speaking up, I Irish exited as the sun was starting to rise.

I made up reasons to not have a vulnerable conversation with Peter. He was too fresh out of a relationship, so new to New York, and definitely in his player stage. But the truth? While I was really good at getting others to open up and wear their hearts on their sleeves, I shielded mine with a thick coat of armor. Keeping my truth suppressed was starting to catch up with me, though. It was causing not only deep emotional pain, but physical effects as well. I needed help, from a professional . . . something.

20

Carl, Hypnotherapist to the Stars

"Jen, I need your hypnotherapist's information—my jaw hurts so bad," I said to my sister on the phone.

"Carl was life-changing," she said, texting me his info as we spoke. "He's the go-to guy for the stars. You're going to love it."

It was about a month after my trip to New York, and my jaw had been bothering me for some time now. My dentist got me a mouthguard, which helped for a bit. But its days were numbered, as I gnawed through it each night.

I not only needed help for my TMJ; I figured it was a good idea to see a hypnotherapist since I was now in school to become a hypnotherapist. Oh, had I not mentioned that yet?! Three weeks after leaving my job, I decided to jump into hypnotherapy school. Fun, right? The program my sister Jen had done was about to begin and I decided that was surely a sign and signed up (all the signs!). When Jen had hypnotized me post-breakup with James, we had joked about becoming the "Hypno Sisters" one day, helping others heal their broken hearts.

Admittedly, part of me signed up for school so people would stop asking what I was doing now that I left my job. I mean, it literally had been three weeks—can't a girl just live?! But the producer in me felt pressure to prove I was doing something productive. I'd become fascinated by the power of the mind during Covid and thought it could be fun to further educate myself while simultaneously fleshing out the million creative ideas running through my head.

In hindsight, it probably would have been smarter if I'd first signed up to see a therapist, hypnotherapist, or some type of expert to talk through everything going on in my mind. But it was on brand that instead I dived into finding a way to help others, before helping myself.

Carl was old school and only did in-person sessions, so I drove to his home office in Studio City. He greeted me at the front gate. He was a short, older, quirky man. He wore high-waisted khakis, a button-down, and a casual L.L.Bean fleece thrown over it. He brought me to his office, which probably hadn't changed since the nineties. He directed me to the recliner, straight out of a 1992 Sears catalog. Judgment ran through me. *This is the go-to guy?!*

As I sat down, the squeak of the chair echoed through the room.

"Would you like some water?" he asked.

"Sure, please," I responded.

As he left to get water, my anxiety heightened. I took in the space around me. It was giving . . . hoarder vibes. Stacks of books, old CDs, and even VHSs were all around me. Piled on the couch were old posters and swag from the peak of his career. His gallery wall brought a whole new meaning to gallery walls, with a variety of mismatched artwork that hung crooked throughout.

He returned with a glass of water for each of us. I took a sip; he took a sip. I put my glass down; he put his glass down. It was a classic neuro-linguistic programming (NLP) move—him mirroring me to subtly build rapport. *I see what you're doing here, Carl.* After all, I was a hypnotherapist in training.

I smiled; he smiled.

After an awkward moment of silence, he spoke. "So, what brings you in today?"

"I have really bad TMJ," I said, matter-of-factly. "I'd like you to help me get rid of it."

He nodded, more silence, and then said, "So tell me, how are you doing?"

How am I doing? I didn't know how to answer that. I'm usually the one asking the person in the chair across from me how they are.

"I'm fine," I said, my eyes wandering off as I played with my hair. He looked at me in silence, waiting for me to expand.

"I just … well …" I got about two words out before the tears streamed down my face. I simultaneously started laughing.

"I'm sorry. I don't know why I'm crying …" *Come on, Julie. You're here for your TMJ, not some major life crisis. Focus on the jaw pain …*

"It's just … this pain is not fun. I mean, I wake up with pounding headaches from all the clenching in my sleep. My mouthguard is pretty much gnawed through, and throughout the day it just hurts, as I catch myself holding tension," I said, visually massaging and moving my jaw as I told him.

"Well, that's no way to live," Carl said.

"I know. I agree!" I stated with wide eyes.

"What's been going on in your life lately?" he asked.

"Well …" The tears came down more now, as I grabbed a tissue from the box beside me. I proceeded to tell him how I was currently in hypnotherapy school after quitting production, but that I was worried about not having a paycheck and wasn't really sure what I was doing. I talked about how hard it was leaving a show so many people loved, and that my identity was tied to. Sometimes I missed it but feared going back would mean I failed. But maybe I should?

After having judged him, I feared he was judging me now, thinking, *This girl wants to be a hypnotherapist? She can barely hold herself together.*

Eventually, he prompted me to recline and look at a painting on the wall. He began his deepening techniques to guide me into hypnosis. I focused on a spot on the wall, opening and closing my eyes as prompted.

Eventually they closed and he guided me down an elevator from the twenty-second floor (my angel number, yay!).

As someone in hypnotherapy school, I sure was critical of the process. My conscious mind was convinced it wasn't working. I began to wonder if I made a huge mistake studying hypnotherapy, resenting this decision that was now taking up way more of my time than I had hoped. My mind was wandering between judgment of Carl, myself, and trying to surrender.

Just as I was finally starting to relax, he counted me out of hypnosis, and we were done. I was skeptical about it all but still bought a package. He had transformed my sister, after all.

When I returned the following week, we worked on releasing the fear, stress, and anxiety I had about my future. I didn't get into the specifics of Peter and me—I wouldn't dare let anyone on the outside world know that! Too risky. *He would judge me* and *What if he knows someone from the show?* is literally where my mind went. Instead, I shared that I was trying to work on activating my throat chakra and speaking my truth.

What do those things have to do with jaw pain, you may wonder? Well, everything. As I was starting to uncover in school, our bodies talk to us. If there is something we're avoiding or suppressing on a subconscious level, it will show up physically. Look at the word *disease*—it literally is *dis-ease* in the body. I thought back to my time at *The Bachelor* and how my body was communicating with me then—large chunks of hair coming out of my scalp daily, my eye twitching for weeks at a time, waking up in a pile of sweat. I'm glad I listened to my body and left when I did, which wasn't the case for some coworkers, who were literally forced to leave due to health problems that unfolded.

I came to realize that my jaw pain was a manifestation of my fear of the future, and my fear to speak my truth, which, ironically, was a necessity for my future. After just three sessions with Carl, my jaw pain was gone. Maybe I was on the right career path, after all?

School became its own form of therapy and self-reflection, as I started to understand the power of our subconscious minds. Formed in our childhood, and shaped by significant life events, trauma, and repeated patterns, our subconscious does all it can to keep us clinging to what is familiar, because familiarity equals pleasure (for better or worse). It's estimated to dictate 88 percent of our day-to-day decision-making. Even if on a conscious level we want to change a habit, or, say, a pattern in our dating life, if we aren't doing the inner work, be it through hypnotherapy or other modalities, the subconscious is going to keep repeating what it knows.

Thanks to hypnotherapy school, I was beginning to tap the surface of the inner work. That's when things really got interesting. Leading with curiosity, I started to embark on a woo-woo journey I never saw coming.

21

Thomas, the Toad

I was resisting the urge to go back to production, but the opportunity for some quick cash got the best of me. I paused my schooling and hopped on a plane to the Dominican Republic to film a dating show about women in their forties dating men in their twenties.

The show I was filming was called *Back in the Groove*, a play on the movie *How Stella Got Her Groove Back*, with none other than Taye Diggs as the host. I truly admired these strong, independent women. They had depth, had been through hardships, and had built lives for themselves. Had they also kissed their fair share of frogs? Sure, but they refused to settle for less than what they deserved. It gave me a fresh perspective on life after forty.

The area of the Dominican we were filming at held a special place in my heart. I had gone there twice in high school to do mission work with my church youth group. We helped build a school and baseball field. It was my first trip out of the country and an eye-opening experience to see such extreme poverty. We brought small, simple gifts for the children—a baseball, crayons, coloring books. Their hearts were full of gratitude. Yet what stood out the most were the smiles on their faces as we played with them, a reminder that material things don't really matter. Maybe that's why I was unfazed when, on my first day there, I plugged in my laptop and fried my Mac, leaving me computer-less for the month. Namaste!

The Love Producer

We stayed in villas that were walking distance from the set. The juxtaposition of luxury built amongst poverty was a humbling reminder of my privilege. One night, I was walking back to my villa at around 3 AM after a long day on set. As I rounded the corner and walked up the steps, I jumped, startled by a figure in front of me. No, it wasn't the hot pool boy on the early shift. It was a giant toad.

"Oh, hello, cute toad!" Yes, I talk to animals sometimes, especially when sleep deprived. "What's your name, little guy?" I asked, watching him swallow like he wanted to reply. I made my way closer.

"I'll call you Thomas. Thomas the Toad," I said, sitting down next to him. He didn't move an inch. I had noticed recently that animals seemed to be drawn to me. It all began a few months back, when I was behind in school and signed up for a Reiki course to earn more credits. Admittedly, I found Reiki strange. People just put their hands over you and help you heal? But in true Julie fashion, I signed up to get trained in something I had never experienced myself.

My teacher said, "You don't find Reiki. Reiki finds you." I didn't understand what she meant by that at the time, but let me tell you, Reiki sure did find me. After the level one and two trainings, all sorts of woo-woo wildness unfolded. I started to see and feel energy. I'd be lying in bed at night, watching static flow between me and the ceiling, almost like the static on a TV screen. I started seeing auras around people. My lights were flickering in ways that felt like hellos from the other side. In yoga, I felt a thickness in my hands as I flowed, as though I were running them through a body of water. My teacher explained that the energy around us is like how fish perceive water; they don't know it's there, but it's there. And now? I was really starting to notice it was there. On set, I would feel the pulsating of energy between my head and the camera next to me. It was wild.

And the animals? In Sequoia National Park, I had a stare-off with a deer and saw a blue glow around it. One day at the park, a bunch of turtles surrounded me, so I started doing Reiki. My friend posted it on TikTok and it quickly went viral, with half the people confirming I was a real-life Disney princess, and the other saying I was delusional, and they clearly just wanted food. I'm going with the princess narrative.

So of course, I did Reiki on Thomas the Toad. I felt tingles in my hands as I sent him positive energy and pet him for a bit before calling it a night. Almost every night after that, whether at 3 AM or 11 PM, Thomas was waiting for me upon my return from the set. We developed what felt like a friendship, with me owning the childless toad lady vibes.

Surely Thomas must be a sign from my spiritual team, but what was the message? My prince was soon to come? Should I kiss the frog? Seriously, I considered it.

In LA, I had met a number of people who had smoked toad venom, which contains DMT, leading to a psychedelic, spiritual experience. I even knew someone who became a physics genius as a result of his journey. True story! Maybe Thomas was a sign from spirit for me to do a toad venom journey? I want to become a physics genius. I googled the type of toad I was seeing, and it sure looked like a cane toad, the kind with DMT. I also realized they were poisonous, so it's a good thing I didn't kiss Thomas. But let me tell you, months on the road without a boyfriend make you consider doing crazy things.

Whatever Thomas was doing there, I was grateful for his company. And whether or not my Reiki attunement is what drew him to me, I can't deny that energy is a thing. Have you ever walked into a party and known someone's energy was off? Or immediately clicked with someone and commented, "You have great energy!" There are all the sayings—*Your vibe attracts your tribe; the energy you put out into the world is what is drawn back to you; positive people attract positive things* . . . and so on.

That got me thinking about what vibe I was giving off to men. While in theory I was on a journey for love, a husband, and the whole thing, I knew I was not embodying wifey energy. If anything, I was giving off "manic pixie dream girl" vibes. I've been told this once or twice, and while I love to offer my light and quirkiness to a man on his journey, what was it going to take to shift my energy to leading lady vibes? SOS: Where was my fairy godmother when I needed her?!

Signs from the universe continued. After filming concluded and I was at airport check-in to leave the Dominican Republic, I lifted my bag onto the scale and said, "I hope it's not overweight. I'm returning home with Larimar crystals." That immediately got the attendee excited, as he started talking to me about energy and the healing power of the local crystals.

"The Larimar stone opens up the throat chakra," he said. "It aids in spiritual growth and healing. I know this stone will be very helpful for you." He gave me a smile that said, *I see you.* He also let the couple extra pounds of weight slide as he put the bag check label on.

When I returned from that trip, I knew my chapter in reality TV was closing. Not because I didn't enjoy it; I still enjoyed many parts of it. Rarely do we end a relationship because the love is completely gone. It's the other things—are our lives aligned? Are they helping me evolve to my highest self? The truth is, I felt something shifting in me. When it comes to energy, my vibration no longer matched the frequency of the chaos of reality TV.

The Aquarius side of me wanted to keep exploring this new spiritual path I was on. The Capricorn side was like, *Don't get lost in space, Julie. You need to stay grounded here on earth, with a job and a paycheck.* It was hard to feel grounded in anything, though. I was still avoiding properly confronting my shame. I was still suppressing my truth. I was feeling this internal anxiety that made it hard to create, write, and produce anything of significance on my own. "I am in school and writing a book," was an easy narrative to tell people. It was true. But I wasn't exactly thriving at either.

I started to reflect on energy more deeply. It wasn't just woo-woo Reiki talk. As Albert Einstein says, *Everything is energy . . . Match the frequency of the reality you want and you cannot help but get that reality.* I was ready to take the steps needed to align my frequency with the reality I wanted. But I couldn't help but wonder . . . How many more toads would it take before I vibrated to the frequency of love?

22

Ayahuasca Bros

While we often think we'll be friends for life with people, we all grow and shift. Most of my friends were now married with kids, and while I'd see them on occasion, our priorities had understandably changed. My friends from *The Bachelor* were always away. Plus, I probably avoided hanging out with them because I was ashamed of where I was at in my life. Then there were the friends who were out partying all the time—something I felt I had outgrown. I was transitioning to an introvert phase of my life, craving solitude and self-reflection.

I had a tendency to attract "energy vampires"—people who left me feeling drained and depleted. I always offered a listening ear as they shared their problems with me. That quality made me a good producer, but it carried over into my personal life as well. I needed to ask myself, *Are they elevating my consciousness? Are they worth keeping in my life?*

I started getting better at setting boundaries with friends that were draining my energy. There was a mourning period after I shed old friendships. While I enjoyed my solitude, I missed having a community. I wanted to call in those that were more aligned with the spiritual journey I found myself on. The universe delivered . . . especially with men. I call them the ayahuasca bros. You can easily spot an ayahuasca bro in the wild; they most likely reside in Venice, frequent the Erewhon off Abbot Kinney, have a picture of themselves on Instagram in a faux fur coat at Burning Man, and have left corporate America to become a life coach.

Admittedly, I was always a bit judgmental of the Burning Man crowd. My assumption was that it's a bunch of people on drugs partying in the desert. Growing up, I was an A+ D.A.R.E. student who barely drank in high school. When I started going out in college, people would ask me, "Do you party?" I'd eagerly respond, "Yeah!" without realizing they'd meant, "Do you want drugs?" They'd pull out cocaine and offer a bump. I'd politely decline.

It wasn't until my junior year of college that I gave in and tried weed for the first time. I wasn't a fan. That same year, I'm sad to admit I tried coke. It was one and done for me, as I passed out and had seizure-like convulsions in the middle of Pink Elephant, the hot nightclub at the time. I'm thankful now that it happened; I learned my lesson quickly. There are very few things I'm more repulsed by than cocaine, as I've seen how addictive it can be. #CokeisGross.

I shocked myself when I decided to try magic mushrooms. They had made a resurgence for their "healing benefits," and since they come from the earth, versus a lab, I was open to trying it. The first time wasn't exactly a healing setting . . . it was while partying in the Hamptons during the summer of 2019. I had a hot make-out session with a vibey artsy man by the bonfire, where all my sensations were heightened. Months later, I accidentally took way too much (It was a chocolate bar, I couldn't resist!) and had a terrible experience where I went into a time loop of the same scene over and over again. It was terrifying and I vowed to steer clear of mushrooms for a while after that.

I was skeptical of these ayahuasca bros, but they started to show up in my life. First, there was Danny. We were set up through a matchmaking service that had recruited me after my spike in Instagram followers. Danny was an ex-sales bro turned sales-bro life coach, thanks to an ayahuasca journey that saved him from depression after his father passed away.

I was shocked when, on our first date, Danny asked me what my sign was. Isn't that what the girl usually asks? When we realized we both had the astrology app The Pattern, he suggested we run our bond—a feature on the app to see how compatible we are based on our astrological charts. Was our connection written in the stars? It sure seemed like it, as the word SOULMATES flashed across our screen.

Both of our eyes lit up. Neither of us had ever seen a soulmate result! Our first date took on a whole new meaning, as we read about why we were so aligned. I did feel an instant connection with him, almost like we'd known each other forever.

On our second date, we went for a hike in Topanga, a mountainous canyon town I was starting to feel drawn to, immersed in nature and solitude yet only a short drive from the city. Afterward, we grabbed a bite to eat, then went back to his place, where he projected the twinkly night sky onto his ceiling to set the mood (so ayahuasca bro of him). We played a card game that helps people connect, called We're Not Really Strangers. He pulled a card and read it aloud: "What have you tolerated from men in the past that you no longer have space for?"

"Hmm. I would say poor communication and not knowing where someone is at. If we are dating and I have to play a guessing game to try to piece together how you feel about me, or when you're going to ask me out again . . . I know you're not my person."

I pulled a card to read to him. "What about you has felt misunderstood by others?"

Danny had grown up Mormon. He left the church, and his successful sales job, to go on a spiritual journey that led him to ayahuasca. His journey was misunderstood by the Mormon community back at home.

"What about you?" he asked.

"Kind of similar to you," I said. "Not the Mormon part. But no one seems to understand what I'm doing right now and why I left a great job. I don't fully understand it myself, but I know I'm on the right path. I know I'm being guided toward my highest truth . . . Does that make sense?"

"Yeah, it does. You're breaking out of the matrix, Jules!" he said with a smile. It felt nice to talk to someone who understood.

Admittedly, after the second date, I was feeling more *I want to be friends for life* vibes versus *This is my future husband*. We communicated honestly and openly with each other and formed a strong friendship that we still have today. I do believe we are soulmates, as I've come to learn that soulmates are simply souls that come into our lives to help us evolve to the greatest version of ourselves, romantic or not.

The next ayahuasca bro was Ben, an ex-finance guy turned healthy pancake entrepreneur, who held our hug a little too long, even for me. Then there was Martin, founder of a community dedicated to curating gratitude experiences. And Charles, who left the tech space to start a company that threw singing events. These sounded like made-up jobs. And yet, here they all were, leaving behind the grind of corporate America to do something they were passionate about. I couldn't help but be intrigued.

Next, there was Albert, who I always flowed next to in yoga class. He would invite me weekly to do ayahuasca in his backyard (I declined). Then Paul, someone I met at a party twelve years prior, who reached out after I came to him in a meditation. How about that for a pickup line? I dabbled with mushrooms again with Bradley, who led curated events where we drank mushroom tea in a ceremonial setting, followed by a guided yoga, breathwork, meditation journey, and cold plunge. I selfishly challenged myself to stay in the cold for ten minutes, wanting to outshine the guy in the tub next to me. The aftereffect? Not so great, as my body wouldn't stop chattering for a good twenty minutes. Lesson learned—everything in moderation.

That was my main takeaway from observing all these ayahuasca bros: moderation. Though I never tried it, I saw the profound, life-altering effects ayahuasca had on some of these men, especially those suffering from depression, PTSD, and deep trauma. I started thinking maybe every millennial and Gen X man should go on an ayahuasca journey; it could help the collective break through the toxic masculine energy they've been conditioned with throughout their lives. But on the flip side, I saw how some people used it as a form of escape, like other drugs. We do need to stay grounded here on earth, after all (says the girl talking to frogs and seeing energy).

Ayahuasca contains DMT (like the bufo toad), said to offer a direct connection to the spiritual world. Some researchers believe humans release DMT naturally, through our pineal gland (aka the third eye), both at birth and death. This may explain the idea that people's lives flash before their eyes at death. It made me wonder—do our lives flash before our eyes at birth too? Through my meditations with Joe Dispenza, I learned that the pineal gland can secrete DMT through breathwork alone. I've had many beautiful meditations where I am almost certain DMT was released, sending me on out-of-body journeys through the cosmos, astral projecting to places around the world, and seeing views into my future and my past. I was unlocking a lot of the same things as ayahuasca bros, naturally—through breathwork, meditation, hypnotherapy, energy work, and so on. Half the time, people think I'm on drugs when I'm completely sober, because I act in awe of the world around us. I'm just high on life. Shouldn't that be the goal?

I went with another ayahuasca bro, Matt, to a tapping event. Tapping, also known as the Emotional Freedom Technique (EFT), stimulates acupressure points while focusing on personal fear, trauma, and stuck emotions. By tapping meridian points on our body while focusing on these feelings, the belief is we can move energy to release what's stuck.

You begin with a setup statement: Even though I feel (insert feeling), I love and accept myself.

As I sat there with Matt and a room full of beautifully diverse misfits, I went along as people shouted out words—stressed, anxious, sad. We all tapped together to release those emotions. I felt a swell rise in my throat as I knew I needed to say the word I had been holding inside for so long. My body clenched as I finally found the courage.

"Shame." I felt my cheeks turn red.

"Shame," the facilitator repeated. As a group, we tapped each meridian point as we repeated phrases around feeling shame.

Tears quickly flowed out of me. A surge of energy pulsated throughout my body, moving from my stomach, up through my chest, and into my throat, where a forced cough felt like I was releasing the silence that had been stuck within me for centuries.

As the tapping concluded, we brought our hands down upon our laps. The tension was now replaced with a sense of calm and lightness throughout my body. I felt free, like I no longer needed to hold everything inside. I could let it flow out of me—through tapping, speaking my truth without fear of judgment, and embodying this new version of myself that was emerging.

Shortly after the night of the tapping event, Danny invited me to Mycelium Festival. The itinerary was right up my alley—daily yoga, breathwork, heart-opening workshops, pool parties, organic meals, and my own little yurt.

I arrived to discover that I was probably the only person there who had never been to Burning Man and didn't live in Venice. I immediately questioned my decision to go but was already there so had no choice but to stay curious. I became mesmerized by the man leading a kindness workshop. He was like a hot fairy with glitter on his face, an exposed chest, piercing blue eyes, and the cutest smile. He carried himself with such poise and grace, speaking so eloquently, I ate up every word. I sipped tea served by a couple wearing animal antlers, ecstatic-danced with divine goddesses in a teepee, and went in for extra-long hugs with strangers as part of a bonding exercise. (Ben would be proud.)

At dinner the first night, I met Greg, an older ayahuasca bro who resided in Venice, used to have a high-pressure corporate career, and is now a life coach. I'm not kidding. Greg went through his rebirth after leaving an unhealthy marriage. The next night, I found myself hanging with him again, by the fireside, under the desert stars, when he asked, "So tell me, what really happened at *The Bachelor*? I know there is something more that caused you to leave."

I paused for a moment, debating how to respond. I couldn't brush off the truth any longer. Tears immediately began trickling down my cheeks. I told Greg the whole story, the real story. He held my hand, listened as I spoke, and allowed me the space to be vulnerable, judgment free. This was the first time I really spoke out loud about Peter, my job, and the real effect it was having on me. And I was telling it to a stranger . . . but I guess we aren't really strangers, are we?

"Ah, you're still in the depths of your journey," Greg said.

Was I? Fuck. This hero's journey thing was no joke. I thought I'd just go on a few dates, find my husband, and call it a day. I had been in denial that I had any real deep wounds to heal. Trauma is reserved for those that had really gone through it, right? I've been blessed with a beautiful life, an amazing upbringing, a dream job, and the courage to move on when I knew it was time.

But the truth? I had never really allowed myself to sit in the pain of losing the identity I'd built over seven years. While I was enjoying the spiritual expansion, I was ignoring some of the deeper stuff.

I'd always been a glass-half-full kind of girl. My boss once said to me, "Wow, I just heard you get verbally abused through the mic and you seem totally okay!" I was always "totally okay." Emotional abuse was just part of creating reality TV, right?

And the Peter stuff? I had still been keeping that chapter to myself, fearful it might somehow get back to my ex-bosses if I spoke it out loud to anyone. But now, I was finally speaking it out loud. And it felt really freeing.

23

My First Love

"All right, Julie, show us the way home!" my dad said.

It was a crisp fall day in Connecticut. My father, sister, and I had gone for a walk in the woods behind our house. All around us were trees and brush; the only clearing was from above, where the sun glistened through the branches.

I closed my eyes and listened. In the distance, I could hear the faint sound of the river flowing to the north of us. My dad's words echoed in my mind from times past: "Whenever you're lost, follow the river's flow and you'll find your way home."

I didn't need to detour to the river, as the sound alone guided me.

"This way!" I said with poise.

My dad and sister followed behind as I trekked with confidence over fallen logs and past moss-covered rocks, listening to the slight crunch of fallen leaves on the spongy forest floor. I always loved that sound.

Eventually, I saw a clearing ahead. When we made our way through the brush and stepped out of the woods, we were standing right where we entered earlier.

"I'm so proud of you! That's my girl!" my dad exclaimed, impressed by my natural sense of direction.

We returned to the house, where my dad shared the story of my impressive navigation skills with my mom.

It's hard to say exactly how old I was when that happened, as I seem to get younger each time my dad tells the story to friends.

"Julie has always had a great sense of direction," he'd begin. "You should've seen her as a kid! When she was just *two* years old, I took her in the woods behind our house and said, 'Julie, show us the way home.' And like it was nothing, she said, 'Follow me, Dad!' With her little footsteps bopping along the forest floor, she got us home with full confidence. I couldn't believe it!"

My dad has always had a knack for storytelling. He has a handful of stories he tells regularly that get more exciting each time you hear them. Soon, I'll have been a baby on all fours, crawling to guide us home.

When the movie *Big Fish* came out, the lead character, Edward, played by Ewan McGregor, reminded me of my father, not just because of the way he might exaggerate a bit to make the tale more exciting, but also because of the joy and childlike wonder he shows when he tells his stories, bringing a smile to my face. Maybe that's where the whimsical side of my storytelling comes from.

Big Fish has always been a favorite movie of mine, but it took on a whole new meaning when my dad was diagnosed with cancer. In the film, Edward is dying of cancer, and his son, William, a journalist, comes to see him and tries to get to know his father better before he passes. They always had a strained relationship because William felt like his dad never told the truth with his tall tales. Ultimately, through their journey together, William comes to discover just how much love and truth were behind each of those tales.

I'm fortunate I've always had a great relationship with my father. I personally don't see the harm in getting a little younger each time I navigate out of the woods, or the fish he caught growing a little bigger with tales of fly-fishing on the Yellowstone. To me, it adds color and excitement. But since his cancer diagnosis, I wonder how I can bottle these stories up and hang onto them forever, ensuring his legacy lives on when he is no longer here. How many more stories can he and I create together? How many of my dad's life stories have I not heard? I want to know them all.

I made a career of digging into other people's backstories, emotions, and feelings of the heart, but when was the last time I asked my parents those same meaningful questions? Life can become so routine—wake up, go to work, come home, ask your spouse or roommate (or plants, in my case) how their day was, watch some TV, go to bed, and do it all over again. Now, I made a commitment to bring my producing skills to the people that matter most—starting with my parents.

Admittedly, I would get triggered when my dad suggested I go back to work at *The Bachelor*; he loved that I worked for the show and was so proud of all I'd accomplished. Tales of Peter, my adventures around the globe, and my stint in the headlines were some of his favorite stories to tell. Anytime I was home and we'd go out to dinner, he'd bring up my job.

"Have you ever watched the show *The Bachelor*?" he'd say to the waitress, excitement in his voice.

Usually, they'd respond with, "Of course! I love it!"

"Well, my daughter here was the senior producer!"

I'd correct him, "Supervising producer, Dad."

"Oh yeah, yeah. Supervising producer. Let me show you photos!" He'd pull out his phone, and with my assistance, would find the cloud folder I created called *Adventures of Julie!* If I wasn't there, he'd call and ask me how to find them.

I didn't mind him bragging about me. All I wanted to do was make my father proud . . . but it also caused an unspoken pain inside of me. It was the pain of not wanting to disappoint my dad. It was the pain of being too ashamed to share the whole story with him. It was the pain of acknowledging that, for the first time in my life, I didn't have a good sense of direction on where I was going.

I remember one dinner visit out with my parents when, after he shared the story of my fifteen minutes of fame, I excused myself to the bathroom, where I sat on the toilet and cried. I debated going back to the table and confessing everything. Instead, I wiped away the tears, cleaned up my makeup, and went back out like everything was okay.

About a month after Mycelium Festival, I finally gained the courage to tell my parents the truth during one of their visits. We were sitting outside at my sister Jen's house having lunch on the patio when my dad brought up Peter.

"There's something I've been wanting to tell you," I said, trying unsuccessfully to hold back tears. I proceeded to tell them everything that happened between Peter and me, and the spiral of emotions that came after. They were the loving, nurturing parents I needed, hugging and caring for me like they always have. It felt healing to get it off my chest, like my scarlet letter was starting to fade. Of course, my dad made a point to say that he always knew there was something between Peter and me. He's always been pretty intuitive himself.

I hoped that now that he knew the whole story, he would understand why I left—and that a big part of it was to be able to spend more quality time with him. I never knew when his health might take a turn for the worse. I debated moving closer to home, but the clock was ticking in another way—I was inching closer to forty. Goshen isn't exactly full of eligible bachelors. This feeling that I was chasing time left me in a heightened state of anxiety.

Would I be able to fall in love, get engaged, marry, and have children before I ran out of time? Would my father be around to witness those milestones? I always pictured my father there on my wedding day, passing me off to my prince. More so, I always hoped I would give my dad his first grandson after being surrounded by women (three daughters and three nieces!).

I've tried my best not to live in fear of the unknown and instead make the most of every moment I have with my father. Yet in the non-duality of life, I feel both joy and freedom while quietly carrying anxiety and fear alongside me.

My First Love

My dad and I recently returned to the Soaring Eagle Lodge in New Mexico, where we went fly-fishing together years ago. That first trip was another one of my dad's favorite stories to tell, as I outfished all the men at the lodge, earning a standing ovation at dinner. The seasoned fly fisherman would set the hook as soon as the fish bit, but I had a bit of a delayed reaction. The guide and my father would see the fish bite and yell, "Set, Julie! Set!" *What? Huh? Oh, okay . . . !* was my thought process before setting the hook . . . which seemed to work in my favor. It became comical as I caught fifteen, twenty—oh, at least thirty—fish! It's hard to remember. The number goes up each time my dad tells the story.

The river flowed in my favor that day, a reminder that we don't always need to have a quick response. Perhaps there is something to be said for taking a moment to pause and reflect before we act. If we set the hook too quickly, we may end up with a fish, a job, or a man that wasn't worth the bite. But if we trust the flow of the river, we'll always be guided in the right direction. It is through the direction of my parents that I've always been taught to dream big, and something tells me a big fish may come my way. Until then, I will continue to follow my dad's words of wisdom, knowing that whenever I am lost, I can follow the flow of the river and trust that it will guide me home.

24

Return of the Exes

My parents set a great example of love for me growing up. So, as I reflected on why I hadn't found my life partner, I knew I needed to look more closely at my past relationships, rather than what was modeled for me. But you all know my dating history—my emotional baggage isn't that intense, right? It must go further back … like, way, way back. That's right, I'm talking past lives.

I dove into the idea of past lives after learning about it in hypnotherapy school. While it was wild to think about at first, the more I studied it, the more I believed in the idea of reincarnation. We are souls having a human experience, traveling with soul families, with each lifetime helping us learn, grow, and evolve to our highest selves.

One night in bed, where all the magic happens (the spiritual kind, not the sexual kind lately), I saw a guided past life regression on my meditation app and decided to give it a try. I was skeptical, but that didn't stop me from being curious about what might come up. I must have been a flapper in a past life, right? Wined and dined with Fitzgerald in Paris?

I put in my wired headphones (I don't use Bluetooth anymore—bad for the brain!), lay on my back with my arms out beside me, and began the journey. I thought I might fall asleep instead, as I listened to the lady's soothing voice bringing me deeper and deeper into hypnosis. I was listening to her prompts, waiting to see what images would come through, but nothing was coming up for me.

Until . . . it happened.

My heart began to race, resistance at the edge of surrender, before I finally let go and entered the theta state. My heart slowed down, and I felt as though I were floating. Suddenly, I was transported back in time. I was sitting on rich oak wood flooring, looking down at an altar of sorts. There were candles, tarot, crystals, a feather, and a few trinkets in front of me that I was waving my hands over. Clearly, something witchy was going on. Clearly, my husband didn't like it . . . I looked up to see him towering over me with anger and rage in his brown eyes that penetrated through his round wired glasses. He had dark hair and a full, thick beard. In his hand was an ax. Before I had time to process anything else, he raised the ax and swung. Everything went to black.

I gasped as my eyes shot open in bed, my heart beating out of my chest. Holy shit! No wonder I block letting love in—my ex-husband literally murdered me! Talk about not feeling chosen. It all made sense now. This may also explain why sometimes I fear going too deep into spiritual things. Clearly, it wasn't accepted in that lifetime—why would it be now?!

I lay in bed processing what I had just experienced. *Was it real, or my imagination?* But even in my wildest imagination, I couldn't have conjured up this scenario. I needed to know more. *I did slightly break the professional rules*, I thought, *listening to a recording instead of seeing a facilitator.* Regardless of what you believe, if you work with a professional, they'll guide you to release what comes through so it can benefit your current life—now. I decided to book a session with Natalia, a medium, hypnotherapist, and energy healer who I met at an event. I was drawn to her; she came off as a cool, normal girl, not one of those esoteric characters you'd see on a spiritual date on *The Bachelor*.

I didn't tell Natalia I specifically wanted a past life regression, but as soon as I walked into her office she said, "I feel a past life regression would be best for you today."

"Yes, I was thinking the same!" I exclaimed. Her office was modern and cool, though the air still smelled of palo santo, and crystals graced the table beside me as I got comfortable and lay down on the couch. I understood that the same past life might not come up, but as she guided me on my journey, I was transported back to that same time period. More details came through this time. I said them out loud as she prompted me.

"My husband's name is John," I began. "We live in a Colonial-style home. I see a big oak tree outside and children playing." I could feel my body starting to clench, a tightness in my chest and an ache in my gut, preparing me for what was coming.

"We have two boys and a young girl." I paused and took a deep breath, my throat tightening. "My daughter and I both have healing gifts with our hands . . . but he doesn't approve of it. And he caught me using our gifts." Suddenly, an electric pulse surged through my body, causing a flood of tears to burst forth as I recounted the night of the murder. My fists tightened. My body trembled. While I questioned if my imagination was making this all up, the visceral reaction was undeniable.

"John's spirit is here with us," Natalia said gently. Her hands were over me now, doing energy work on my body. "He wants to apologize for what happened. He didn't know then what he knows now. He'd like to help guide you in this lifetime."

Tears continued to flood out of me as Natalia guided me through releasing the energetic imprint in my body. A cool tingle ran through me. My body was working through all the stored trauma, and letting it go. My muscles eased, my hands opened, and I relaxed. Behind closed eyes, I saw a wave of light. I felt warmth. I felt love. It was raw, emotional, and healing.

Ultimately, I accepted John's apology. I mean, I've never been one to hold grudges! John may have murdered me in a past life, but now that we made up, I looked forward to seeing what our future could hold. Whatever supporting character John was playing for me, I was glad we were able to put the baggage behind us, break the karmic cycle, and bring me one step closer to a sacred love during this lifetime.

Unfortunately, John wasn't the only ex in the spirit realm. I swear, when I began this journey, I had no intention of interacting with dead exes, but soon after my past life regression, there was another one to add to the list.

I was in the car driving when I got the call.

"Hey, Leah!" I said, turning off the music.

"Julie, did you hear?" Her tone was somber. "Dominic died."

My heart dropped.

"What? No . . . no," I said in disbelief. "Dominic?" I felt numb as I spoke his name.

"Nikki just saw on his Facebook page . . . I'm sorry. It's so awful."

"Thanks for telling me, but I can't process this right now," I said abruptly. I was about to lead a mindfulness group at a teen treatment center my sister Janelle and her husband had opened. "I'll call you later. Love you."

I hung up, parked my car, and disassociated for the next couple of hours as I led a group of teenage girls through a hypnosis journey. I was almost done with school and had started bringing what I was learning out into the world. But that night when I returned home, I couldn't stop crying as I sat with the news.

It had been years since we had seen each other, but Dominic was one of only three men I'd ever expressed my love to. He had been my safety blanket as I navigated life in a new city during my early years in Los Angeles. His passing left me crushed and confused.

I knew Dominic wasn't my person, yet as I reflected on my relationships of the past, every guy I had been with had betrayed me in some way. Every guy . . . but Dominic. He loved me so damn much, he would've done anything for me. I was resistant to that love then, and I'd been resistant to it all these years since. Now that he was gone, I longed to feel that kind of love again.

But if there is one thing I was starting to uncover on this journey, it was that he didn't need to be here in the flesh for me to feel his love. That night, as I was crying in my bed, I felt a tickling sensation on my feet. Dominic used to love to tickle my feet.

"Hi, Dom," I said, laughing through the tears. I could feel his spirit all around me, comforting me in his love. I felt that same warmth of comfort at his service, as I noticed a light in the corner of the church flickering throughout the Mass.

I truly believe our loved ones who have crossed over are always communicating with us. If you start asking for signs and open your eyes and senses to the magic of the universe, you, too, can experience their unconditional love and presence. It may be through a flickering light, a brush of warm or cool air, a familiar scent, feathers, coins, or even animals sent our way.

Speaking of animals, I looked back on Instagram to see our last communication with each other. It had been a few months prior, when I posted the video of none other than Thomas, the Toad. He wrote, "Kiss him, maybe you'll get your prince." I couldn't help but smile and cry. Of course, that was our last exchange together. Trust me, Dom. I thought about it.

On this journey within, I realized I had been drawing in men who were emotionally unavailable, because I wasn't emotionally available. I've always kept men at an arm's length. I was attracting Peter Pans because, let's be honest, I was a Wendy. I would never fully admit I wanted a relationship. Sometimes, I wasn't sure whether I did; I've always had a fear of losing my independence, and losing my youth. But on a deeper, subconscious level I knew this was a block from the pain of my past.

Now that I was bringing awareness to my patterns and working through them, I thought to myself, *I am ready for someone who makes me feel safe, seen, and heard as my authentic, weird self.* I was ready for a love that went beyond space and time.

"I want to do a session to call in love," I declared to my hypnotherapist, Katt, a few weeks later as we began our video call. "I really feel like I'm ready now."

"Okay, great. We can work on that," she said. "What are you looking for in a partner?"

"I want a love that just clicks and feels right, you know? That's passionate and romantic," I emphasized. "Someone loyal and caring. I want to feel comfortable in their arms—safe, appreciated, like I can fully be my authentic self. They need to be adventurous, fun, and spontaneous like I am. Protective, but still give me my freedom and independence. We support each other's goals and build one another up. Trustworthy. Growth mindset. Good communication. And a little bit of edge," I said with a smile. "Oh, and funny."

"You got it," Katt responded. "I can't guarantee the timing of the universe, but we can definitely work on opening your heart to draw in that loving partner you desire." She guided me through a hypnosis journey, and I came out of it with my heart chakra wide open, vibrating to the frequency of love!

A few weeks later, I flew to New York for a quick production gig. The next day, I met my last standing college friend still living in the city, Paige, for lunch. We chose a chic Mediterranean spot in Midtown for mezze, Chablis, and boy talk.

"I've decided I'm ready for a boyfriend," I told her.

"Wow, Julie, I don't think I've ever actually heard you say that," she said with surprise.

"I know! I'm just so over these noncommittal LA hotshot types who think they are so cool," I stated. "The guy I was just hanging out with literally has viral videos on the negative effects of ghosting. Know what he did? He ghosted me! Such a fraud. I just want something real this time, you know?"

"I think that's great," she said, smiling. "I'm rooting for you."

A few days later, I headed to Connecticut, where I shared the same sentiment with my family and friends. For the first time in a long time, I was verbally and energetically expressing my desires for a loving partnership. I could feel the shift within, no longer pretending I didn't care.

As I started to rewrite the script of my past, the universe listened. After having sorted through my fair share of "wrong reasons" men, I was finally about to meet my front-runner.

25

Henry, the Leading Man

My one saving grace living in West Hollywood, an area that had become too chaotic for me now that I was actually home for more than a month at a time, was my wellness sanctuary, Artha. Walking through the doors is like entering every Goop reader's dream oasis. There are rows of infrared sauna rooms and float tanks, cryotherapy (cold temperature therapy), and a spa that includes electromagnetic body sculpting and endermologie (mechanical massage). The space is modern, sleek, and sensual in design. It became my home away from home once I fully embraced the LA-girlie-on-a-spiritual-journey-post-entertainment-industry burnout.

One day, after my morning yoga class, I stripped out of my sweaty clothes, wrapped a towel around myself, and sat in the infrared sauna to sweat some more. The heat caressed my body as I soaked in every bit of the anti-aging remedy. After a half hour of sweating, I stepped inside the cryo chamber in just my towel to freeze my butt off for three minutes.

A cool chill spread throughout my body. I did a kundalini exercise with my arms raised to try to generate heat, all the while thinking, *Don't let the towel fall . . . and if it does, I hope no one's watching through the glass window!* While it was iced up for me, I knew onlookers could see from the outside.

I listened as the calm female voice counted down through the speaker . . .

Two minutes remaining . . .

One minute remaining . . . My breathing became more rapid now.

Thirty seconds remaining. I was almost there.

Fifteen seconds remaining . . .

I brought my hands down over my heart, took a deep breath in, and exhaled slowly, my breath visible in the chilled air, just as I heard the voice say, "Therapy complete."

As I stepped out, the mist from the cool air flowed out with me, creating a fog that gave the room an ethereal feel. I felt like a hot mess version of Elsa from *Frozen*; the sweaty hair strands that previously graced my face were now icicles, and my arm hairs looked like snow had fallen upon them. Little did I know, I stepped out of the cryo chamber and straight into a fairy tale.

Through the mist, a figure emerged—a tall, handsome man with a chiseled jawline and light brown hair that cascaded around his face in soft waves. We stood there, frozen in time, as our eyes locked. His piercing blue eyes, a mirror image of my own, reached deep into the seas of my soul. As the mist began to evaporate, I couldn't help but gaze down at his washboard abs, as he was in nothing but a towel as well.

Heat suddenly rushed through, accompanied by excitement and nerves. He gave me a sweet, welcoming smile. I smiled back.

"Great job in there!" he said. I fell even more into my daydream, now that I discovered he had an English accent.

Back to reality. "Oh, hi, thanks!"

"I'm Henry," he said.

"Julie. Nice to meet you," I said with a smile.

"It's my first time trying cryotherapy—any tips?" he asked. I gave him a few pointers, and almost asked if he wanted me to join him . . . but I held back, not wanting to be too obvious about my desire to know him.

He was there with a friend, who I spoke with as we cheered Henry on in the chamber. I'd felt an instant connection when we were chatting; a feeling I hadn't felt in a long time. I was hopeful he'd ask for my number when he came out. When he reemerged through the mist, shivering with a big smile, we continued our conversation.

"I just got back from Burning Man," he said. "Have you heard of it?"

Ah, another ayahuasca bro, I thought to myself.

"Of course! Was it fun?" After some small talk about his desert adventures, he told me he was from London but moving to LA. He was in town for the next couple of months to work on his visa. It sounded promising.

Before leaving, he asked for my . . . Instagram. *Dammit, he must be a Gen-Zer*, I thought, noticing his youthful appearance. Though I'll admit, it was nice to go home and immediately stalk his page. I was happy to discover he worked in tech, not as a life coach.

He DMed me later that same day . . .

Great meeting you Julie. I'm still fresh to LA, but would love to grab a drink sometime if you're free.

A big smile came across my face. I loved that he was direct and to the point. We exchanged numbers and he texted me soon after, asking if I'd like to go to LACMA on Friday night. A cultured man who loves art? Yes, please. They also have jazz on Fridays, my favorite. And with that, we locked it in—our first date! After years of producing other people's love stories, spending lonely nights in hotel rooms, and kissing one too many frogs, something told me my leading lady dreams were about to come true.

Date Card: Let's Paint the Town

I was giddy getting ready for our date. I sent outfit options to my girlfriend to help me decide what to wear. I opted for a short black dress that I kept casual with kicks and a denim jacket since we'd be walking around the museum.

Henry picked me up, like a true gentleman. I stepped out of my apartment to see him waiting outside the car with that charming smile. He wore a colorful button-down shirt that hinted at his adventurous spirit, paired with loafers like a proper English gentleman. I was drawn to both sides of him.

"Hey, you," he said, opening the car door.

"Hi there." I smiled, giving him a quick hug before stepping in. My pulse fluttered with excitement for the night ahead.

My nerves vanished as I internally laughed over Henry's not-so-smooth driving skills, navigating the opposite side of the road than he was used to back in England. It felt like we were on a bumper car ride. I found it rather endearing, even if I did jolt forward at every stoplight.

When we arrived at LACMA, we grabbed a glass of wine and sat outside, enjoying the jazz band as the sun set upon the city. We chatted with the band's entourage next to us, feeling like we had been transported to the early days of jazz in New Orleans. Henry seemed to be able to naturally spark conversations with just about anyone. I loved that about him.

As we got up to make our way into the museum, Henry grabbed my hand and spun me to the music. We danced in the courtyard to the soulful sounds of saxophones and trumpets. Our bodies flowed, as if we'd danced together before. We had similar energies, making things feel natural, effortless, and fun. The last time I had felt this way was, well, with Peter.

As we wandered around the museum, Henry impressed me with his knowledge of art, not in a pompous way, but in a way that kept me intrigued. He was the perfect blend of intelligence and fun. We posed like various art pieces and played hide-and-seek around sculptures. We were silly and flirty, like Ferris and Sloane at the art museum in *Ferris Bueller's Day Off*. I immediately regretted not wearing my fringe leather jacket to truly embody Sloane.

As night fully arrived, we went back outside. We strolled hand in hand to the iconic Urban Light fixture, a collection of 202 cast iron streetlamps that once graced the streets of Los Angeles in the 1920s and '30s. (Also, a popular spot for proposals.) We weaved in and out of the lamps, dancing, twirling, flirting, and striking poses. It was playful and romantic, and I felt our connection grow stronger with each moment. This was the part of the date when the producer in me would want to yell from behind the camera,

"Kiss her already!" Without needing my cue, Henry leaned in for the kiss, filling my heart with the warmth of possibility.

And the night wasn't over yet. I had been ignoring my phone; when I finally looked, I saw that my friend Adam had called three times and sent me a text . . .

> Babe call me. I have 2 extra tickets to the Abba Tribute Band at the Hollywood Bowl. Bring your date and come meet us! We just got here.

I turned to Henry. "Do you like ABBA?"

"Do I like ABBA?" he exclaimed. "I'm European—of course I like ABBA!"

"Great! Want to go to another iconic LA landmark, the Hollywood Bowl, and meet my friends?" I asked.

"Uh, yeah!" And with that, we raced back to the car and drove straight to the Bowl.

Walking into the Hollywood Bowl always fills me with a rush of excitement. That excitement was amplified, now that I had a hot date by my side. We grabbed a bottle of wine at the concession stand and climbed the sloping path to the outdoor amphitheater. We weaved through the buzzing crowd snacking on Trader Joe's charcuterie spreads and sipping wine out of plastic cups. When we arrived at our seats, Henry immediately hit it off with my friends.

We all sang and danced the night away under the stars to ABBA's greatest hits. It felt so natural, easy, and comfortable as Henry held me in his arms. My heart was warm and buzzing with excitement for what could be. If I was the dancing queen, I think I may have found myself a king.

Date Card: Is It Written in the Stars?

Dusk was upon the city as Henry and I strolled hand in hand, past tourists and couples picnicking on the grounds of Griffith Park Observatory. Perched on the hills of Hollywood, the iconic art deco landmark is a celestial dream, where Tinseltown meets the cosmos. It was the idyllic setting for our second date together.

"Do you think we could be twin flames?" Henry asked as we cuddled under the starry sky and crescent moon, night upon us now.

"Yeah, for sure," I replied, excited he was the one bringing up twin flames.

"I've never felt such a strong connection like this, so instantly," he said.

"I feel the same," I whispered, looking up into his eyes as I lay in his arms. My heart felt such comfort and ease as he leaned down and gently kissed the top of my head.

Henry and I had spent the whole day together after our first date the night before. He had an LA bucket list of things he wanted to do, and I was all in on the journey. I felt like the Bachelorette in my own city, seeing the sights from a new perspective, with Henry by my side. Can you believe I had never actually gone inside the observatory before? Crazy, given my fascination with the cosmos and aliens. Stepping through the doors of the giant dome had been like stepping into a scene from *La La Land*. We circled around each other at the Foucault pendulum, levitated to the cosmos in the planetarium, and studied the star charts above.

Now, as we picnicked under the night sky, we talked about our hopes and dreams for the future. I was happy to discover Henry was not a Gen-Zer. He was thirty-four, just three years younger than me.

Lying side by side, he looked at me and asked, "Do you want kids?"

I paused. I had never had a guy ask that so soon.

"I mean, I always pictured myself as a mother, and I love kids . . ." I said softly. "But, ultimately, it depends on who I end up with and what's best for us."

I still found myself a bit aloof with my response to that question. I know this feels like an oxymoron to the through line of my story. Thus is the complexity of being human; I feared men would think I was on a tight schedule.

"I want kids," he said, looking into my eyes.

"Oh, great!" It brought me comfort hearing him say that. "How many?"

"Ideally, three," he said, giving a thought-out explanation as to why.

"Well, we better get to work, then!" I joked, leaning in and kissing him. Maybe I was on a tight schedule.

There was a comfortable silence between us as we walked to the car. On the drive back to my place, Henry queued up his playlist. The song "Wild Love" by James Bay came through the speakers. I felt like stardust was sprinkling over my body, filling me with wonder at what was unfolding.

I turned to him in disbelief. "I used to listen to this song on repeat every day."

He glanced over from the driver's seat with a tender smile. "Me too."

We played the song on repeat the whole drive home, the lyrics striking a chord in my heart. Could the universe have been conspiring all along to deliver us the wild love we both desired? As I gazed out the window at the stream of lights on Sunset Boulevard, it was as though all my wishes upon a star had led me to this very moment.

My logical mind wanted to take it slow and not rush something I saw long-term potential with. Yet, all logic went out the window as James Bay reminded me to *lose a little guard, let it down, we don't have to think it through* . . .

And we didn't. As we arrived back at my apartment, we barely made it to the bedroom before our clothes hit the floor. Henry caressed every inch of my body like he had known it for lifetimes, kissing me and pleasing me in a way no man had before. We made wild love that was passionate, intimate, and cosmic. I'd always told men I wasn't a cuddler, but as Henry and I lay in bed afterward, curled up with each other, our bodies felt so good melted together.

Then, I noticed something. As Henry was drifting off, I felt a wave of energy between our bodies, as though our hearts were beating in sync with each other, pulled by a magnetic force beyond our control. My bed really was where all the magic happened, as I felt there was some merit to the whole twin flame thing, after all. Twin flames are supposedly two people who share the same soul, and in this moment, our souls felt like one.

Date Card: Love is a Wild Ride!

The cinematic landscape of Universal Studios was a perfect blend of Hollywood thrills and inner child adventures. Kids were running around with Harry Potter wands in hand, Minion plushies, and reusable souvenir cups filled with Coca-Cola. Screams, laughter, and "Hedwig's Theme" filled the air.

It had only been a day since Henry and I had last seen each other, but we kept our *Bachelor*-style dates going with a day at Universal Studios. We ran through the park like we were on an episode of *Amazing Race*, trying to get as many rides in as we could. We turned into wizards at Hogwarts, conquered "The Transformers," and returned to "The Mummy." Henry was a huge *Harry Potter* fan, while I geeked out as we strolled through Krustyland.

"I was obsessed with *The Simpsons* as a kid," I exclaimed as we sat for lunch at Moe's Tavern, a re-creation of the iconic dive bar on the show. "I had all the dolls, dressed up as Lisa for Halloween, and loved Nintendo's *Bart vs. the Space Mutants*."

Henry smiled as I told him about my childhood, taking sips of cola in between bites of his burger.

"What were you like as a kid?" I asked.

"I was always curious and independent in nature," he said. "We moved around a lot so I kind of had to be."

While Henry considered England home, his childhood had been shaped by constant movement, ping-ponging from one country to the next for his dad's job. Admittedly, I had to look a few of the countries up on a map. He had such a different upbringing than I had, but I admired his worldly charm and intelligence. He wasn't as close with his parents now, having had to set his own boundaries around some of the more complicated family dynamics. I admired that he was doing the inner work to break the patterns of his family's past, yet still spoke about his parents in a loving, compassionate way. He seemed to be on a similar journey as I was, focused on inner growth, purpose, and curiosity about the meaning of life.

He was a gentleman the whole day, refusing to let me carry my backpack. It was hard at first to accept that simple gesture; throughout the day I kept saying, "I can carry my bag now if you'd like. Are you sure you don't want me to take it?" I had gotten so used to doing everything myself that it was hard to lean back and embody feminine energy. It was such a stark contrast to my last relationship; James would walk five feet ahead of me in his warm jacket while I shivered behind him. It felt really nice to be taken care of and seen as my authentic, silly self.

The next day, Henry was leaving for a trip to Vancouver but then would return to LA to buckle down and sort out his visa. Wanting to spend every moment together, I eagerly volunteered to drive him to LAX. Anyone who has been to LAX knows I must have been crushing hard to make that gesture.

We talked regularly while he was away, counting down the days until his return. I had never had such consistent, honest communication with a man. He made it clear he was all in, and I did too.

One night while FaceTiming, he gave me a smirk and said, "So . . . I have to admit something. I've already been referring to you as my girlfriend to all my friends."

"Oh, have you now?" I said with a coy smile. "I mean, same—but in a playful, wishful-thinking way."

"I'd love nothing more than to be your boyfriend, Julie," he said without hesitation.

"Really?" I asked, a bit bashful now.

"It would make me the happiest man in the world." I could hear the sincerity in his voice.

"Does that mean I have a boyfriend?!" I smiled, feeling the same thrill as when my middle school boyfriend asked me if I wanted to be his girlfriend, through a passed note. (Circle yes or no.)

It felt so good to have no question marks or mixed signals. And with that, we made it official. For the first time in over five years, I HAD A BOYFRIEND! It felt thrilling, exciting, a bit too soon and nerve-racking, but also totally right.

While Henry planned to get an Airbnb when he returned from Vancouver, after looking at a few places, I told him he should just stay with me. We always wanted to be together anyway. So, he moved in with me for the month. In the past, I usually hung out with a guy for months before we put a title on it. Often, it would be weeks between a first, second, and third date. But with Henry? We met, he became my boyfriend, and moved in with me within a few weeks! Honestly, I shocked myself. It was so out of character and went against all logical thinking. But I was leading with my heart, and for once, I didn't question it.

Henry brought me coffee in bed every morning. He loved to cook and even did the dishes afterward. He would leave sweet notes for me to find in my bag, just like my mom used to do when I was a kid. He knew how to work with his hands, fixing things around my place. He did the laundry and even enjoyed cleaning. Are you kidding me?! I wondered when I was going to wake up from this daydream. I had manifested my dream man!

We got into a routine together, going for workouts, working side by side at the library, making dinner, and making sweet love. We continued to have *Bachelorette*-style dates, finding ourselves in Chinatown having dim sum one day, and sailing with friends in Marina del Rey the next.

While Henry was not an ayahuasca bro, he had been through his fair share of therapy and was on his own healing journey. During our dinners (and breakfasts / lunches / fantasy suites), we would have deep, vulnerable conversations, opening up about our patterns of the past, heartbreak, trauma, and issues we were still working through. He was the first romantic partner I shared the details of my Peter saga with.

As they say in Bachelor Nation, we wore our hearts on our sleeve. And my heart was falling, fast. Henry had certainly received my first impression rose, and I was beginning to believe he may get my final rose as well.

26

The Warning

The bounce of the gravel road below the tires brought a slight bob to my body, causing me to awaken from my slumber. I was fully sprawled out on the back seat of my Uber, head resting on my curled-up jacket after a sleepless red-eye from LA to Nashville. I rubbed my eyes open and sat up. As I gazed out the window, I felt wrapped in the amber, red, and orange hues of the leaves dancing along the tree-lined street outside.

"Good morning, Sleeping Beauty," my driver said with a smile. "We've arrived."

Shoot. I missed the last Starbucks stop on the drive, I thought to myself, my head pounding from lack of caffeine and sleep.

The road widened as we drove past a sign that read WELCOME TO THE ISHA INSTITUTE OF INNER-SCIENCES. As the car pulled up to the welcome center, I stepped out and took a deep breath of the crisp fall air to waken me.

"Thank you. Have a great rest of your day," I said to my driver as he handed me my luggage. I took in the grounds of the ashram, nestled amongst the mountains of the Cumberland Plateau. In the distance I could see the magnificent dome-shaped meditation center, the copper-toned roof glistening from the sun beaming down upon it.

I was there for a weeklong retreat with the world-renowned guru Sadhguru. In the midst of my whirlwind romance with Henry, I had been invited to attend what I thought would be a restful retreat. It felt like a once-in-a-lifetime opportunity to learn from a guru I admired, so I eagerly agreed to join.

While I was looking forward to a week of spiritual growth and reflection, Henry was nervous. He had an ex who once went to a wellness retreat and dumped him upon return from her soul searching. I assured him that wouldn't be the case as I kissed him farewell at the airport the night before.

I'd been to my fair share of retreats, so I assumed this one would be a walk in the park. But the universe had other plans, and it all began with my cup of joe (or rather, lack thereof). At check-in, I was relieved to see a large carafe labeled COFFEE. Except, upon taking a sip, I discovered it wasn't coffee. It was an herbal concoction said to serve as a natural stimulant. Apparently, they didn't believe in caffeine at the ashram. Now, had I done my research, I would've known that and weaned myself off it for the full experience, but I was too in my love bubble to think about research, especially with a hottie bringing me coffee in bed.

My head was pounding harder now, with no Tylenol in sight. I pulled out my phone to text my friend Benedict, who was arriving later that day. *SOS. There's no coffee! If you find instant on the drive up, can you grab for me?!*

Sadly, Benedict didn't have any luck, so I was stuck with "Ashram coffee" for the week ahead, along with a daily wake-up call of 5:15 A M! The Inner Engineering Retreat I eagerly agreed to was no luxury retreat, but a week of intense training and long days. Next time, I'm checking into the White Lotus Koh Samui.

Trying to stay positive, I arrived at class with my water bottle and notebook in hand . . . only to discover those weren't allowed either. As a water-holic and someone who needs to write things down to remember, I was pissed. I could feel the blood boiling within me. The one plus was that rule helped with the next rule: We could only use the restroom when we had a break.

I tried my best to surrender to Sadhguru's rules, but the head throb and dehydration weren't helping. Then, one day at lunch, I found my saving grace. In the pile of tea bags, I discovered two caffeinated green teas. I wanted to scream with joy, but contained myself, not wanting the others to see what I was doing. I quickly tucked them into my tote like I was sneaking drugs into a party. Namaste.

There were about twenty of us there, learning how to inner engineer the body to reach enlightenment. We were an eclectic group of "perfect strangers," including pro athletes, entrepreneurs, and influencers. Our days were filled with long educational videos, talks, exercises, and learning a twenty-one-minute meditation sequence. I felt like I had skipped over the basics in my spiritual journey, so I was grateful to learn something that could ground me in my daily practice. Also, all the volunteers kept talking about this "life-changing" initiation we'd experience on the final day. I was curious.

By the time that last day arrived, my headache had finally disappeared. I felt mentally refreshed and ready for the day to come. We began the morning meditation as a group, then had a silent break before the initiation would begin. And that's when my final trigger kicked in . . . All I wanted to do was go for a walk around the building, but I was physically blocked by a volunteer. Apparently, I was walking past the "boundaries." My throat tightened as I held in my frustration, holding back tears. I was so annoyed by another damn rule! I made my way to a nearby tree. It was technically a few feet off the boundary path, but I couldn't help myself—let a girl hug a tree!

I stood there with my arms wrapped around the trunk, enjoying a moment of calm and serenity as I closed my eyes and took in the senses around me—the bark against my palms, the soft breeze on my face, the scent of fall in the air. It was grounding . . . until I felt a tap on my shoulder. Seriously, again?! Was I about to be grounded now? The lump thickened in my throat as I was filled with more internal rage than I understood. I quickly turned around, annoyed, to discover the tap was simply my cue to go inside. We were about to begin.

But I wasn't over the frustration. I barely made it back to my cushion before the tears came flooding down. What was it about rules and boundaries that triggered me so much? The rules of the ashram, the rules of society, feeling like I always needed to follow the rules. I was the good girl, the people pleaser, the person who did the right thing. Here I was, trying to break free from the boundaries of my life, only to continuously feel blocked. Why couldn't I just drink the damn coffee, write in my notebook, fuck who I want, leave my job, and walk around the building? Why did I always have to be the girl that followed the rules? Why did I feel so much shame when I broke them? What would it take for me to finally feel free?

As the tears purged out of me, I noticed a shift. Built-up anger, tension, and hurt was purging out of me as well. My body felt lighter, my mind calmer. The tears slowed down. As I opened my eyes to watch the final video, I noticed a box of tissues someone had placed beside me. I blew my nose and wiped my tears away. I felt better already.

Now time for our attunement. I crossed my legs, adjusted my butt cheeks, brought my pointer fingers and thumbs together on my knees, and rested my eyes. The music began. Sounds of drums, rattles, and nature echoed through me. Sadhguru's voice guided us, and it didn't take long for me to feel out of body (I guess that just comes with the territory). Euphoria swept through me as I felt a sense of oneness, my breath pulsating in unison with the energy field around me. I felt extreme gratitude and love for this precious life, my family, and for Henry. Tears streamed down my face again—this time, happy tears.

When the attunement was complete, we had one final step to conclude the program. One by one we walked up to the altar and were handed a single rose. Yup, a rose. There was no doubt in my mind, this was a little Easter egg from the universe, confirming what I already knew in my heart to be true. Henry was it. Henry was the final rose on my journey for love. I couldn't wait to return home and tell him. My happily ever after was coming true. The portal to my heart was wide open now.

As we were all saying our goodbyes to one another, one of the ladies in the group pulled me aside to chat. It felt right on cue, almost like a producer had sent her in to speak to me. Let's call her Liz, The Psychic.

"You smile and radiate joy on the outside, but on the inside, there is a lot of hurt," she said. "Know that when God takes someone away from you, it's for your highest good."

What the fuck?

She continued, "Tomorrow, your boyfriend will pick you up from the airport. He'll take you to a nice dinner where you'll sit by the candlelight. He'll share his desires for the future. When he does, look into his eyes and you will know whether he is right for you. Don't be afraid to express your feelings. But look into his eyes—you will know . . . Oh, and don't rush into marriage!"

Seriously?! Way to burst my love bubble, Liz.

I immediately googled the restaurant Henry said he wanted to take me to. I didn't notice any candles in the Yelp photos. I tried to laugh off her warning. Still, the suspense was killing me.

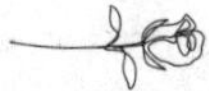

Henry greeted me at LAX with flowers in hand. All I had ever wanted during my five years with James was for him to pick me up with flowers in hand, just once.

"I missed you," he said, wrapping his arms around me.

"I missed you more." I felt safe in his embrace.

We drove to the Italian restaurant. When we arrived, I didn't notice any candles on the table. But they only had seats at the bar available . . . As we rounded the corner and were seated, there it was—a single flickering candle between us. Cue the dramatic music.

Henry said a toast. "Julie, you wonderful marvelous human. I'm so grateful you've come into my life. Your being away has only solidified my feelings and how much I'm falling for you."

"I'm falling for you too," I said. "I know you were worried about me going on this retreat, but if anything, it only confirmed how grateful I am for you, for us." We toasted, eyes locked in.

In *The Bachelor* world, there are a few phases of falling in love—there is the *I'm totally falling for you* phase (which producers see as a cop-out—just say the "L" word!), the *I'm falling in love with you* phase, and finally, the *I love you* phase. Henry and I were tottering on the lines. While the producer in my head said, *Just tell him you are falling in love with him!*, the warning I'd received earlier held me back.

Right on cue, like we were on a *Bachelorette* date, Henry immediately dived into the important conversation he wanted to have. Henry had a deep appreciation for the way he grew up, living in various countries and being exposed to different cultures at such a young age. He told me he enjoyed that lifestyle, and wanted to craft a life where we had the freedom and flexibility to move around every few years—maybe Vancouver, London, New York, LA, Dubai . . .

Excuse me . . . Dubai?

I told him part of why I left *The Bachelor* was to craft a lifestyle where I had the freedom and flexibility to work from wherever, whenever, and that travel would always be important to me. While I was open to living in other cities, I craved a home base, somewhere we could always come back to, where we have community. And I definitely didn't see myself living in Dubai.

He agreed, a house would be nice. And Dubai didn't seem to be a deal-breaker.

We seemed to meet somewhere in the middle . . . I guess that's what you call compromise? I stared into his eyes, glowing from the candlelight, searching for answers. For the first time since having met Henry, I was starting to have some doubts. I could feel that deep pinch within me, weighing at my heart.

I didn't dare tell him about Liz. While Henry appreciated my spiritual side, he did not like psychics. His mom used to get wrapped up in their every word and he saw them as manipulative cons.

Maybe he was right? You know who else wasn't a fan of psychics? Sadhguru.

One of the biggest takeaways from the retreat was not to worry about the future; all you have is this moment right now. Right now, I was happy. Right now, I was falling in love. I decided to stay in the present and fully lean into my happiness. Besides, love conquers all, right?

27

'Til Death Do Us Part

Halloween was fast approaching, and Henry was excited to experience his first American Halloween. Apparently, the Brits don't get nearly as into it. I was excited to finally have someone to do a couple's costume with.

We went to Goodwill for inspiration—another American favorite of Henry's, as England's charity shops don't come close in comparison. Nothing stood out, so we went around the corner to the Council Thrift Shop. And that's when we saw it . . . a blood-splattered wedding dress, on display in the window.

"That's it!" said Henry. We had thrown around the idea of going as a dead bride and groom, and now we had the perfect dress—Zac Posen, my size, and only twenty dollars. I began to wonder if I could get the "blood stains" out somehow.

The night of the party I slipped into the dress and had Henry zip me up. As he stood behind me, his gaze caught mine through the mirror in front of us. The unspoken thought of future possibility communicated through our eyes. He leaned in and kissed the side of my neck, sending a gentle shiver down my spine.

"You look beautiful," he whispered.

Henry pieced together a tux between his thrift shop finds and wardrobe. We then coated our faces with ghostly makeup, and I put on my alter ego wig—a short black bob. Throw in a dead flower bouquet, and we were ready to hit the town as dead newlyweds.

We went to a party in the Hollywood Hills, a first for Henry. After grabbing drinks, we walked to the edge of the property to take in the sparkling views, then wandered into the home, which was decked out like a haunted house. Henry met more of my friends as we mixed and mingled and danced to the DJ holding it down outside. Everyone loved our costumes, commenting on what a great bride and groom we were. I couldn't help but think the same. We even acted out a fake wedding ceremony with a "priest" at the party.

As the night wound down, Henry and I found ourselves alone on the dance floor, his arms around my waist, mine around his neck. We slowed down our dance moves as we gazed into each other's eyes, swaying under the night sky.

"Julie Emily LaPlaca," he said. "You brilliant, beautiful soul. I know we've only been together a short while, but I want you to know . . . I have fallen madly in love with you." His words echoed into my heart as I was overcome with joy, warmth, and safety in his arms. I had craved feeling this kind of love for so long.

"I love you so, so much, Henry Evans," I replied, holding back the tears behind my smile. There was a poetic beauty to the expression of our love, said while embracing each other in ghostly makeup and dead bride and groom attire. It was a love that transcended time and space and went beyond 'til death do us part. It was a love that felt eternal.

So much so that we decided to lock it in at the courthouse the next morning! That's right, Henry put his tux back on, I my bloodstained wedding dress, and we went to the Beverly Hills Courthouse to seal the deal. Love makes you do crazy things, right?!

Just kidding . . . did I get you?

I may be crazy, but I'm not that crazy. We did, however, put our outfits back on and stage a full-on wedding photo shoot around Beverly Hills, with my friend Allie as our photographer. I was getting a good taste of Henry's humor, as he thought this would be a fun prank to play on friends. He could have been a Bachelor date producer, as wedding photo shoots are right up the show's alley.

The photos came out great. We were one good-looking bride and groom. Once turned to black and white, we could barely notice the red marks. That's when prankster Henry got to work, leading friends to believe we'd actually gotten married. I wasn't able to commit to the bit, cutting right to the chase after sending photos to friends.

My mom was in town, so we showed her, my sister, and my nieces the photos in person. They had . . . mixed reactions. I think it was a bit too on the nose, with him needing a visa and all. And it was definitely out of character for me. Then again, this whole whirlwind romance was out of character for me, usually being the slow and steady one.

Getting married may have been a joke, but the romance, love, and joy I was feeling were very real. The limited number of days left on Henry's visa was also very real. You know what that means, right? That's right. It's the part of the journey where we are going to say goodbye to Los Angeles and take this love international!

Coming up—We are going to a city where romance fills the lamplit streets, time stops beneath Big Ben, and your Notting Hill dreams come true. There is no shortage of palaces, because this metropolitan city is made for queens and kings. Ladies and gentleman, pack your bags, because this journey for love continues in London!

Will Henry's and my love continue to flow like the Thames, or crash and burn when Big Ben strikes midnight? Stay tuned to find out!

Three weeks later, I was on a plane to London. It was early December, and I'd be spending my first Christmas away from my family to be with Henry and his. I'd always fantasized about spending the holidays in London, and now I was about to live out my real-life *The Holiday* meets *Love Actually* dreams. I rewatched both in preparation, obviously.

This is the moment in a rom-com where we would cue up a montage of Henry and me prancing around London doing all the magical, romantic things we picture a couple in love doing around the holidays. We ice skated at Somerset House, caroled on Columbia Road, caught a show on the West End, and wandered through festive markets along the Thames. We decorated a darling tree, got lost in museums, strolled the Tower Bridge, and had high tea at Harrods, with crumpets galore! For New Year's, we took a road trip to the Cotswolds in the beautiful English countryside. I'm happy to report that Henry's driving was much better now that he was on the right—well, left—side of the road.

We arrived at the manor house where we were greeted by Henry's friends, now mine as well. The house was straight out of a movie, with gorgeous stonework covered with climbing ivy. Every corner offered a peek inside the owner's imagination—little trinkets, quirky artwork, and multiple reading nooks I wanted to get lost in with a book.

We dressed up on New Year's Eve and played silly English games, wore marvelously ridiculous hats, and were served an exquisite meal. We danced, laughed, drank champagne, and counted the clock down to midnight.

"Happy New Year!" we all cheered, voices filled with joy. Henry swept me into a dramatic dip, kissing me like the leading lady I was. If Nancy Meyers had zoomed out on our story there, we'd be giving Amanda and Graham a run for their money. But was it *The Holiday* we were emulating, or *Notting Hill*? The next night, while relaxing by the fire and watching some TV, we flipped the channel just in time to catch Julia Roberts declaring to Hugh Grant that she was "just a girl, standing in front of a boy asking him to love her."

It was then that I noticed the uncanny resemblance between the young Hugh Grant and Henry. While I'm no Anna Scott, I was a girl from

Hollywood who, after one too many Hollywood playboys, had found herself a kind, charming, humble English man like that of William Thacker. My story was unfolding beautifully.

Henry and I continued our whirlwind romance by flying to Paris for my birthday a couple weeks later. It felt like a full-circle moment from the last time I'd been there, a week after James and I broke up. What a joy it was to be in the city of love while in love! We savored all the crêpes, danced around the Louvre, and kissed under the Eiffel Tower. *La vie en rose* . . . Henry was my final rose. Wasn't he?

Perhaps now is the time I should switch from working on that fictional rom-com book to the nonfiction, real-life rom-com I was creating for myself. It felt like I was living the Hollywood ending I'd always dreamed of. While I wanted to continue living *la vie en rose*, seeing life through rose-colored glasses, the producer in me knew that it couldn't all be rainbows and butterflies. Oh, no. It's now time to send in the villains and stir up some drama.

28

The Villains

I think a lot about the stories we share. We live in a world of likes and curated profiles, where everything appears to be rosy. We see picture-perfect displays of a couple's love and fun adventures. We censor ourselves when sharing stories, depending on who we are speaking to. Like an editor in the edit bay, we cut out specific details that may not be great for the plot, depending on the audience and what story we want to craft. A story I tell my best friend may be completely different than the version I share with my dad. They're a different target market, after all.

The stories I share about Henry and me falling madly in love and our whirlwind adventures around the world are all very true. I could just leave it at that. The love I felt was undeniable … so much so that I justified all the things that were starting to irritate me.

In reality, there was another version of the story unfolding simultaneously. It wasn't the version I wanted to tell. For starters, I quickly discovered that my Prince Charming didn't exactly come from royalty. For the first time in a long while, I was beginning to worry about finances, as my savings was starting to deplete. Henry, too, was in a transitional phase. He worked in tech but didn't enjoy it, and seemed to be doing the bare minimum to get by while figuring out what was next for him.

His anxiety amplified my anxiety, as my typical abundant, positive mindset began to diminish. He would regularly take deep, loud inhales through his mouth when thinking about something, causing a tinge of anxiety in my stomach every time. We were so entangled that my stomach literally absorbed his anxiousness. And as someone with self-diagnosed misophonia, trying to co-work beside him—with his heavy-handed typing punctuating his every thought—was a recipe for disaster.

Also, I had just graduated from hypnotherapy school before going to London, so I was trying to sort out what the hell I was doing with my life. Should I take the next practical step and launch a business, go back to a production gig, or follow my heart and continue working on the story I was crafting? I was attempting to write my novel while in London...when I had time to write, that is.

Problem was, all these fun, *Bachelor*-style dates Henry and I went on didn't slow down. He filled our social calendar almost every night. I loved meeting his friends and immersing myself in his world, yet our workflow wasn't meshing. He was an early riser, whereas my creativity sparks at night. I shifted my schedule to match his, even though it didn't suit me.

I felt pulled between trying to be present with the man I loved, while also figuring out the next chapter of my life. We couldn't keep ignoring reality in our little love bubble like we were on one long vacation or reality show, could we?

I started to suspect that the filling of Henry's social calendar was his way of avoiding stillness and internal reflection, while I felt called on the path of stillness and internal reflection. Speaking of stillness, out the door went my daily meditation practice. Sleeping in bed with someone else really messed up my routine. How do people do it?

Henry and I were two anxious humans trying to find our passion and purpose in life instead of staying on the hamster wheel. We were each other's biggest cheerleaders! We were also each other's biggest distractions and triggers. He was full of ideas and enthusiasm, but follow-through didn't come easily. I started to wonder if he would ever be able to focus on achieving his goals so I could trust in the life we were imagining together? *Oh wait...* would I ever be able to focus and achieve my goals?

The Villains

Also, I quickly remembered why I had moved to Los Angeles. While my fantasies of winter wonderlands in London and Paris were magical in theory, it was cold, like, really cold. *Midnight in Paris* strolls were replaced with dashing from place to place to stay warm. And, as it turns out, Henry doesn't like Paris. That hate was only amplified when he was pickpocketed an hour after we arrived. Talk about ruining the romance.

You know who else was in Paris while we were there? None other than Hannah Brown. I DMed her: *Hey! We'll be in Paris this weekend for my birthday!* She saw the message and didn't reply. I don't know why that triggered me so much, but it did. It's not like I necessarily wanted to meet up with her—I was looking forward to my romantic getaway. But to see the message and not even respond with a *Have a great birthday!*? It felt as cold as the Paris air.

It could have been an oversight, but as I scrolled back, I realized she hadn't responded to any of my DMs or birthday texts, for over a year. This got me back in my head, wondering if she knew about what happened with Peter and was upset with me. Why did I care so much? Why was I trying to maintain a relationship with someone who once caused so much stress in my life? Why did I always want everyone to like me? As much as I was trying to let go of the past, I still felt so entangled in it. I had a deep need to feel appreciated for all I had done . . . for all the hours and years of my life I had thrown out the door for the success of others. I had also created this belief that everyone knew about Peter and me and was judging me.

Around this time, I started the audiobook version of *God Bless This Mess*, Hannah's memoir. I was quickly hooked as I listened to her book while jogging around Hyde Park. I saw a lot of parallels in our journeys for love and self-discovery since leaving the show. I also pieced together that she and Peter likely slept together the same week he and I had. Talk about taking Eskimo sisters to a whole new level.

Luckily, I was so in love with Henry that, instead of being bothered, I laughed at the absurdity. It seemed like Peter, in his hot mess desperation for a happy ending, had slept with all the options to see what stuck! I don't blame him. Of course, it was the one who wouldn't put out, Madison, who he longed for in the end. I could hear my dad's constant advice in my head: "Julie, remember. You need to always make the guy wait."

Shortly after returning to London, I attended a writing workshop at Soho House. We did an exercise on jealousy as a creative tool and were prompted to write down someone we were jealous of. As much as it pained me to admit it, I wrote down none other than the hot mess express herself, Hannah Brown.

I was jealous when I saw she was staying at a nicer hotel than me in Paris and flying first class.

Jealous she was a *New York Times* bestselling author, ten years younger than me.

Jealous that she could do one post on social media and survive for the year.

Jealous she was making a living by being unapologetically herself—weird, quirky, and messy.

Jealous she got to be the Bachelorette and I didn't.

Jealous that part of my personality shined through her, while I stayed in the shadows.

It wasn't just Hannah. It was all the cast members who came on the show, got a following, and used their platform for something awesome. Why did they get to shine bright in the spotlight while I rotted away in the background? How did Nick Viall become an expert on dating?!

And yet, I'd been handed a platform, too, when the Peter rumors swirled. I could have easily leaned into that following to share my voice with the world. But I didn't. You know why? Because the villains got in the way. My villains weren't Hannah, Nick, Peter, or my old bosses. It wasn't an ex from Henry's past. It wasn't a witch with a poisonous apple or an evil pair of stepsisters. No, it was much worse than all that. The villain on my journey for love . . . was me.

My ego, jealousy, shame, and negative self-talk were getting in the way of my happiness.

All of it was tied to fear.

Now, from the outside looking in, people see me as fearless. I've done the world's tallest bungee jump, after all. But if you heard the internal dialogue of my mind these past few years, it would tell a different story. My mind said: *Go back to what you know—you can't write. You need a regular job. How's that scarlet letter? You have nothing to show for yourself—what are you doing with your life? You're not spiritual. You can't even quiet that mind of yours . . .*

The fearful thoughts continued to build up—fear of failure, fear of disappointment, fear that I was in the wrong relationship, fear that I was in the right relationship, fear of settling, fear of being alone, fear of aging, fear of not being talented enough, fear of my dad dying, fear of running out of money, fear of running out of time, fear of judgment, fear of sharing my truth, fear of being seen . . . and fear that the negative thoughts that passed through my mind would become my reality, because I understand the law of attraction!

Deep breath, Julie. Deep breath . . .

How could I tap into my social media platform when I was hiding behind a giant lie? I felt like my followers were there just because of my ties to *The Bachelor* franchise and Peter rumors. Who was I without that? How could I embody this new version of myself that was unfolding without sharing my backstory and my truth?

There was another voice in my head through all of this. It was the voice beneath all the worry and fear. It was the voice that whispered . . . *Share your truth.* That message kept coming through. It came to me in meditations, through my inner knowing, and through intuitive guides that showed up along the way. *Share your truth with the world, and the rest will unfold from there. Share your truth. Share your truth. Share your truth.*

For someone who spent her career behind the camera, shielding her truth while drawing it out of others, to be vulnerable, show my imperfections, my mistakes, and that I don't have it all together . . . that was scary.

Exposing myself instead of hiding behind the shame? It was easier to produce a fictional rom-com novel buttoned up with a happily ever after.

But there's a reason I got into reality TV instead of scripted. It's the real human experience that has always fascinated me. It's the story behind every smile, tear, and outburst. It's the journey that led an individual to be sitting in front of me in the interview chair, standing next to me in line for coffee, or meditating alongside me at an ashram in Tennessee. We're all full of stories wanting to burst out of us. As I witnessed while producing reality TV, it can be deeply healing to share our story out loud. It frees us from the pain of holding it inside.

If I wanted to fully heal and embody this new version of myself, I needed to free myself from the fear and shame holding me back. With that, I put the novel version of my story to the side and began letting the truth spill out onto the page. I wasn't sure if I would have the courage to do anything with what I wrote, but I discovered that writing was one of the deepest forms of healing. It was a way to release what was being held inside of me.

And where did Henry fall within all of this? Well, it's said that relationships are our greatest teachers, offering a reflection of what is going on within ourselves, bringing to the surface our deepest wounds, fears, and insecurities. These were all coming to the surface for me now.

Henry and I did our best to work through our wounds and fears together. But along with our internal villains, external drama was starting to unfold as well. It was the type of drama made for a reality show.

29

Drama and Decisions

"If you say you're working on your visa, then work on your visa." I was back in California, and on the phone with Henry. "We can troubleshoot if you don't get accepted. If you need me to move to London for a year, communicate that and I'd probably move. But you've been saying you're working on it since the day I met you six months ago, and I don't think you've even clicked one button on the visa website!"

"You're right. I haven't," he admitted. I could feel the frustration bubbling up inside of me. "I'm just feeling so much pressure. And I know you want to get married and have kids soon . . ."

Hold up. The marriage and kids thing? He was the one who love bombed me with all that talk early on. I liked it, yes. Was it kind of a lot so soon? Yes. But why was he now backpedaling and projecting onto me? I was confused.

As it turned out, Henry was doing some deep thinking about whether he had the capacity to be close and loving in the way I needed him to be. He sent me the book *Attached: The New Science of Adult Attachment and How It Can Help You Find—and Keep—Love,* ostensibly for me to better understand him. One of the styles the book talks about is "anxious-avoidant" (also called fearful-avoidant), where someone craves intimacy but also fears it, leading to push-pull dynamics, anxiety about abandonment, and withdrawing when things get too intense. The pattern was familiar … He was all in early on, but was now entering avoidant territory as things became real. I appreciated the self-awareness, but it didn't make matters easier. While in the past I had avoidant tendencies, I was happy to discover—through the book's quiz and Henry's validation—that I had a secure attachment style.

It had been nearly two months since we'd seen each other. When I left London at the end of January, he told me he'd come back in about a month's time. It was difficult being apart for so long, with no understanding of when he would return. And now that I felt him pulling back on his excitement for the future, he sure was starting to remind me of someone else … James.

Sounds like it's time to SEND IN THE EX, wouldn't you say? Yup, it's the part of my journey where my ex, James, returned. He was moving out of Los Angeles and wanted to meet for lunch before he left. As we sat across from each other, I noticed something different in James. He was speaking in esoteric ways, telling me about recurring dreams he'd been having of us with children. He referenced the movie *Everything Everywhere All at Once*, saying maybe in another lifetime, our souls would come back together and have a family. Tears fell down our cheeks as he spoke. James talking about reincarnation? Maybe he had evolved.

Why was he suddenly saying all the things I wanted to hear so many years ago, while Henry was pulling back and emulating young James? Talk about everything, everywhere, all at once … What was happening?!

I knew in my heart James wasn't my person. Yet, our conversation did have me thinking long and hard about what's important in a life partner. I loved Henry, deeply; I wanted our love to conquer all. But the bubble around our journey had popped. We had real-life things to think about … like the fact that we lived in different countries, for starters; or that Henry wasn't anywhere near ready to get married and start a family. I was also noticing a lack of action behind his words.

After all this personal growth, why did it feel like I was moving backward? Speaking of moving backward, after London, I left LA for two months to move in with my sister Janelle, in Riverside County. She was going through a divorce, dealing with her own drama more complicated than a reality show. While that's her story to tell, I ended up moving in with her and her daughter for a couple months to help them get back on their feet.

My sister was working at the teen treatment center our family had helped open, where I led groups from time to time. They were short on staff, so she asked if I would help out full-time while staying with her. I decided it would be a good opportunity to gain experience with the modalities I had learned, help my sister, and hopefully make a positive impact on these teen girls' lives.

One day, I was doing Reiki on one of the girls. I felt a trust forming between us. She was being vulnerable with me, wanting my help. I sensed I was getting through to her, like I might have a positive impact on her broken soul. The next day, that all changed.

While she was at an outing with the other girls, I went to her room to check on some things and found vapes she had stolen. I texted my co-worker about the vapes and told her that I'd confiscated them. She must have found out, because when the group returned, she burst through the door with rage. Before I could process what was happening, she stormed at me. She gripped my hair with one fist, pulling my head back and throwing punches with the other. Punch after punch, over and over, harder and harder each time. My body tightened in defense, clammed up like a shell in freeze mode. *I might die*, I thought, as nobody stepped in to help and there was no sign of her slowing down (my sister wasn't there that day). The sounds amplified, her screaming voice, the pound at impact. My vision started to blur, everything slowing down as I disassociated, floating somewhere else. She dragged me down the stairs and slammed me into a wall, something I didn't remember but heard about afterward from onlookers.

It wasn't until one of the other clients pulled her off me that I was able to finally escape. I dashed for the door, ran across the driveway, and hopped a fence to hide until the cops arrived. My heart was pounding through my chest, and I prayed the cops would show up before she found me again. Fortunately, they arrived soon after.

"Would you like to press charges?" they asked while taking my report. I didn't know what to do. The new manager was now on scene and shook his head at me, as if to say, "This is par for the course in the industry."

"No, I guess not," I responded, defeated.

"If you change your mind, you can always follow up with me," he said. My empathetic side didn't want to put her through that, yet as I sat with it over the upcoming days, I felt I should. What if it's worse for the next person? How will she ever learn her lesson if she continues to get away with it? By the time I called the cop with my change of heart, however, she had already been released from the hold at the hospital and was back in her home state on the East Coast, making a legal battle too complicated.

Ladies and gentlemen, I experienced my first ever physical GIRL FIGHT, like a true reality star. But let's be honest . . . it was more like flight. I left that experience with my first black eye, a fractured nose, physical therapy for my back, and questioning whether going into a career to help others was the right move for me. And with that, I finally found myself a therapist.

Why did it feel like life was throwing me jabs, literally and figuratively? How could I be so in love and such a mess? It felt like I had lost a game of Jenga, and all the pieces were scattered in front of me. I was always the half-glass-full kind of girl. Why was my glass feeling so empty?

Hannah once said to me, "Why are you always so happy, Julie? You don't need to be so positive about everything." At the time I felt like she was trying to dim my light. My persona has always been the bright, positive, vibrant soul . . . even when there was hurt inside. But we all have a shadow self behind the persona. Maybe Hannah hadn't been dimming my light at all. Maybe she was actually a mirror, reflecting the anger, messiness, and emotional truth I had learned to bury beneath the smile. Maybe I just needed to SCREAM!

I thought I left my job to be the leading protagonist on a journey for love. Yet somehow, without even realizing it, I jumped from being the producer to the helper and healer for everyone else. My shadow self said, *It is safer to support others than take up space. Swallow your shame, control the narrative, stay hiding in the shadows, keep your voice small. You don't want to be too much.*

But my wounds were coming to the surface, aching for attention. Especially once Henry entered avoidant territory. Questions arose in my heart . . .

What if sex was the leading drive of the relationship, and now that things were getting serious, I wouldn't be chosen?

Was I abandoning my needs, like I did in past relationships?

What if my heart had never fully healed from the shame of my past? What if the wounds couldn't be resolved until I radically embraced my truth, was vulnerable, and confronted the hurt that still held a piece of my heart?

What if Henry isn't my person? What if I got it wrong? What if . . . I am still holding onto the what-ifs with Peter?

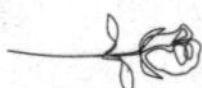

Right as my black eye was healing, there, in the shadows of a honky-tonk at Stagecoach, I was forced to confront my shadow self, face-to-face.

There, in front of me, was . . . Peter.

As soon as I saw him, all the wounds and unresolved feelings came back to the surface. I could feel the magnetic pull of my heart as we danced with each other. I realized in this moment I could continue to suppress my emotions, or I could finally let down my guard, be vulnerable, and share my truth with Peter. Not just because I was holding onto the what-ifs, but because if I wanted to continue to grow and evolve, I needed to purge what I was holding inside. As Brené Brown discusses in her book *Daring Greatly*, speaking one's truth is intrinsically linked to authenticity, which is key to overcoming shame and living a more fulfilling life.

I knew a festival in the desert while partying with friends wasn't the right setting to have the conversation, however. I wanted to be mindful and respectful to Henry, while still being honest with Peter. A month after Stagecoach, I was traveling to New York, where Peter lived. I scheduled a dinner with him. I rehearsed the conversation in my head so many times of what I would say. But then, on the actual day, Peter texted me:

Jules! My buddy Ted who you met at Stagecoach is still in town staying with me. Do you mind if he joins us?

Clearly, this dinner didn't hold the same weight for him.

Of course not!

I ended up inviting my friend Paige along and it turned into a fun group hang, but not the setting to spill my heart. This was probably another blessing from the universe, seeing as I still had a boyfriend back in London.

There was a moment, though, when it was just Peter and me talking at the dinner table. A candle flickered between us in the dimly lit tapas bar, casting a warm glow on the exposed brick wall—and on Peter. We were reminiscing about our fun adventures during his season. He paused for a moment, reflecting.

"I have absolutely no regrets about doing *The Bachelor*," he began, leaning in toward me now. "Honestly, Jules, when I think back and reflect on the whole experience . . . the best part of it all . . . was you."

His words sent a ripple through my heart—both validating and confusing. If he felt that way, why didn't he pursue me?

"Aww, really?" I said nonchalantly, like I hadn't conjured up an entire imaginary proposal speech in the past where he said this exact thing.

"A hundred percent," he confirmed. "The experience wouldn't have been the same if you weren't there. My favorite memories from the season were when we were together."

"We really did have a great time, didn't we?" I said, a soft smile on my face. "If I'm being honest, you were the best part of all my years working at the show too. It didn't feel like a job with you."

He took in what I was saying, then remarked, "You know, they really messed up not making you the Bachelorette. I would've totally come back for the season."

His tone was playful. I couldn't tell what he meant. Come back to offer advice as my friend? Or come back to date me? The not knowing pained me; I was dancing between the lines of catching up with an old friend I hadn't seen in a while . . . and wondering if there was something more in the unspoken vibration I felt between us.

"Their loss!" I exclaimed, taking a sip of my cabernet. I bit my tongue, refraining from further comment. I wanted to spill my heart, yet remained protective of Henry's. I also didn't want to cry, changing the mood of our fun group dinner.

What I really needed was a producer . . . someone to talk through my complicated feelings with. Our conversation would have gone something like this . . .

JULIE'S ITM (TV lingo that stands for "In The Moment" interview):

PRODUCER: How are you feeling right now?

JULIE: I'm feeling confused. Part of me feels like if I confess my love to Peter, he and I would end up together. Like, I was the best part of his entire Bachelor experience? That has to mean something, right? The truth is, when I reflect on my seven years producing the show, I, too, feel the best part of my time there was with Peter. Sometimes I wonder if my whole journey working on the show was to bring us together. But I've never been vulnerable with Peter in terms of telling him how I really feel. I wonder if it might be too late. And I don't want to risk losing a good thing with Henry.

The Love Producer

PRODUCER: *Where is your head at with Henry right now?*

JULIE: I'm so deeply in love with Henry. From the beginning of this journey, he has left me with no question marks about his love for me. He has been vulnerable, worn his heart on his sleeve, and I know he is here for the right reasons. We've had such a fun journey together, exploring the world with childlike wonder. He has challenged me to be vulnerable and share my heart and truth. I've grown a lot while with Henry. That is what you want in a partner, right?

PRODUCER: *Yes, absolutely. But I sense some hesitation. What are your fears with him?*

JULIE: Well … there are some red flags I've been ignoring. While this hot and heavy, all-in romance was new for me, I realize it may be a pattern for Henry. I'm in a transitional/hot mess phase of my life right now, but I realize that, too, may be a pattern for him. That doesn't make me feel very safe and secure. I do know he would be an amazing father. I know our life would be full of fun adventures, magic, and love. But now that he has been pulling back in all the grand talks of our future, family, and kids, I fear we may not be in the same place in our lives, both literally and figuratively.

I'm also noticing he seems more concerned about making sure his visa is figured out for Burning Man than he does about figuring it out for us and our relationship. Sometimes I think he loves that festival more than me. I mean, I know that's not true … but it feels that way.

Oh, and have I mentioned I've never seen Henry cry?! I used to pull tears out of people professionally for a living, and with Henry I just can't. It's driving me crazy. Maybe it's an English thing?

PRODUCER: *That must be hard, especially as you've become so vulnerable on your journey. Is there anything else coming up?*

JULIE: Yeah . . . over the past couple of years I have felt my connection with God—or the universe—heighten. Intuitively, I feel I'm meant to keep exploring this . . . but it freaks Henry out. I'm like, *hellooo*, of course the lamp flickering is an angel communicating with me. He'll smile and laugh but then go on some scientific rant or tell me to replace the light bulb. I've been holding back from talking to him about things I sense and feel because I can tell he is skeptical. I'm not saying I have the answers, but I wish he'd be more open and curious about what all *this* means (*hands waving in the air*). Can't he at least be one woo of the woo woo? In the past I didn't care as much, but as I'm growing spiritually I realize it's important to be with someone who believes in something greater than just us. Does that make sense?

PRODUCER: *Of course, spiritual alignment with a partner is important. It feels like you are beginning to sense that, while you love Henry, your futures don't really align?*

JULIE: Yes. I also don't want to hold him back from living a nomadic life. I fear he would always hold resentment if I did. I know I was warned about this during our first month together, but I desperately wanted to believe we would figure it out. But the more I think about it, the more I realize how unsettled I'd feel with that lifestyle. I want to set roots somewhere. I want a house with a big yard we can raise our children in. I love to travel and will always go on fun adventures, but the older I get, the more I realize the joy of coming home.

PRODUCER: *It's okay to honor your needs. Is there anything else?*

JULIE: Yeah . . . Most of all, I fear if I stay with Henry, I will always wonder if I missed a chance at what could have been with Peter.

PRODUCER: *You really can see you and Peter together, can't you?*

JULIE: I mean, yeah. It just makes sense. I know he plans to move back to California soon. He wants to have a family near his family. I can see how beautifully our lives would align, with similar family values and ideas on how we'd raise our kids. We would spend summers on the East Coast. We could travel whenever we wanted because he is a pilot! I think we would have a special life together; our energy just complements each other.

PRODUCER: *Am I also sensing some fears with Peter?*

JULIE: Well, there's a good chance he's just not that into me and I've completely fantasized and idealized this life together. He seems to be more into brunettes. He did once say if I dyed my hair dark I'd look like Megan Fox. That's just about the greatest compliment.

PRODUCER: *He clearly is attracted to you.*

JULIE: Yeah, but I'm aging . . . I fear I'm too old for him now. I hate that that's a thing, but it's the reality. I think at one point he said he wanted four kids so they could each have a partner on the roller coasters. I'm definitely not having four kids . . . but two would work for that, right? I fear he might not be ready for a relationship. He's currently living his best single life in New York, as he probably should! He has all these hot young influencer girls flaunting themselves at him . . . Why would he be interested in me? He says he is ready to settle down and start a family, but is he really?

Also, what Peter did post-show really hurt me. He hooked up with me and, just a few days later, was with someone else, with no heads-up, no text or call. In many ways, maybe that should've been clarity enough for me? If a guy isn't going to choose me off the bat, why should I pursue him? I don't know why I'm feeling the need to in this case. I guess I'm just following my gut, knowing that regardless of the outcome and hurt it may cause, in order to move on I need to be vulnerable and share what's on my heart with him. Ugh, why is love so complicated?

PRODUCER: *I see some emotion coming up. What are you feeling?*

JULIE: Why does it hurt so bad to love so hard? Why does it have to be so complicated? Why did I have to develop feelings for both of these men? Why am I crying as I write this all these years later? (For real.) Do our hearts ever heal from heartbreak? Do our hearts ever heal from breaking another's heart? I'm feeling so many emotions all at once.

PRODUCER: *What are you going to do?*

JULIE: I'm in love with two wonderful men. I'm not sure how this journey is going to end for me, but I know what I need to do . . .

30

The Breakup of Our Burning Love

I'd like to say I immediately spoke to Henry about everything going on in my mind, but he had finally booked a flight back to Los Angeles, so I waited. Naturally, our reunion sparked passion and delayed the hard talk.

Eventually, we scheduled a chat, and both "prepped" for the conversation. I showed up with scribbled notes all over a giant sketch pad. Henry had a neatly typed-out list of things to discuss. During our talk, I admitted seeing Peter had brought up unhealed feelings. On his list of concerns about me? That I was too wrapped up in the story of us. Umm, what? I'm a storyteller, Henry. Sorry if I get excited sharing the details of our meet-cute worthy of a modern-day *Frozen* remake. (Wait until he reads this book.)

We talked through everything like two mature adults who loved each other. It felt good to be open and honest with one another, and it felt clear that, while we loved each other, our futures weren't aligned. Still, he was in town another few weeks, so we stayed together, almost like we were bottling up the time we had left. We decided we would consciously uncouple, as Goop loyalists would say. And what better place to do that than … Burning Man?

Yup, I went to Burning Man. Henry really wanted me to experience it with him. I hesitantly agreed and we locked in tickets. Every part of me wanted to bail now that we were breaking up. But as the producer in me says, it's good for the plot! Maybe I am too wrapped up in the story.

Still conflicted, I went to my go-to resource for advice—my oracle deck. You know what card fell onto my lap? *The Horned Cactus.* The description read, "The Horned Cactus thrives in the barren desertscape, offering you the gift of water when all appears to be dry . . . a symbol of resilience, of resourcefulness, of your needs being met in spite of appearances to the contrary . . . dig deep below the less than friendly surface that hides a rich underground world."

I don't think a card could get more literal than that . . . to the desert I went! We loaded up the car and road-tripped to Black Rock City, the made-up desert town of art and self-expression. Upon arrival, I immediately regretted it. I had landed at a giant adult playground, and it was the last place I wanted to be. Not because we'd be roughing it in a tent, using port-a-potties, and dealing with excessive heat, but because I was now getting the impression that Henry had no desire to hook up with me. Huh? I thought Burning Man was about being free and in the moment? It was our last hoorah together, and we hadn't even kissed!

Suddenly, my deepest fear came flooding to the forefront: being undesirable. Sex was the one thing I always knew men wanted from me. And now, the person I'd spent the past year with didn't even want that. Fear he was going to hook up with other girls swarmed through me, as he bounced around camp like a social butterfly. I didn't feel like being social. To add to the burn, after setting up and loading the tent, we were told we needed to move it three feet. Another place with dumb rules.

That first night, we went out with Henry's friends from the camp. I may as well have not been there, as I felt like he ignored me all night. This isn't how conscious uncoupling is supposed to work, is it?

The next day, while I enjoyed exploring, something felt off. Like I was just there, following Henry around and doing whatever he wanted. I went to bed early, convinced everyone was on drugs and judging Burning Man for all the reasons I always judged Burners.

The Breakup of Our Burning Love

I woke up early to use the bathroom. As I stepped out of the tent, I saw the sun rising over the playa. I rode my bike to the closest porta-potty, passing others cruising around from the night before and hearing the distant sounds of the clubs still going strong.

Off toward the horizon, I saw the silhouette of a giant heart as the sky behind it started to glow a soft orange. It moved me. I wrapped myself in my surroundings, acknowledging that I was in a beautiful place full of so much love and creativity. I knew that I needed to change my perspective if I was going to get through a week here. There was magic and mysticism to the land I was on. I just had to be open to receiving it.

While in the porta-potty, I saw an event flyer on the door. There was a workshop that afternoon called "I'm My Healer, I'm My Lover." I decided I would attend, solo.

As the rest of the camp awoke, I began speaking to a girl named Uma. When she asked how I was liking things, I began to cry, admitting how difficult and hard it was . . . not because of the conditions, but because of Henry.

"Why don't we go explore for a bit?" she said.

"Yeah, I think some time away from him would be good." I told Henry I would be back later, and Uma and I embarked on a girls' adventure.

We landed at Rumi's Tea House, passing through rich red and gold flowing fabric, into a tent that offered an oasis of the great Rumi's poetry, tea, and soulful nourishment. I made myself comfortable on the cozy Persian rugs covered in pillows and poofs. I grabbed one of Rumi's poetry books, closed my eyes, took a deep breath, and flipped it open to see what wisdom would land before me. As I began to read the page I turned to, I didn't know whether to laugh or cry. Of all the great Rumi passages, the one I opened up to was . . . about a man getting an erection, the energetic connection during sex, children, and how, just as quickly, the man loses his desire to be with the woman? Way to read into my soul, Rumi.

But, upon deeper reflection, I understood the message. Sex isn't just sex. It's two souls coming together. Even when we think we're just having fun, there is an energetic entanglement that happens. I've heard the womb can absorb men's energy for up to seven years after intimacy!

According to Taoist and Tantric philosophy, women are yin, receptive, while men are yang, projective—meaning the energy is flowing more easily from the man into us. We can absorb their problems and trauma on a somatic level, blocking our own creativity, sensations, and ability to move on. No wonder I still felt so entangled with Peter's chaos—there was a lot going on at that time! And, upon reflection, I could see how I was absorbing a lot of Henry's anxiety and fears as my own. My womb had been whispering this to me. Finally, I was ready to hear it.

I have a strong appreciation for the liberation and sexual freedom women of my generation have embodied, leaning into our masculine energy and not feeling "attached." But at the same time, we can't deny that we are wired differently. Our wombs are an energetic vessel, the center of creation. While I wasn't about to become a born-again virgin, I was able to reframe my thinking. Henry not wanting to sleep with me wasn't about me being undesirable. It was a form of protection as we disentangled as lovers and moved forward as friends.

I knew Henry's bopping around talking to everyone stemmed from his own insecurities of wanting to be loved and accepted. Maybe it bothered me because I wanted to be loved and accepted. But I loved and accepted Henry, and myself, for where we were on our healing journeys. As Rumi says, "the soul of life is playful," and I wanted to bring that energy back for my final days with Henry.

He was grateful for my return to camp later that afternoon, saying he had missed me. I told him I had felt unwanted, and he assured me all he wanted to do was be in this together. As early evening approached, we rode our bikes to an art installation called the Elder Mother, a large metal tree sculpture that moves to the wind, illuminates colors, and whispers various fairy tales throughout. It was inspired by Hans Christian Andersen's fairy tale of the same name, which is a story of love and nostalgia that blurs the line between reality and dreams. I cried in Henry's arms as we reflected on the past year, my dreams of that fairy-tale ending, and the reality that we'd never become the elder couple in the story, and in my imagination not long ago.

Our story would be told a little differently now. It would be a story of fun adventures, passion and chaos, vulnerability, confronting our shadows, working through the fear and shame, and growing together through it all. It would be a story of two people who wore their hearts on their sleeves and showed up for the right reasons, as they say in Bachelor Nation. Because of that, we were able to discover a deeper understanding of ourselves, our truth, and of love.

While I've learned that love doesn't conquer all in terms of finding a life partner, I agree with Rumi that love is "an alchemist that makes alchemists." I believe each experience of romantic love can transform an individual. My relationship with Henry helped me confront my shadows, face my inner villains, and gain a deeper understanding of myself. I'll forever be grateful for our time together and the personal growth I gained.

Henry and I spent the rest of Burning Man like two young kids exploring all that was possible. We zip-lined, ecstatic-danced, climbed towers, rode unicorns, and let ourselves get lost to be found. I was even starting to get a bit sad about the week ending.

Then, as the oracle card declared, The Horned Cactus offered the gift of water when all appeared to be dry. Rain poured down on the barren desert, trapping us in Black Rock City due to the mud. Ahh, universe, come on. I wasn't *that* sad!

I guess we needed one more challenge thrown our way, symbolic of how messy and unpredictable the journey for love could be. And while at times I had felt stuck in the muddy terrains of my heart's desires, I felt something blooming within me. Like the lotus flower that emerges from the mud, I was closing this chapter with Henry less attached to what could have been and awakening to the love within.

I'll take that over a rose any day.

31

The Not So Hollywood Ending

This is the moment of a romantic comedy where one leading man or woman runs after the other, confesses their love, and the two take off into the sunset to live happily ever after. In the case of *The Bachelorette*, it's when the final man magically picks the dream ring, gets fitted in a dapper suit too hot for the tropical location, and walks up to a platform adorned with clay pottery, lanterns, and a single rose, with a picturesque backdrop behind them. The leading lady and man each express their love, prompting viewers at home, and producers behind the cameras, to cry sweet tears. We then see the man get down on one knee and ask for the Bachelorette's hand in marriage.

Seeing as I'm not the Bachelorette, I dreamed up ways of how I'd express my love to Peter. I wanted it to be in person . . . perhaps my excuse for waiting so long. I imagined us walking the Brooklyn Bridge over to DUMBO for pizza at Grimaldi's, then walking to the water's edge at sunset to sit on a perfectly placed bench to chat. Seeing as Peter is a pilot, I also dreamed of the classic run-after-him-at-the-airport scene. This felt achievable given the circumstances. If I'd had the courage, I would've done it.

I saw Peter for a quick hello while in New York for a gig after Henry and I broke up. It was a group setting, right before a red-eye I had to catch. He expressed wanting to do a weekend trip to Goshen, even texting my dad a picture of us, saying a trip was definitely happening soon (to which my dad again replied, "That's a good-looking couple!"). I imagined what that weekend would look like. We'd lie in the grass and see a shooting star, a full circle moment to the shooting star he saw before his *Bachelor* journey. He'd meet the rest of my big Italian family and fall in love with the idea of us. Maybe his parents would join, not wanting to miss the coming together of our families. I didn't technically have a trip planned to Goshen for a while. I debated booking one, with the hopes that Peter would join.

More time passed as Peter went to film *The Traitors*. He knew I was single now. If he was interested, he'd pursue me, right? I went back to my old ways of thinking, wanting to avoid the vulnerable conversation, maybe because I knew what the outcome would be and wanted to skip the hurt. Yet the more I avoided it, the more it consumed my mind. My inner voice grew louder. *Have the conversation, Julie . . . for your own closure, healing, and growth.*

Admittedly, it wasn't until the tabloids speculated that Peter was seeing Ekin-Su from *The Traitors* that I gained the courage to reach out. The rumors brought up old wounds from the headlines with Kelley. I assumed they were true, and decided I just needed to get the words out of my mouth before it went public so I could move on.

I texted, asking if we could talk. We planned a call for the following day. The date was March 15, 2024, just about four years to the day since the last time we'd hooked up. Four years—it took me four years!

"Jules! How are you?" he asked when I called.

"Hi, Peter. I'm pretty good—how have you been?" I asked.

After some small chat, I got into it. "You know, I spent years as a producer getting you and other contestants to be vulnerable and share your truth. Yet, when I reflected on my own life, when it comes to love, I always had a shield up. It's been a form of protection, due to hurt in past relationships. Over the past few years, I've been on a bit of my own journey to work through that. So, Peter, I'd like to practice what I preach, be vulnerable, and share my heart with you."

"All right, Jules. I'm your producer now," he said. "Tell me, how are you feeling?"

I went on to tell Peter everything. Well, the CliffsNotes version of this book with fewer details from my crazy internal dialogue. Ultimately, I admitted that I loved him, and feared if I didn't tell him I would always wonder "what if."

He seemed shocked by this revelation. He admitted that he had thought about it as well, but had to pick his words carefully. He had just started seeing someone he saw potential with (not Ekin-Su) and wanted to be respectful of that.

"Why did you wait until now to tell me?" he asked.

"Oh . . . you know, I made up excuses in my head," I said. "I really wanted to do it in person when it was just you and me. Yet somehow, over the past four years, we haven't had that. Then you were with Kelley, then I was with Henry . . . and time just seemed to pass."

"I guess the timing has always been a bit off with us, huh?" he said.

"Yeah, I guess so," I reflected. "Timing really is everything."

We ended up talking for a couple of hours, catching up on life and family, and reminiscing. I let him know my love was unconditional, and I was glad he found someone he could see a future with. When I hung up, it was like a giant boulder that had been weighing me down was suddenly lifted. I felt so much lighter. I felt free.

Have you ever seen the docuseries *The Rehearsal* with Nathan Fielder? In the first episode, Nathan helps the trivia-obsessed Kor rehearse how he will have a difficult conversation with his teammate, admitting he lied about something early on in their friendship. Through the brilliance of Nathan, they stage a replica of the trivia bar, hire actors, and play out all the possible scenarios of how the conversation may go, so Kor can get over the fear of sharing his truth. The real-life interaction is a lot more anticlimactic, with his friend being totally understanding.

I think a lot about that episode. While ridiculous, it brilliantly illustrates the torture we put ourselves through as humans before having an uncomfortable conversation. Sometimes fear stops us from having the conversation at all. Some couples get married despite a deep inner voice that says not to. Some couples get engaged because they've been together so long, only to later have their relationship blow up because they were too scared to admit they had grown apart. I hear stories of the one that got away, yet they never told the one that got away. There are people with lifelong crushes who have never told their crush they're crushing!

Tell your crush you're crushing. Tell the person you love them. Tell the person you don't. Those conversations you've been rehearsing in your head? Speak them out loud. You have no idea how freeing it will be to speak your truth and share your heart, even if it feels scary and hurts in the moment. The timing is never going to be "just right."

While Peter and I aren't destined for that Hollywood happy ending I thought I so desired, I have no regrets for the wild journey our relationship, or lack thereof, catapulted me into. Rejection never feels great, but I was quite happy after speaking to him, finally getting the closure and clarity I needed.

Honestly, I don't know that I was even hoping for Peter to confess his love and for us to be together. I think I knew deep down we were on different paths in our lives, and that the call was for my own release and healing. Peter's life in New York City is what my life was ten—shit, twenty—years earlier. I think there was a part of me trying to hold onto those old versions of myself . . . the Wendy in me not wanting to grow up, the girl fearful of aging. But the truth was, I was glad I had evolved past those days; my priorities had shifted once I embarked on my journey.

Looking back, I think I romanticized my happy ending with Peter as a way to justify what happened between us. I thought that if we ended up together, the shame would go away. But now I realize I can rewrite my relationship with shame; I can have compassion for it, and speak it out loud. When you speak it out loud, something powerful happens. Like magic, the grip it had on you disappears.

32

My Final Rose

Growing up, I heard tales of princesses and princes and happily ever afters through Disney classics like *Cinderella*. Those were then replaced with rom-coms, with stories that were buttoned up with a happy ending that left you feeling hopeful. From there, I went on to land my dream job, creating real-life rom-com versions of these fairy tales I so desired.

How could I not imagine and hope to get that Hollywood happy ending for myself? How could my mind not wander to thoughts of my dream man and dream proposal? As women, we are conditioned all our lives to desire this type of love.

I once came across a quote that said, "It is our imagination that is responsible for love, not the other person." Sometimes I wonder if I made this all up in my head. Maybe I was too tied to the story of what could have been versus the reality of what was, both with Henry and with Peter. I wanted so badly to get my happy ending, feeling like I was chasing time.

The truth is, while we think we want the stories told to us through the screen, we don't really see what happens after "Happily Ever After." I mean, how many words did Cinderella actually exchange with the prince? He could end up being a complete dud, for all we know! I had my *The Holiday* happy ending, kissing my version of Jude Law at midnight, but we all know long distance rarely works out. Only on reality TV do we get to see the bubble pop, with most couples not lasting once back in the real world.

Does that mean the journey wasn't worth it? No. I think it's the opposite, actually.

I think whenever we feel called toward an adventure, or a certain person, it is worth following that calling. I've seen cast members come out of their experience on *The Bachelor* with a profoundly deeper understanding of themselves. I've witnessed them share personal, often traumatic stories they've never spoken out loud, helping heal wounds within them. They confronted their fears and villains in ways they never would have had they not come on the show. For many, time spent in the interview chair is the closest form of therapy they will ever experience, unlocking parts of themselves they wouldn't have tapped into if something hadn't called them to go on that journey. Cast members who don't have a great experience are usually those who keep their walls up, resist vulnerability, and let fear of judgment get in their way. That used to be me.

While I was hoping to create my happy ending, I realize now there was another story unfolding all along. It was the story of a girl who felt stuck and stagnant in the routine of her life, craving a deeper understanding of herself, her purpose, and love. It was the story of a soul who wanted to be guided toward her highest truth. While I may not have ended this journey with a man by my side, I gained something much more profound. After years of putting everyone else's needs before mine, I have finally chosen myself.

In choosing myself, I also acknowledge my current truth . . . I'm not anywhere close to being ready to have children. Shortly after Henry and I broke up, I attended my family-friendly twenty-year high school reunion. I was the only one there without a significant other or kids. While I admired the families that had blossomed since graduating all those years ago, I didn't look around and desire that for myself. It was quite the opposite. I felt extreme gratitude for the freedom and independence my life offered. While sometimes you can't help but question whether you did it all wrong, I knew in that moment I did it all right, with no regrets for the unconventional life I've led.

I'll also admit this—I cried afterward. I do want children someday, just not yet. Why do women have to deal with the clock striking midnight on their fertility, causing the internal pressure to "settle down"? I feel like Tick-Tock the Croc from *Peter Pan* has been following me around, sounding the alarm to the fertility farm. I don't ever want to settle just because I'm of "that age." I've come too far to settle for less than what I deserve.

I took matters into my own hands to relieve some of the pressure I was feeling as I approached the last year of my thirties. Being with Henry had made me seriously consider freezing my eggs, since I knew he wasn't ready to have children anytime soon. And quite frankly, neither was I. I met with my gynecologist and had bloodwork done to check my numbers and was relieved to learn they were still really good.

Admittedly, I had a lot of fear around freezing my eggs. I hate needles . . . like, pass-out-when-I-get-a-shot hate. Remember the Botox story? How was I supposed to inject myself with needles on the daily? Luckily, thanks to my spiritual journey, I knew I had tools to help me through it. My hypnotherapist worked with me to get over my fear of needles. I listened to a recording every night leading up to the start of the injections. I also had my sister do an emergency hypnotherapy session the day of the first procedure.

Spanning fourteen days, I injected myself with thirty-two needles all on my own. As I lay in bed each night, I did Reiki on my womb while listening to a follicle growth meditation and visualizing a specific number of eggs. I had high hopes, with a number more than three times higher than the fertility calculator predicted, given my age. I literally felt the souls of my future children moving around as I went woo-woo on my womb. I kid you not—I really felt them. Life and spirit are so wild. The final shot before my retrieval landed on my thirty-ninth birthday, bringing a whole new meaning to birthday shots.

As I was coming out of anesthesia the day of the retrieval, the nurse told me the number of eggs they collected. It was the exact number I'd visualized. This was yet another reminder from spirit that the universe had my back—well, and my womb—on this journey through life. Another weight was lifted from my shoulders, knowing my babies' souls are with me and will come when the time is right—if the time is right, in this lifetime.

I truly believe it was because of my holistic approach and mindfulness practice that I was able to have such success. I share this not to brag, as I know it can be a very painful experience for a lot of women. If you're struggling, my heart is with you. I understand the importance of the connection between the mind, body, and soul, and pray fertility clinics bring more awareness to this deeper connection going forward.

That is what my journey has really been about—connecting with myself in a deeper way. I confronted parts of myself I had never looked at before. I had to let go of the stories of the past that wanted to shape my future and release the fears of what that future may be. I had to change the story women have been led to believe their lives must look like by a certain age. I found ways to reconnect with my body, mind, and soul. I found my voice. I now understand why my wounds, insecurities, fears, and patterns in love needed to come to the surface. It wasn't a setback; it was a clearing—creating space for me to feel whole and secure within myself.

My journey may have ended with some eggs in the freezer rather than a ring on my finger, but I wouldn't have it any other way. I always hoped that for one season of *The Bachelorette* we'd have a lead who, instead of leaving engaged, chose herself. Network television hasn't caught up with the times. But in my story, I'm happy to say the final rose is going to me.

Often when contestants would first arrive in Los Angeles, excited and nervous for the journey to come, they'd ask for my advice. I always told them to be unapologetically themselves, lean into it all, be vulnerable, and share their truth. While the odds of them ending up with a husband were slim, by giving themselves over to the process and feeling through all of it, they would grow and form a deeper understanding of themselves, and of love. I'm grateful I finally took a bit of my own advice.

As humans, we are the producers, writers, and stars of the movie of our lives. We get to choose how it unfolds. We can continue to hold onto the stories of the past and repeat the same patterns, or we can go on the journey within, and rewrite how our story looks going forward.

Throughout my journey, I became a curious observer of what was happening around me and within me, noticing the signs and messages from the universe. One of many mystical experiences came to me after doing the dishes. I saw a small floating soap bubble and put my hands out, thinking it would land and pop. Instead, it began to dance with the movement of my palms, gracing the edge of my hands but never landing. I laughed with awe and amusement, then tucked my hands away and watched the bubble float upward. Just as it was about to hit the ceiling, I yelled, "Come back!"

Right on cue, the bubble curved away and back toward me. I watched with wonderment and put my two palms out. This time, the bubble landed ever so gently. I stared into the sparkling crystal ball of soap and made a wish. Then, it popped, sending a wave of energy throughout my body. I brought my palms together in prayer. I whispered, "Thank you, angels, for showing me there is magic everywhere."

A few days later, I watched the Disney movie *Wish* with my niece. I didn't know the plot, but it quickly caught my attention when the characters formed bubbles on the palms of their hands to make a wish! I mean ... weird, right? The evil king took the bubble wishes from the people for his own power and control, before the leading protagonist, Asha, was able to retrieve them and return the wishes to their rightful owners. In the end, Asha became the fairy godmother of the land.

That's when it clicked. We girls were led to believe we want to be princesses, seeking the external validation of a "prince" who will give us the love we desire. But what if we were told the wrong story? What if we were actually the fairy godmothers all along? What if the key to finding love is unlocking the magic that is already within us?

When we stop searching externally for someone or something to save us, love us, or bring us joy, and instead awaken to the love within us, that is when the magic truly happens. That is when we become producers of love in all that we do. In doing so, that love radiates right back to you.

As I finished writing this chapter, I stepped outside to watch the lunar blood moon eclipse. I took in the marvel of the red-hued moon. As if that weren't magical enough, I said out loud to the universe, "It would be really cool to see a shooting star right now."

Seconds later, a star shot across the night sky under the red moon. Tears streamed down my face. This time, they were happy tears. They were tears of gratitude for the love and magic I've discovered on my journey. My wish? My wish is that by sharing my story, others are inspired to embrace the leading lady role of their own lives.

Don't be afraid to follow that inner calling, step into the unknown, share your truth, and unlock the love and magic that lives within you. And if you need a love producer to help along the way, I'm your girl.

Epilogue

A few months before my fortieth birthday, I went on a date with a guy named Colin. Toward the end of dinner, he made an observation.

"I go on dates with a lot of women your age and their focus is one thing and one thing only—marriage and kids. But you, your focus is on expansion." He brought his arms out wide. "You've been going through a rebirth."

I did all I could to hold back tears. I didn't hear from Colin after that date, but I got the message I needed. It's hard to see while going through it, but as the great poet David Whyte says, "You know you are on the right path when the path disappears and you enter the black contemplative splendours of self-doubt." Admittedly, the second half of my thirties were some of the most difficult as I shed my old identity. Reflecting back, I hold so much compassion and empathy for that version of myself, admiring the strength I had to follow the intuitive voice within that whispered, "Keep going. You're unlocking parts of yourself that have been suppressed."

When I stopped letting fear hold me back, things began to unfold. I finally put the stories of my past behind me and embraced the new story I was creating. I knew I would no longer suppress my truth, play small, or dim my magic. I even committed to sharing my story, the unscripted version, with all of you.

I made other changes too. After seven years in my rent-controlled

West Hollywood apartment that I felt trapped in—the one I moved into after my breakup with James—I finally left and followed my inner calling to be in nature. I spent time in a secluded yurt in the redwoods before finding myself a literal fairy cabin in Topanga to begin this next decade in. My inner child's heart is full being back in her element, sitting by the stream and catching frogs. I've found a community that aligns with the path I'm currently on and am so grateful for new, blossoming friendships.

And yes, I'm forty now. Admittedly, I cried a lot the last day of my thirties. Like—a lot, a lot. There was immense grief as I bid farewell to a decade full of growth, success, and heartbreak. I hold space for this grief now, allowing myself to feel the full range of emotions with compassion. Simultaneously, in the non-duality of life, I also feel so much love, joy, and gratitude. I step into this next decade with a deeper understanding of myself and my purpose going forward. I also understand why I haven't found my life partner yet. I needed to connect with myself first. In doing so, my desires for a partner have changed, and I trust that we will be brought together when the timing aligns.

To quote another Disney classic, "Mirror, mirror on the wall ..." I've learned that everyone that comes into our life is simply a mirror, there to reflect parts of ourselves back to us. My goal now? To be a producer of love; to reflect love back to you.

To be a producer is to bring something into existence. I'm grateful for the years I spent bringing love stories to the world through the screen. But to me, that was just tapping the surface of the love stories I hope to bring into existence going forward. During my journey, I learned the tools needed to break through the subconscious blocks, limiting beliefs, negative patterns, and false stories we tell ourselves. I became a certified life coach and hypnotherapist, and studied a number of healing modalities including energy work, tapping, and intuitive development.

These modalities have helped me on my journey for love, and I now guide others on their journeys as well. Through my business, The Love Producer, I work with women who are ready to break through the stories of their past, step into their truth, and write their own love story. It all starts with you, as they say on *The Bachelor*, following your heart. On the other side of doubt and fear is the ever-present energy field of love ready to guide you.

I am not perfect, but one thing I do know is that in a world full of so much anger and sadness, there is something powerful that happens when we connect with the love that's available to each and every one of us. When I finally stepped away from the noise of the city and spent time in nature, I entered a meditative state, took my pen to paper, and asked my higher self about love. My hand started moving faster than my mind could process, as a poem came out onto the page.

And so, as a teaser of what's to come "next season" on this journey for love, I'll leave you with this message from my higher self…

The journey for love is something we are all on in this lifetime

Though some may not admit it or may try to deny it

Shielding their heart from all of life's hurt

Or by looking for love in all the wrong places

People continue old patterns conditioned from the past

Latching onto "love" something they know won't last

We all search and search and may even go on a show

In hopes to find that love made for a fairy tale

The journey often feels long and hard

But the reality? Love has been there right from the start

When we are born into the world as a young vibrant soul

Love is truly all that we know

Then life happens and things get in the way

Conditioning your mind with egocentric ways

You learn right versus wrong, good versus bad, normal versus weird

When to worry, what to fear

That you must go to school and get a good job

Work really hard so you can buy a new car

Epilogue

Get married, have a baby or two
You are at that age so it's what you should do
But let me ask you … how much have you connected with you?
And really discovered what is real, what is true?
I am here now understanding all of this
Love isn't just in the kiss
Close your eyes and make a wish
To feel love unconditionally …
I now have come to discover, love is in everything
In the air we breathe, in the birds that sing
In my pen that writes what comes to my mind
Through a more powerful source, through the divine
For the divine is here, I feel it all around
The divine is our guide and wants you to know
That we are all one and we are all love
We are all connected to everyone
When you look at your neighbors with loving eyes
The same way you look at a stranger, perhaps to their surprise
Look at them with love and the other ones too
Can you feel a piece of you?
In him, in her, in they, and in them?
The divine feminine and her intuition is here and ready to lead
To bring this world to ascension and bring man to his knees
Ready to open his arms, release the ego and receive
All of this love that is in everything
When this happens, the world will ascend
A beautiful balance of masculine and feminine
We will elevate our consciousness and get rid of all war
Love will prevail, it will, it will …
Right now, it may feel heavy and dark
As we fight through the weeds and dark energies
But soon goodness and joy will supersede

Epilogue

So, what can I do now? you may ask
The answer is simple—it's one little task
Be a producer of love in all that you do
And the divine light will shine through you
And through your sisters and brothers too
All of God's children playing on this earth
What do you say? Want to make it more fun?
It will be when we lead with LOVE

May you live happily ever after, and realize there is no such thing as The End.

Resources That Supported My Journey

If parts of my story resonate with you and you're curious to keep exploring, below are some of the books and tools that helped guide me along the way.

Books

Atlas of the Heart: Mapping Meaningful Connection and the Language of Human Experience by Brené Brown

Attached: The New Science of Adult Attachment and How It Can Help You Find—and Keep—Love by Amir Levine and Rachel S. F. Heller

Awakening the Heroes Within: Twelve Archetypes to Help Us Find Ourselves and Transform Our World by Carol S. Pearson

Be Still and Listen: A Guide to Unlocking Your Intuition by Jeff Bomberger

Becoming Supernatural: How Common People Are Doing the Uncommon by Joe Dispenza

Big Magic: Creative Living Beyond Fear by Elizabeth Gilbert

Daring Greatly: How the Courage to Be Vulnerable Transforms the Way We Live, Love, Parent, and Lead by Brené Brown

Eastern Body, Western Mind: Psychology and the Chakra System as a Path to the Self by Anodea Judith

Inner Engineering: A Yogi's Guide to Joy by Sadhguru

Many Lives, Many Masters: The True Story of a Prominent Psychiatrist, His Young Patient, and the Past-Life Therapy That Changed Both Their Lives by Brian L. Weiss

Proof of Heaven: A Neurosurgeon's Journey into the Afterlife by Eben Alexander

Soul Boom: Why We Need a Spiritual Revolution by Rainn Wilson

The Artist's Way: A Spiritual Path to Higher Creativity by Julia Cameron

The Celestine Prophecy by James Redfield

The Creative Act: A Way of Being by Rick Rubin

The Power of Now: A Guide to Spiritual Enlightenment by Eckhart Tolle

Card Decks for Deeper Connection

The Life Story Interview Kit: Crafted question cards to help uncover stories.

The Shaman's Dream Oracle: A 64-Card Deck and Guidebook by Alberto Villoldo & Colette Baron-Reid: A great resource to receive guidance from your guides above.

We're Not Really Strangers: A card deck designed to foster vulnerability, connection, and meaningful dialogue.

Acknowledgments

I can't believe I wrote a book! What felt like a pipe dream not that long ago actually happened, and it wouldn't have been possible without the love and support of so many.

I'd like to start by thanking you, my readers. Whether you've been following me since my time at *The Bachelor* franchise or are new here, thank you for taking an interest in my story. I hope you found a bit of yourself through my words.

To Bachelor Nation

To my Bachelor Nation family—including the fans and friends behind the scenes and in front of the camera—I wouldn't trade my years at the show for anything. Those experiences helped shape who I am today, and I'll forever cherish all the memories, sleepless nights, and wild adventures we had together. To EPs 1-9 and all my producer friends—leaving you was the hardest breakup of them all! I'm so grateful to have worked alongside such talented, kind humans.

Chris Harrison, thank you for your friendship, guidance, and continued support. You are loved by so many and the best at what you do, even holding me through the tears, judgment free, as I shared my truth with you.

Acknowledgments

Mike Fleiss and Rob Mills, thank you for seeing my leading lady potential before I saw it in myself.

To My Family

My parents: I count my lucky stars to have been blessed with the most supportive, generous, compassionate, loving parents a girl could ask for. Thank you for giving me the strength and courage to follow my dreams, no matter how crazy they may seem. Mom, you are a literal angel on this earth. I love you as much as all the stars in the sky and flowers on my wallpaper. Dad, you are a warrior. Your grit, resilience, and determination motivate me every day. Together, may we continue to create our own luck for years to come! To know both of you is to know love.

To my sisters, my best friends: Jen, I will always look up to you and don't know where I'd be without you guiding the way. Who knew jumping into hypnotherapy school would lead to this? Thank you. Janelle, my wish came true when you were born. Your patience, resilience, and continued support are appreciated more than you know. I can't wait to see what unfolds on your journey.

To my nieces: Siena, Riley, and Teegan. You are my greatest teachers. Never lose your magic. My favorite compliment is when you say Auntie JuJu is a kid! This is true, and yes, I am a fairy too.

To my nana, cousins, aunts, uncles, and extended family: Thank you for being my biggest cheerleaders and filling my belly with lots of love and pasta.

To All the Men Who Became My Muse

I believe every relationship, romantic or not, is there to help an individual evolve to their highest self. While some of you didn't make it past the edit bay, you know who you are. Thank you for being a supporting character on my journey for love.

Peter: I've come to realize we have multiple soulmates in our lives, often showing up when it's time for something to crack open within us.

Acknowledgments

Thank you for seeing me, appreciating me, and being the catalyst for my journey toward awakenment.

"Henry": My twin flame, whether you like it or not. You'll forever have a piece of my heart. Thank you for your unconditional love.

"James": We were young and growing together. I'll always cherish our time together, in this lifetime, and those to come.

Dominic: My angel surfing through the clouds above.

To My Team

Amanda Bernardi, my agent: Thank you for believing in my story and vision. I appreciate your guidance, hand holding, and support through it all. May this be the beginning of a magical journey together!

Rebecca Pillsbury, my editor: As soon as I read your memoir, *Finding Ecstasy*, I knew the universe had brought us together for a reason. Thank you for pushing me to go deeper and explore parts of myself I had been avoiding. This book wouldn't be what it is without you. I'm forever grateful.

The BenBella family: Thank you for bringing my story to life and for making me feel like a part of the team. My senior editor, Rick, who helped me laugh through the process; cover design magic from Morgan and Sarah; production editor Kim; marketing director Lindsay—let's have a party! Glenn, Susan, Claire, Alicia, Madeline, Monica, Jennifer, Rachel, Adrienne, and Ariel. You all get my final rose!

To My Friends

Thank you to all my friends, old and new, who have held space for my tears and danced alongside me with no fear. Natasha: You were family before you joined me at *The Bachelor* family, Adam: My favorite plus one, Allie, Jane, John, Benedict, My FIT/NYC girls, all the magical fairies that have come into my life—in Topanga and beyond.

To all the talented authors and friends who read an early copy of the manuscript and offered their endorsements, I'm forever grateful. Thank you from the bottom of my heart.

Acknowledgments

To My Love Producers

To all the healers, therapist, coaches, yoga teachers, gurus, and lawyers (ha!) that helped guide the way. Thank you to my teachers at HMI, my wellness sanctuary Artha (extra big hug to John San Juan and Christian), Natalia Ochoa, Bibi Caspari, Amy Schmidt, Kate Yamamoto, Niki Payne, Mimi Magnuson, Jen Pastiloff: It was at your retreat I realized I'm the villain! Kindbody for keeping my baby eggs safe . . . and all the love producers that have crossed my path. They are everywhere, when your heart is open to receiving.

Katt Lowe: My mentor, hypnotherapist, Reiki extraordinaire, and intuitive guide. I don't think you realize what a big role you had on this journey of mine and making this book actually happen. Or maybe you do, because you just know things! Thank you, thank you, thank you . . . and so it is.

Jeff Bomberger: My spiritual coach. It was you, who I first met while visiting Topanga for a mini retreat, that told me that I needed to share my truth. I was still overcome with fear, but thanks to your spiritual guidance along the way, we have arrived.

To God / the Universe / the Divine . . . and, more specifically, to my spiritual team, ancestors, and loved ones on the other side. This book was a collective creation, something I never could have done without you by my side. May we continue to co-create together, allowing me to be a vessel of your love to the world.

Julie LaPlaca is a seasoned television producer, with over two decades of experience working in the entertainment industry. Most notably, she spent years crafting some of reality TV's most iconic love stories as a supervising producer on *The Bachelor* franchise. Julie is an author, a life coach, hypnotherapist, and founder of The Love Producer, a personal development brand devoted to helping others produce the love they desire in their lives (TheLoveProducer.com). Now she's flipping the script, guiding others (and herself) on the greatest journey of all, that of finding the love within.